THE NEW CLASS?

THE NEW CLASS?

Edited by

B. Bruce-Briggs

* * *

Robert L. Bartley
Daniel Bell
Peter L. Berger
Nathan Glazer
Andrew Hacker
Michael Harrington
Jeane J. Kirkpatrick
Everett Carll Ladd
Seymour Martin Lipset
Kevin P. Phillips
Norman Podhoretz
Aaron Wildavsky

Transaction Books
New Brunswick, New Jersey

Library of Congress Catalog Number: 78-62999
ISBN: 0-87855-306-1 (cloth)
Printed in the United States of America

Library of Congress Cataloging in Publication Data

Main entry under title:

The New Class?

   Includes bibliographical references.
    1. Social classes—United States—Addresses, essays, lectures.
2. Intellectuals—United States—Addresses, essays, lectures.
3. Professions—Addresses, essays, lectures. 4. Right and left (Political science) I. Bruce-Briggs, B.
HN90.S6N5   301.44'0973   78-62999
ISBN 0-87855-306-1

in memory of
MAX NOMAD
(born Nacht)
1881-1973

· ·

Jeremiah 8:8

To the conservative property-owners:

Gentlemen, I have lived long among scholars and artists, and have carefully observed them in private, and I can assure you that these people will push you until you resolve to sacrifice your pride and set their leaders in the highest rank of esteem and provide them with the wherewithal they need for the complete development of their plans. I would be exaggerating if I led you to believe that I have discovered this precise intention in the minds of the scholars and artists. No, gentlemen, I can even tell you that it is merely vague, but, from long observation, I am certain of its reality and of the influence that it exerts on all their ideas.

Henri, Comte de Saint-Simon (1803)

In this very simple way does the value of our educated class define itself: we, more than others, should be able to divine the worthier and better leaders. The terms here are monstrously simplified, of course, but such a bird's-eye view lets us immediately take our bearings. In our democracy, where everything else is so shifting, we alumni and alumnae of the colleges are the only permanent presence that corresponds to the aristocracy in older countries. We have continuous traditions, as they have; our motto, too, is *noblesse oblige*; and, unlike them, we stand for ideal interests solely, for we have no corporate selfishness and wield no powers of corruption. We ought to have our own class-consciousness. *"Les Intellectuels!"* What prouder clubname could there be than this one . . . .

William James (1907)

Plainly the middle-income skill groups have not yet found a common name; nor have they discerned the inner principle of sacrifice on which their unity depends; nor have they risen to the full comprehension of their historic destiny.

Harold D. Lasswell (1936)

. . . it is quite possible that the great new "isms" of tomorrow will be ideologies about knowledge. In tomorrow's intellectual and political philosophies knowledge may well take the central place that property, i.e., things, occupied in capitalism and Marxism.

Peter F. Drucker (1968)

CONTENTS

A PREFACE ON PURPOSE AND ORGANIZATION

"The New Class." This term has begun to appear with ever-increasing frequency in discussions of the contemporary American scene. Its usage expresses the view that a new important class, or a new dominant class, or even a new ruling class, is emerging. Those who use the term are usually hostile to the group they so label: the New Class is regarded as ominous, even sinister, undemocratic. As we shall see, its first American usage in its present form was largely politically motivated. If polemics were all there was to the idea, we could inter "the New Class" in the graveyard of catch phrases along with "egghead," "extremism," "new left," "radical right," "hardhat." But there is more to the idea than that. Those who have employed the phrase have a grounding in contemporary scholarly ideas of how society is organized and where it is going. The New Class portends fundamental changes in the structure of our economy, society, polity, and culture, many of which are subsumed under another currently popular term—"the post-industrial society."

As I understand it, the idea of the New Class attempts to relate those trends to one another—to connect the changing economy to a changing occupational structure, which, in turn, is related to a changing society and changing dominant political, social, and cultural ideas. In particular, the New Class hypothesis tries to account for the prevalence of radical/reformist ideas among members of our society who would appear by any objective measure to be favored in income, status, freedom, power, and other presumed benefits of life. The conventional view of the world, buttressed by historical experience, is that the less privileged orders should be the least enthusiastic about the *status quo*, while the better-off should be conservative. Today, it appears that these attitudes are largely reversed—the working people and even the poor, however defined, have conventional ideas, are "bourgeois," "square," and strive for a larger slice of *status quo*, while individuals who are dissatisfied with the existing order, are "alienated," and even hold radical views regarding economic organization and cultural values are most likely to be found among the highly educated, highly paid, and highly regarded. That seems odd.

Having followed the evolution of the idea of the New Class over the past decade (and even contributed very slightly to its development), I thought that now might be an appropriate time to initiate a serious, in-depth study relating it to the overall evolution of American society. The idea of a major study was conceived in 1976 because, in a considerable sense, the New Class was no longer political news in that election year. Many of the participants in this study will refer to the period 1966-1973, in which the idea of the New Class developed from the obvious political circumstances, which have substantially changed since then. So the New Class is today no longer a subject of intense partisan dispute and therefore may be looked upon somewhat more coolly. While the term "New Class" was intended to be pejorative, so originally were "Whig," "Tory," "democracy," "liberal," "capitalist," and "meritocracy." Perhaps, like them, it may attain a neutral connotation.

Although my ideas were well developed (but ill formulated), I thought the role of entrepreneur more appropriate than undertaking a study independently. After conceiving the study, I made an outline of relevant topics and recruited the participants listed on the following pages. They were intended to represent a variety of scholarly disciplines and contemporary political/ideological viewpoints. Nevertheless, as the reader, especially the skeptical reader, will notice, the majority of the participants are drawn from the group of scholars and publicists that has lately been labeled "neo-conservative"; that is, individuals who once were identified as liberals and many before that as socialists or communists, but who have moved to the Right and/or seen the Right move left and embrace them. This selection was deliberate, for several reasons: the most banal is that these people were known to me and I highly respect their talents. More important, they are the very people who have identified and discussed "the New Class" (although not always under that label*). "The New Class" is in a considerable sense a neo-conservative formulation. Nevertheless, as we shall also see, one version of the idea was generated by the extreme Left, and

---

*Indeed, there is not even agreement on the style of the term—"the new class," the new class, or the New Class. I use the last, but have not imposed that version on other contributors.

some of the neo-conservatives have brought it over to the Center, while other writers on the Left who have retained its more or less original form are also represented in the study, as are a scattering of other viewpoints as well as some who deny the idea altogether.

I initially decided to recruit approximately thirty participants for the study, and to include about ten essays, with commentaries by the advisors to the study.* Fortunately, the idea for the study was enthusiastically received, and more than ten papers were commissioned. Unfortunately, some of those papers did not materialize before the deadline for the study, so it was not possible to use the services of the advisors as internal critics as much as had been planned.

Some topics are missing: a commissioned paper on journalists failed to appear; although the subject appeared innocent to me, several advisors enjoined me to stay away from the question of ethnicity; the right person could not be found to write on the federal bureaucracy (I hope to do this myself at some future date); I considered trade union staffs a minor group (that had in any event been nicely covered by Harold L. Wilensky's *Intellectuals in Trade Unions*). Moreover, I did not think it was the best investment to include ideological/ political points of view that necessarily deny the idea of a New Class—orthodox Marxist, orthodox laissez faire, idealistic, or (left- or right-wing) populist conspiracy theorists. Since so many of the contributors are expressly hostile to contemporary liberals, serious but unsuccessful attempts were made to recruit spokesmen for the following positions:

"This so-called 'New Class' is a reactionary slander on America's most thoughtful and concerned citizens."

"Yes, there is something that might be labeled "the New Class"—and it is a good thing, too, because we will run this country infinitely better than those dolts who have preceded us." (Particularly regretted was John Kenneth Galbraith's inability to participate, but his refusal was expressed in such exquisitely gracious terms that receiving it was almost a pleasure.)

Doubtless, some of the reviewers will more than repair these omissions.

---

*One criterion for the selection of contributors was their demonstrated ability to write English, because it was intended that the study might be both enlightening to scholars and instructive to the general educated reader. So the contributors were enjoined to eschew excessive scholarly apparatus or jargon.

But this goal was not quite achieved. The lay reader especially will note a wonderful flutter over the employment of the word "class." A proper understanding of this agitation requires a grounding in the history of social science and of Marxist thought, in which the notion of "class" performs a role similar to that played by "the church" in Christian theology. To write of a New Class that is not found in Marx's system is to question the happy ending of history promised by Marxism, so Marxists must be mollified with "stratum." And for "bourgeois" sociologists, haggling over "class" has been a rewarding bone of contention for nearly a century.

The study was limited to the United States. Obviously, most Third World countries are ruled by tiny, Western-educated elites (but drawn mostly from the former ruling classes). Europe and Japan are far more advanced than the United States in converting a system of privilege via family property to one of privilege via formal education (Canada is also farther down the New Class path), so the foreign reader will likely see in this volume further evidence of Americans' peculiarity.

Here then is an examination of the idea of the New Class by a group of distinguished scholars and social commentators, all of whom are members of the New Class—if there is a New Class.

—BBB

NEW CLASS STUDY PARTICIPANTS

PROJECT LEADER AND EDITOR

B. Bruce-Briggs. Historian and policy analyst. Author of *The War Against the Automobile*, and coauthor of *Things to Come* and *Canada* Has *A Future*. Contributor to many journals. Former city planner and foundation executive. Consultant to U.S. and Canadian government agencies. Formerly on staff of Hudson Institute and Commission on Critical Choices for Americans. Senior research associate, Center for Policy Research.

CONTRIBUTORS

Robert L. Bartley. Editor. He has spent almost his entire career with *The Wall Street Journal* and has been editor of its editorial page since 1972.

Daniel Bell. Sociologist. His many works include *Marxian Socialism in America, The End of Ideology, The Coming of Post-Industrial Society*, and *The Cultural Contradictions of Capitalism*. Chairman of the American Academy of Arts and Sciences Commission on the Year 2000. Member, President's Automation Commission. Former editor, *New Leader, Fortune*, and *The Public Interest*. Professor of sociology, Harvard.

Peter L. Berger. Sociologist. Author of *Invitation to Sociology, Pyramids of Sacrifice, Facing Up to Modernity*, and several other works. Formerly with the New School for Social Research and Brooklyn College. Associate editor, *Worldview* magazine. Professor of sociology, Rutgers.

Nathan Glazer. Sociologist. Author or coauthor of many books, including *The Lonely Crowd, The Social Basis of American Communism, Beyond the Melting Pot,* and *Affirmative Discrimination.* Former editor, *Commentary,* Doubleday, and Random House, and currently coeditor of *The Public Interest.* Former professor of sociology, University of California—Berkeley. Professor of education and sociology, Harvard.

Andrew Hacker. Political scientist. Author of *Political Theory: Philosophy, Ideology, Science; The End of the American Era;* and *Free Enterprise in America,* among others. Regular contributor to scholarly journals and general magazines. Former member of the Cornell government department. Professor of political science, Queens College of the City University of New York.

Michael Harrington. Political analyst. Author of *The Other America, Toward a Democratic Left,* and *The Twilight of Capitalism,* among many other works. Former editor, *The Catholic Worker* and *New America.* Former national chairman, American Socialist Party. Chairman, Democratic Socialist Organizing Committee. Professor of political science, Queens College.

Jeane J. Kirkpatrick. Political scientist. Author or coauthor of several books, including *Political Woman* and *The New Presidential Elite.* Consultant to many government agencies. Active in national Democratic Party. Resident scholar, American Enterprise Institute. Professor of political science, Georgetown University.

Everett Carll Ladd, Jr. Political scientist. Author or coauthor of many works, including *Negro Political Leadership in the South, The Divided Academy: Professors and Politics,* and *Transformations of the American Party System.* Professor of political science at the University of Connecticut and director of its Social Science Data Center. Currently acting director of the Roper Public Opinion Research Center.

Seymour Martin Lipset. Sociologist. Author of *Political Man, The First New Nation;* coauthor of *The Politics of Unreason* and *The Divided Academy,* among numerous other works. Formerly at Berkeley, Columbia, and Harvard. Professor of sociology and political science, Stanford University and the Hoover Institution.

Kevin P. Phillips. Political analyst. Author of *The Emerging Republican Majority* and *Mediacracy.* Former special assistant to the U.S. attorney general. Syndicated political columnist. President, The American Political Research Corporation. Editor and publisher, *The American Political Report*.

Norman Podhoretz. Literary critic and editor. Author of *Doings and Undoings* and *Making It*, and articles and reviews in most of the major American magazines. Contributor to many anthologies. A leader of the Coalition for a Democratic Majority. Editor-in-chief of *Commentary* since 1960.

Aaron Wildavsky. Political scientist and educator. Author or coauthor of *The Revolt Against the Masses, The Politics of the Budgetary Process, Implementation, Presidential Elections*, and many other works. Former professor at Oberlin and Berkeley. Former dean, Graduate School of Public Policy, Berkeley. Former president, Russell Sage Foundation.

ADVISORS

David T. Bazelon. Lawyer and educator. Author of *The Paper Economy* and *Power in America: The Politics of the New Class*. Professor at Buffalo State University.

Amitai Etzioni. Sociologist. Author of *The Active Society* and many other works. Professor of sociology, Columbia. Director, Center for Policy Research.

Stephen Hess. Political analyst. Author or coauthor of *The Republican Establishment, Organizing the Presidency*, and other books. Senior Fellow, The Brookings Institution.

Irving Louis Horowitz. Sociologist. Author or coauthor of many works, including *Ideology and Utopia in the United States, 1956-1976*. Professor of sociology and political science, Rutgers. Editor, *Society*.

Irving Kristol. Social critic and editor. Contributor to the *Wall Street Journal* and many other periodicals. Coeditor, *The Public Interest*.

Harold D. Lasswell. Political scientist. Author of an enormous contribution to social science. Professor emeritus, Yale.

Clare Boothe Luce. Journalist, playwright, and politician. Former editor, *Vogue* and *Vanity Fair*. Author of *The Women* and other plays. Former U.S. ambassador to Italy and congresswoman from Connecticut.

Bayless Manning. Lawyer. Former law professor, Yale and Stanford. Consultant to many government agencies. Former president, Council on Foreign Relations.

Daniel Patrick Moynihan. Political scientist and politician. Holder of high federal office under Presidents Kennedy through Ford. Author of *The Politics of a Guaranteed Income* and many other works. Former member of the Harvard faculty. U.S. Senator from New York.

Dick Netzer. Economist. Author of *The Subsidized Muse* and several other works. Former economic analyst, Federal Reserve Bank. Professor at New York University and dean of its Graduate School of Public Administration.

Peter C. Newman. Canadian journalist. Former editor, *Financial Post* and *Toronto Star*. Author of *The Canadian Establishment* and other books. Editor, *Maclean's* magazine.

Arthur Schlesinger, Jr. Historian. His many works include *The Age of Roosevelt*. Assistant to President Kennedy. Albert Schweitzer Professor of Humanities at City University of New York.

Roger Starr. Urbanologist. Former New York City housing administrator. Author of *America's Housing Challenge* and other works. Member, editorial board of *The New York Times*.

Gordon Tullock. Economist. Author or coauthor of *The Calculus of Consent* and other works. Professor of economics, Virginia Polytechnic Institute. Associate director of The Center for Study of Public Choice.

Ben J. Wattenberg. Political analyst. Former aide to Democratic politicians. Author or coauthor of *The Real America* and other works. Fellow, American Enterprise Institute.

James Q. Wilson. Political scientist. Author or coauthor of many works, including *Thinking About Crime*. Consultant to several U.S. government agencies. Professor of government at Harvard.

Charles Wolf. Economist. Author or coauthor of many works, including *Rebellion and Authority*. Head of the economics department of The Rand Corporation and director of the Rand Graduate Institute.

Michael Young. English sociologist. Author of *The Rise of the Meritocracy* and other works. Formerly with the research department of the Labour Party. Director of the Institute of Community Studies, London.

STAFF

Associate Editor: Robert Asahina. Former managing editor of *The Public Interest*, now with *Geo* magazine.
Assistant Editor: Steven D. Lagerfeld. Assistant editor, *The Public Interest*.
Research Assistants: Dell Wasserman.
Elizabeth Bowman.

All institutional affiliations are listed for identification only.

THE NEW CLASS?

1

AN INTRODUCTION TO THE IDEA
OF THE NEW CLASS

B. Bruce-Briggs

While many earlier writers have casually used the phrase "a new class" to describe some emerging social group, its general American usage derives from Milovan Djilas' *The New Class*, published in English in 1957, which described the Communist elite of Yugoslavia as a new class that had emerged from the proletariat. It was a "class" because it possessed political control over the means of production. But Djilas specifically limited his analysis to underdeveloped countries; indeed, the historical function of his new class was to modernize backward economies. While the term "the new class" was suggested by Djilas, no serious American writer has claimed that any group here is comparable to the Communist party bosses of Eastern Europe.

The version of the New Class that provoked this study first appeared in 1972, when three very influential American intellectuals adopted and developed the term. The first, as far as I have been able to determine, was D.P. Moynihan, writing in *The Public Interest* about the education lobby, in a subsection titled "The new class":

The social legislation of the middle third of the century created "social space" for a new class whose privilege (or obligation) it is to dispense services to populations that are in various ways wards of the state [his emphasis].[1]

He linked direct economic interest with ideology, quoting Samuel Gompers, who wrote in 1916, "There is a very close connection between *employment* as experts and the enthusiasm for human welfare." But Moynihan was careful to avoid a cynical interpretation: "the self-interest of the new class is merged with a manifestly sincere view of the public interest." Yet,

> the increasingly corporate nature of the American social structure means that fierce, organized pressures will be brought to bear to raise expenditure, and that these will be supported by a civic culture that sees increased expenditure as a general public good. Anyone who on any grounds opposes such an increase opposes the interest of a class, and the preconceptions of the culture.

Shortly after, the editor of *Commentary* magazine, Norman Podhoretz, then writing a regular column, commented upon an essay in the same issue by Michael Novak, who used the term "the New Class." Podhoretz deployed the term politically:

> The nature of the New Politics movement is easy enough to describe in sociological terms. The movement is made up largely of educated, prosperous people, members of the professional and technical intelligentsia and their wives and children, academics and their students: the group, in short, as Michael Novak reminds us, that David T. Bazelon presciently identified as a New Class long before it came to consciousness of itself as a class and as a potential political force.

Later that year, Podhoretz addressed the work of the novelist Philip Roth:

> A remarkably similar species of snobbery and self-righteousness is, of course, one of the distinctive marks of those members of the professional and technical intelligentsia in America who make up what has come to be known as the New Class. And indeed, there is an intriguing parallel between the ethos of the New Class and the attitudes embodied in the work of Philip Roth. The New Class sees itself, in the words of one of its member-admirers, as a "conscience constituency" motivated only by ideas and ideals, whereas others are driven only by baser impulses and issues "of the stomach." Just so, the authorial point of view in the work

of Philip Roth claims for itself a singular sensitivity to things of the spirit . . . whereas others are represented as altogether blind to things of the spirit and as caring only for lesser things of the flesh like food and money and material possessions. Or again, although the New Class—as Penn Kemble and Josh Muravchik [in the same issue of *Commentary*] show in careful and elaborate detail—is capable of supreme ruthlessness in its pursuit of power, it has consistently given its own ambitions, not only for power but for status and wealth as well, the benefit of every conceivable doubt while excoriating or making fun of the needs and wishes of others and putting them always in the most highly unfavorable light.

It does not strike me as fanciful to suggest that Philip Roth owes his centrality to the fact that he so perfectly embodies the ethos of a group which began coming to consciousness of itself as a distinctive social class around the time Roth first appeared on the scene and which has become numerous enough and powerful enough in recent years to move from the margins of our culture into the very mainstream of our political life. The New Class, in short, now constitutes a mass audience in its own right and Roth is the New-Class writer par excellence.[2]

As we shall learn from Podhoretz's essay in this volume, his interpretation was informed by the concept of "the adversary culture," identified and labeled by his teacher, Lionel Trilling.

Writing in the November 1972 *Commentary*, Irving Kristol, the editor of *The Public Interest*, attributed the appearance of the issue of economic equality to a wider problem:

The trouble is that our society is breeding more and more "intellectuals" and fewer common men and women.

I use quotations around the term "intellectuals" because this category has, in recent decades, acquired a significantly new complexion. The enormous expansion of higher education, and the enormous increase in the college educated, means that we now have a large class of people in our Western societies who, though lacking intellectual distinction (and frequently even lacking intellectual competence), nevertheless believe themselves to be intellectuals . . . the figure would easily cross the million mark! And if one also adds the relevant numbers of college students, one might pick up another million or so.

In the course of the essay, Kristol also labels this group the "intelligentsia" and "this 'new class' of the college educated."

> We have a "new class" of self-designated "intellectuals" who . . .
> pursue power in the name of equality. (The children of this "new class,"
> however, seem divided in their yearnings for suicide via drugs and their
> lust for power via "revolution.")

It is opposed by "the American working class" and is "engaged in a class
struggle with the business community for status and power." In the *Wall Street
Journal* in 1975, Kristol wrote more on "Business and 'the New Class.'"

> What is commonly called a "bias" or an "animus" against business is
> really a byproduct of a larger purposiveness. There are people "out
> there" who find it convenient to believe the worst about business because
> they have certain adverse intentions toward the business community to
> begin with . . . . These people constitute what one may simply call, for
> lack of a better name "the new class."

> This "new class" is not easily defined but may be vaguely described. It
> consists of a goodly portion of those college educated people whose skills
> and vocations proliferate in a "post-industrial society" (to use Daniel
> Bell's convenient term) . . . . It is, by now, a quite numerous class; it is an
> indispensable class for our kind of society; it is a disproportionately
> powerful class; it is also an ambitious and frustrated class.

Then he corrected Kevin Phillips' recently published *Mediacracy* by maintaining, "Members of the new class do not 'control' the media, they *are* the
media—just as they *are* our educational system, our public health and welfare
systems, and much else." And:

> "The intellectuals" . . . are the ancestors of our own "new class," very
> few of whom are intellectuals but all of whom inherit the attitudes toward
> capitalism that have flourished among intellectuals for more than a
> century-and-a-half.

> The "new class"—intelligent, educated, energetic—has little respect for
> such a commonplace (business) civilization. It wishes to see its "ideals"
> more effectual than the market is likely to permit them to be. And so it
> tries always to supersede economics by politics—an activity in which *it* is
> most competent, since it has the talents and the implicit authority to shape
> public opinion on all larger issues.

The idea is so associated with Kristol that it is instructive to list all the groups
he includes in the new class:

scientists, teachers, and educational administrators,
journalists and others in the communications industries,
psychologists, social workers, city planners,
lawyers and doctors who make their careers in the expanding public
    sector,
sociologists,
criminologists,
scholars, intellectuals, publicists,
''the most part'' of the population of foundations and universities,
those who created and populate the new regulatory agencies (EPA,
    OSHA, CPSC),
the upper levels of the government bureaucracy.[3]

It is this sense of the New Class that has been widely circulated. For example, it appears not only in the writings of neo-conservatives,[4] but also in the work of a broader spectrum of opinion, including, among others, Ken Auletta in *The New Yorker*, Carl Gershman in the social democratic *New America*, Lewis H. Lapham in *Harper's*, Albert Sommers of the Conference Board, and various writers on the Right, such as Kevin Phillips and Patrick Buchanan.

Drawing upon the above sources, especially Kristol, as well as the much earlier writing of Max Nomad (discussed later), the proposal for this study offered this hypothetical description of the New Class:

> It comprises a large part of academia, the bureaucracy, the media, and related occupations and institutions [and it may] be defined in terms of high or potentially high (i.e., including students) formal education, professional occupational status, high (but not the highest) income, usually from non-market sources—government or non-profit salaries, grants, and contracts, and relative youth . . . .

> It could be maintained that the New Class largely controls or dominates: the humanities and social science faculties of prestige private and state universities, professional schools, and teachers colleges; most of the national media organizations—the prestigious daily newspapers, much of the periodical press, the book publishing industry, the commercial television networks, recording, films, and most educational media; the fine arts; the establishment foundations and other non-profit eleemosynary institutions concerned with influencing public opinion; research organizations; a good part of congressional staff; the federal social welfare bureaucracy; and the government regulatory apparatus. It is

thought that New Class values and sensibilities are penetrating into: the natural science faculties; the business schools; the rank and file of school teachers; state and local government bureaucracies; the clergy; advertising; trade union staff, especially of government and white collar employees; salaried professionals of all kinds; and even business corporations, especially in public relations, long-range planning, and internal education programs. These disparate groups have this in common: they are staff, not line, and they produce or deal in "ideas" or words and hold their positions by virtue of possession of analytical and literary skills usually obtained through formal education.[5]

As they say, "it is no accident" that the idea of the New Class first appeared in 1972. In that year, *the* book under serious intellectual discussion was John Rawls' philosophical defense of equalitarianism, *A Theory of Justice*; income redistribution was emphasized by George McGovern; and, perhaps most important of all, the New Politics elements described by Podhoretz had taken control of the Democratic Party. Moynihan, a nominal Democrat, had served President Nixon and believed that his pet policy initiative, the Family Assistance Plan, had been sabotaged by New Politics forces; Kristol was an avowed Nixon supporter; and Podhoretz was among the implacable defenders of the former New Deal-organized labor liberalism, later institutionalized in the Coalition for a Democratic Majority.

But the McGovern nomination was merely the political culmination of a longer sequence of events—the crushing of the Right in the Goldwater debacle of 1964, the reappearance of a vigorous radical Left, its diffusion and popularization in the New Politics, campus unrest, black ghetto riots, the drug-rock-sex counterculture and its diffusion in "liberated lifestyles," the appearance of environmentalism and consumerism, and, of course, the growing opposition among educated Americans to U.S. involvement in the Indochina wars. One result of these events was that the tiny New York "intellectual community," once a tight-knit, albeit squabbling, "family," became divided. So the appearance of the New Class might be interpreted as one clique of literary intellectuals bad-mouthing another. But the concept has survived, and has been circulated among wider constituencies ignorant of or indifferent to these quarrels.

More important, the centrist use of the idea is not a recent innovation; the mainstream of analysis of the New Class has come from the Left. Interestingly, the neo-conservative usage derives from an apparent misinterpretation. In the 1972 *Commentary* essay that stimulated Podhoretz's discussion of the topic, Michael Novak referred to the concept of the New Class offered by David T. Bazelon (and by Michael Harrington, who borrowed it from Bazelon). In 1967, Bazelon devoted the better part of a political analysis of the United States to the subject of the New Class. He did not limit the term to those groups identified above, but included in it almost the *entire* American salariat—that is, not merely social workers, city planners, professors, and the like, but corporate managers and others in Kristol's "business class." In other words, just about anyone not owning productive property but with sufficient education to read this book would be part of the Bazelonian New Class.

Bazelon did, however, identify "liberals" as the left-wing of the New Class, as its most *class conscious* part, as its vanguard; Michael Harrington related this part to "the conscience constituency" then rallying to the presidential candidacy of Senator Eugene McCarthy.

Bazelon, a long-term New York intellectual (and lawyer) wrote *Power in America: The Politics of the New Class* while he was a fellow at the Institute for Policy Studies (the "pink tank"). He was then sympathetic to the movements of the 1960s; while considerably disillusioned *circa* 1978, he still considers himself a man of the Left. To him, the New Class was:

> *Working intellectuals* ... non-property holding individuals whose life conditions are determined by their position within, or relation to, the corporate order .... people gaining status and income through organizational position. They achieve their positions—or at least are permitted to enter the race—mostly by virtue of educational status.
>
> People who mostly organize and administer, and criticize and comment on, the activities of others ... technologists and administrative intellectuals.

Most important, "Education, like capital in the past, is now a manipulable and alienable property."

Bazelon saw the New Class as frustrated, despite its various attempts to adjust to the wider society, including "professionalism," and "irrelevant Washington jobs." He identified the growth of the New Class with the professional and technical sector of the labor force:

> The education of the New Class member—an electronics engineer or a systems research analyst with a Ph.D. in sociology or a physicist working for the RAND corporation or an economist dealing with manpower programs in the Department of Labor—is an application of training *to think ahead*. These people administer and they plan—indeed, it is impossible to administer without becoming engaged in some form of gross plan, at least a "plan" for resolving the conflicts among the interests you are administering. So it strikes me as distinctly possible that *all* the education of all the members of the New Class has a common denominator—namely to plan something.
>
> The whole theory of rule by property was that the accompanying Competition [sic] dispensed with the need to plan, and thus dispensed as well

with "planners" (intellectuals) and the state (the primary planning agency).

The "liberal," although an acute minority of the New Class, is the most fully achieved and self-conscious form of it, to date.[6]

While his was an ingenious elaboration, he did not invent the New Class. Credit for the first American usage of the term must go to John Kenneth Galbraith, who, in 1958, wrote in *The Affluent Society* about "the emergence of this New Class . . . . to which work has none of the older connotation of pain, fatigue, or other mental or physical discomfort."
For these people:

> Pay is not unimportant. Among other things it is a prime index of prestige. Prestige—the respect, regard, and esteem of others—is in turn one of the most important sources of satisfaction associated with this kind of work. But, in general, those who do this kind of work expect to contribute their best regardless of compensation.

Galbraith did not delineate the New Class, but included within it college professors, school teachers, surgeons, most of those who pay income surtax rates, and politicians. But,

> overwhelmingly the qualification is education. Any individual whose adolescent situation is such that sufficient time and money is invested in his preparation, and who has at least the talents to carry him through the formal academic routine, can be a member. There is a hierarchy within the class . . . an electrical engineer is on the lower edge; his son who does graduate work and becomes a university physicist moves to the higher echelons; . . . In early nineteenth century England or the United States . . . it consisted only of a handful of educators and clerics, with, in addition, a trifling number of writers, journalists, and artists. In the United States of the 1850s it could not have numbered more than a few thousand individuals. Now . . . undoubtedly in the millions.

And Galbraith proposed a public policy initiative.

> The further and rapid expansion of this class should be a major and perhaps next to peaceful survival itself, *the* major social goal of the society. Since education is the operative factor in expanding the class, investment in education, assessed qualitatively as well as quantitatively, becomes very close to being the basic index of social progress. It enables

people to realize a dominant aspiration . . . . Were the expansion of the New Class a deliberate objective of the society this, with its emphasis on education and its ultimate effect on intellectual, literary, cultural, and artistic demands would greatly broaden the opportunities for membership.

The identification of a class by the criterion that it enjoys its jobs cannot endure serious scrutiny, because almost all work contains an element of play. And the New Class does not appear in Galbraith's later works. Instead, *The New Industrial State* (1967) divides it into two elite groups: "the technostructure" of corporate managers and their apologists, hangers-on, and henchmen in government; and "the educational and scientific estate," of scientists and academics called into being by the technostructure's need for trained talent, yet uneasy and straining at the golden cords of the industrial system. Galbraith obviously intends to encourage their restlessness. While the goals of the two men are quite opposite, the analyses of Galbraith and Kristol are remarkably of a type; the technostructure is very similar to the business class, as is the educational and scientific estate to the new class.*[7]

The year 1967 was particularly fruitful for the subject of this study because, in addition to Bazelon's *Power in America* and Galbraith's *New Industrial State*, there was Daniel Bell's first major display of "post-industrial society," in which the central theme is the primacy of theoretical knowledge, possessed by a group that Bell has differently labeled the "knowledge class" and the "professional and technical intelligentsia." The Bell scheme and nomenclature are certainly the most influential current intellectual view of the future of advanced societies and directly influenced Kristol and Podhoretz. But since Bell summarizes its latest version in this volume, elaboration would be superfluous here.

While the *term* is a recent innovation, the idea of the New Class has an ancient lineage. To trace its provenance and pedigree would require volumes. How-

---

*Pointing to parallels does not mean to imply pillaging. While most of the people discussed here read one another, they read incredible amounts, and cannot be expected to remember exactly where and how an idea came to them. Also, they have stood on the shoulders of the same giants—e.g., both Kristol and Galbraith have thoroughly ingested the work of the Austro-American economist Joseph A. Schumpeter, who wrote that capitalism inherently generated a poisonous intelligentsia. Schumpeter will be cited frequently in this volume. In any event, in 1967 Kristol wrote of "an intellectual class" that presages his later "new class."

A long memo on the history of the idea of the New Class was circulated to the study participants, and I detected more than a hint of annoyance when some learned that antecedents of what they considered their own original ideas were in books that they had read, sometimes even by authors whose ideas they abhorred.

ever, a *very* cursory outline (which can be further abbreviated because several of the contributors have discussed their antecedents) may promote a better understanding of the notion. Very crudely, the idea can be tracked on three lines—those who saw its potential as beneficial, those who feared its emergence, and those who considered it inevitable. The first two lines started with berserk noblemen.

Henri, comte de Saint-Simon, was a madman with a powerful idea: Society needed to be reorganized. After the French Revolution, authority had to be reestablished to achieve social justice. Unlike many of the eighteenth century philosophers who admitted the possibility that all men could become enlightened, St.-Simon saw the necessity of an educated elite. His scheme for social order was hierarchy with the industrialists at the peak, but with "savants" playing a leading role as the moral guardians of society. He was consciously imitating the medieval polity, with industrialists as the barons and the savants as the clergy. St.-Simon originally saw science as the unifying "religion," which, like medieval Christianity, would be thoroughly understood by the elite and superstitiously followed by the mass. Later he considered this formulation inadequate and contrived a "new Christianity," which sounds identical to twentieth century Unitarianism.

St.-Simon's disciples, most notably Auguste Comte, systematized and elaborated his ideas, emphasizing even more the power of science to inform and control the society, as compared to the "anarchy" of laissez-faire, and exhibiting greater indifference to the forms of private property. Much of this program was spun out in detail that sounds ridiculous today—Comte even designed a flag for a united European state—but a strong case can be made that the basic principles of what for lack of a better term, I call "social positivism" have been a central body of ideas among educated people for the last century.

The German "academic socialists," the Fabians, the progressives, the Technocrats, the American liberals of the 1920s and 1930s—all took for granted the central social-positivist ideas: the inevitability and desirability of scientific and technological advance; the beneficial effects of applying science and reason to the economy, society, and polity; the superiority of purposeful collective action over tradition or the sum of individual actions; and the "waste" of competition, merchandizing, and finance. All these ideas were supposedly so self-evident that they could be achieved by a program of education, not revolution; indeed, "reform" is the necessary alternative to social upheaval, and discord is de facto evidence of a failure to carry out the program adequately. Edward Bellamy's *Looking Backward* (1887) is the most famous American expression of this attitude. What I call "social positivism" can be summed up in two words—"education" and "planning."

This tradition is by no means limited to the genteel Left; it is central to twentieth century corporation managerialism as well, beginning with the idea of "scientific management." This notion was given great impetus by Adolf A. Berle's thesis that great corporations were increasingly controlled by their managers, not by their nominal owners, the shareholders. Berle was a member of the original band of upper-class, highly educated liberals in close contact with and heavily influenced by the English Fabians, one of whose objectives was to transform industrial control, in R.H. Tawney's words, "to turn it into a Profession . . . a body of men who carry on their work in accordance with rules designed to enforce certain standards both for the better protection of its members and for the better service of the public."[8] Berle elaborated his views for thirty years and must be considered one of the founding fathers of the idea of competent, socially responsible, but *independent* professional management developed by corporation theorists such as Peter F. Drucker and taught at graduate business schools.

While Marx attacked such "bourgeois socialism," a naive social positivism is the official domestic ideology of the Soviet Union, and its diluted version has been so dominant among Western scholars that in the 1950s, their consensus was that other thought systems (labeled "ideologies") were exhausted. What I call social positivism is so pervasive and so taken for granted by most educated people that it has no modern philosopher and lacks a serious historian.[9] One could write a fat book about efforts to justify the privilege and dominance of those first labeled "brain workers" (in German, literally "head workers") and more recently "knowledge workers," and about ingenious, usually unconscious attempts to obscure the privileged position assigned to the learned in the improved social order of the future.

The second major line in the history of the idea of a new class regards its emergence not positively, but negatively. This is the analysis of heretical critics of mainstream Marxism, and is usually traced back to the fantastic Russian nobleman Michael Bakunin, who characterized the Marxist "dictatorship of the proletariat" as rule by "a new class, a new hierarchy of real and pretended scientists and scholars . . . the most distressing, offensive, and despicable type of government in the world." This analysis became conventional among anarchists and anarchosyndicalists. And the role of what were later called "intellectuals" in the presumably proletarian socialist movement was always the subject of intense internal debate. Indeed, it was a standard procedure in doctrinal disputes within socialist parties to characterize opposing positions as deriving from the nonproletarian ("petty bourgeois") origins of their advocates.

Interesting hints of the idea of the New Class can be found as well in the diffuse writings of Marx and Engels. Their texts were elaborated when it became apparent, toward the end of the nineteenth century, that something other than the Marxist projection of increasing bourgeois-proletarian polarization was occurring. Intermediate groups were appearing: salaried workers, owning no productive property, but relatively well-paid and enjoying considerable status. In Germany, these came to be labeled "the new middle class," and in America, "white-collar" workers. Marxist theoreticians wrestled mightily with these unforeseen groups, and the solution was to identify them as "a stratum" not "a class," and to label them "the intelligentsia," a Russian word that first appeared in the 1880s to identify the tiny group with a (Western) formal education, most of whom were employed in precapitalist Russia as teachers or bureaucrats.

Appropriately, an unwilling Russian subject, the Polish revolutionary Jan Waclaw Machajski, made the educated classes the keystone of a thoroughgoing critique of socialism. While exiled in Siberia, he produced what might be called a Marxist interpretation of Marxism. Socialism was the ideological instrument of the class interest of the "white-hands" (i.e., white-collar workers)/the intellectual workers/the intelligentsia who wished to replace the capitalists as the exploiters of the workers:

> By attacking the factory-owner the socialist does not touch in the slightest the salary of his manager and engineers. The socialism of the past century leaves inviolate all the incomes of the "white-hands," as the "labor wage of the intellectual worker," and, in the words of Kautsky, it declares that "the intellectuals are not interested in exploitation and are not taking part in it."

This theory created enough of a stir in revolutionary circles to warrant somewhat nervous attacks by Leon Trotsky. But Machajski's ideas and tiny revolutionary organization were blown away by the Russian Revolution, and he died in 1926 as a minor Bolshevik functionary. In any event, history proved him wrong. During the period 1918-39, the white-collar workers of Europe did, as projected by Machajski, Karl Kautsky, and the American Marxist Louis Boudin, turn away from laissez-faire capitalism (and its political counterpart, parliamentary government)—not toward socialism, but rather toward those illiberal movements called "fascist."

Machajski's ideas are only known today because of the work of his disciple "Max Nomad" (né Nacht), an Austrian subject involved in revolutionary work before World War I who fled to the United States in 1913.[10] Nomad expanded on Machajski's ideas, offering a division within the intelligentsia that roughly anticipated Galbraith, Bazelon, and Kristol:

> In short, formally "employees," the "ins" are in fact, due to their higher educational qualifications, *minor partners* of the capitalists as a whole: the lesser nobility, as it were, within the great bourgeois aristocracy of the

modern age. And in proportion as the *major partner*, the capitalist, becomes a mere consuming parasite, leaving most of the functions of technical and commercial management to his "paid employees"—in the same proportion these "employees" become the potential successors of their employers. But, being satisfied with their social position, they are naturally a conservative element; they are not in a hurry to dispossess their masters (or major partners); for any serious interference with the property relations may disturb the social peace and endanger their own privileged incomes.

Against these defenders of the status quo are arrayed the "outs," the unemployed or underpaid journalists, lecturers, college graduates and undergraduates, "lawyers without clients and doctors without patients" (Marx), educated ex-workers in search of a white-collar position—in short all that motley army of impecunious or starving intellectuals, near-intellectuals and would-be intellectuals, who are dissatisfied with the existing system and are very often militantly active in the various radical or fascist movements. It is the members of this group who have the ambition of eliminating the capitalist class of parasitic consumers and of establishing their own rule in a system based on government control or ownership of industries, and an unequal distribution of incomes.

Nomad identified the Soviet system with the class rule of the intellectuals:

That system has evolved an enormous hierarchy of intellectuals who are bureaucrats at the same time; administrative office-holders, technical managers and engineers, judges, savants, journalists, writers, professors, higher transport and postal employees, Marx-theologians, army officers, actors, singers, scientific spies, bank accountants, trade union and sports organizers—all of them government employees who owe their bourgeois comfort to the labor of the uneducated workers and peasants . . . . The badge of admission to this new privileged class is a certain amount of education or training exceeding the average level of the manual workers . . . this class which, being identified with the government, has become the collective owner of the country's socialized economy—its industries and its land.

However, he did not believe that the ambitions of intellectuals *necessarily* lead to Soviet socialism.

A system embodying the mastery of the office-holders' class is just as compatible with a Paretist-Mussolinian aristocratic nationalism and its

> glorification of the "élite," as it is with the Marxist-Leninist "proletarian internationalism" with its no less aristocratic "proletarian vanguard," or with . . . democratic socialism which takes for granted the higher incomes enjoyed by men of "achievement" and "prestige." [11]

Although he had become disillusioned with his master, Nomad introduced Machajski's ideas to American intellectual circles in the 1930s. An enthusiastic reader was the political scientist Harold D. Lasswell, who wrote in 1935 about "symbol specialists":

> The "capital" of the intellectual is his learning, and he may be considered to be in competition with landowners, business enterprisers, and manual workers, for safety, income, and deference in society.

At that time, the tiny band of American Marxists who had split from the Communist Party was embroiled in a fierce internal debate over the nature of Stalin's Soviet Union. It was evident to them that a regime that so obviously oppressed the workers could not be properly described as a "dictatorship of the proletariat" nor could it be called "capitalist," since private ownership of the means of production had not been restored. But then, what was it? To the exiled Bolshevik Leon Trotsky, the U.S.S.R. was "degenerated" and ruled by a bureaucracy, but it was a workers' state nevertheless, deserving of the support of true Marxists against capitalist powers. But many of his followers were not so sure—perhaps the Soviet Union was *something else*.

So long as Trotsky lived, his authority kept the dissidents under control, but with the Hitler-Stalin pact and his assassination in 1940 the breakup was inevitable. The leader of the opposition was Max Shachtman, whose writings demonstrate enormous erudition and who, by every account, had great ability in debate and immense personal appeal—all of which made him the pied piper to the young New York Trotskyist intellectuals, whom he took with him to form a tiny Workers Party that was relabeled the Independent Socialist League, until it folded into the Socialist Party in 1958, where Shachtman continued his influence over the Young Peoples Socialist League until his death in 1972.

This tiny splinter group was to be enormously productive of leading intellectuals. The first fruits of the Shachtmanite faction appeared almost immediately. One of its theoretical leaders, James Burnham, immediately broke with Marxism in his *The Managerial Revolution* (1941), which claimed that it was not the proletariat, but the salaried industrial managers who were historically destined to be the heirs to the capitalists, and that Soviet Russia, Nazi Germany, and to a lesser degree, New Deal America, were managerial states. [12]

The main Shachtmanite line, however, is summed up in the term "bureaucratic collectivism." Shachtman described Soviet Russia as "a new type of slave-state, with a new type of ruling class." The Stalinist Communist Party "is a *new party*; it speaks for a *new class*, it is the political organization of the new bureaucracy that overthrew the workers' state."

> The new bureaucracy was born, grew, and took power in response . . . to the organic needs of a backward, isolated country, existing in unique and unprecedented world conditions. The new class satisfied these needs (more or less), but by its very nature, by the nature of the conditions of its existence, it accomplished the task in a reactionary way. It converted backward Russia into modern Russia, made it a powerful, industrially-advanced country.[13]

This is so similar to the Djilas thesis that it seems incredible that the Yugoslav could not have been aware of it (although he does refer to American texts obviously influenced by Berle and Burnham). One can understand why *The New Class* was so enthusiastically received by the Shachtmanite remnant in America.

The last generation of Shachtman's progeny are well represented in the AFL-CIO staff and front organizations, the Coalition for a Democratic Majority, and the staff of Senator D.P. Moynihan, and a list of ex-Shachtmanite party members, sympathizers, and hangers-on-the-periphery would be a roster of renowned American intellectuals, including David T. Bazelon, Michael Harrington, S.M. Lipset, and Irving Kristol. In the 1978 preface to his *Two Cheers for Capitalism*, Kristol wrote: "There is no such thing as socialism . . . only versions of more or less coercive, more or less bureaucratic collectivism."

The third major line can be described more briefly. Beginning with the Italian political scientists Vilfredo Pareto and Gaetano Mosca, a body of "elitist" thought has held that a small group has always been on top and almost certainly always will be, so democracy and socialism merely express the "circulation of elites." Elitist theory has had a heavy impact on many socialists (e.g., Sorel, Michels, and Burnham) and social scientists (e.g., Lasswell, Mills) and much twentieth century thought has wrestled with the not entirely contradictory but difficult to reconcile concepts of "class" and "elite," resulting in such formulations as "power elite" and "ruling class." Perhaps it is by now unnecessary to note that this is the line I find most congenial.

Fifteen years ago Daniel Bell wrote of

> the preoccupation that has attended the rise of sociology since its beginnings in the nineteenth century: namely, the scanning of the historical skies for portents of "the new class" which will overturn the existing social order.

The old classes that were to be replaced were, of course, the "feudal" aristocratic military landowners and the capitalist factory-owning "bourgeoisie." The former never existed in North America (outside Quebec); but the latter, until recently, was considered to be the most privileged and powerful class in America. It is striking how much writers of different disciplines and objectives agree that the capitalists are on the way out. But there are several candidates for the succession:

I. *The New Middle Class*: the white-collar workers, or salariat, who have no productive property but enjoy relatively high income and physically non-demanding work, usually in offices pushing paper, and who have gained access to their position largely via education. The growth of this group is copiously documented, and projections of its further increase are, I believe, plausible and universally accepted. But, of course, its growth must stop at some level— someone has to do the physical work.

Therefore, to the degree that the United States (or any other nation) is politically democratic, the white-collar workers will increasingly be the electorate, and to the degree that private economic choices are permitted, the new middle class will be the market for goods, services, *and ideas* (or words).

But most of this mass is modestly paid and without substantial "power," however defined. Within it are two more interesting groups:

II. *The Managers*: those industrial officials having "power without property," not to mention very high incomes and considerable perquisites, who now control almost all industrial and financial enterprises that matter. How to define "managers" is a difficult problem. All writers would include the titled executives of privately-owned corporations, but consensus is progressively lost as administrators in government and other "nonprofit" organizations and staff and lower ranks in the corporate hierarchy are added.

But the expectations of writers like Veblen and Burnham that managers would become a revolutionary force have come to naught—they are pillars of "The Establishment." However, the remaining entrepreneurs and active rentiers (who do indeed have "class consciousness") would agree with writers like Boudin and Galbraith that managers are wishy-washy and unreliable defenders of the "rights" of property.

III. *"X"*: a group that makes its living by the use of learning, especially the ability to use words. Members of this group do not own anything but personal private property, and to the extent that they directly control and/or are responsible for anything, they are "managers." They are "staff," or teach or do research or write about things, make calculations, give advice, sometimes have "pretentions of being the critical conscience of society" (F. Castro).

Defining this group is also very difficult. Most who accept the notion would include, I believe, such types as professors at prestigious schools, highbrow journalists ("intellectuals"), and government lawyers, but presumably not physical education instructors, Defense Department operations researchers, or society page editors for provincial newspapers. Like "managers," the size of this group, and therefore its power in the marketplace of goods, services, votes, and words, depends largely on how its boundaries are established. However defined, it seems to be growing rapidly (see the appendix).

In the past, the most widely used terms for this group were "intellectuals" or "intelligentsia," but they have not been acceptable in America, I believe for two reasons: 1) the literary and academic intellectuals who dominate these sorts of macrosocial analyses (e.g., most of the contributors to this volume) are loath to grant what they deem their noble appellation to mere traffickers in words and numbers; 2) the popularly unacceptable implication of special capacity or "intelligence" inherent in the word. "Knowledge workers" would seem a more promising label, but do not farmers or skilled blue-collar workers employ "knowledge?" And what "knowledge" is produced by the bulk of journalists, foundation or government bureaucrats, or professors of education? Hence, I believe, the need for the term "New Class."

Early in the study I circulated this schema of the problem to the participants:

A	B	C
rentiers	salaried managers	"intellectuals"
business owners	engineers	salaried professional
"free" professionals	profit sector	nonprofit sector

A is the traditional bourgeoisie. B is the managers. C is "X."

C is the neo-conservative New Class. B and C together are the leftist New Class.

To my mind, the fundamental questions of the study could be reduced to testing the schema. Here are three conjectural elites/classes/strata—or are they two? Is Kristol right in opposing the business class (A & B) to his New Class (C), or was Bazelon right in opposing his New Class (B & C) to the traditional capitalists, or are writers at the extreme Left and Right correct in viewing the whole lot as an interrelated "elite" sufficiently united to thwart the legitimate objectives of the American masses? Or is it all nonsense?

NOTES

1. D.P. Moynihan, "Equalizing Education: In Whose Benefit?," *The Public Interest* (Fall 1972). "It could be I was the first to use 'The New Class' in the sense which appears to have found acceptance over here. It seemed to me that Djilas was simply discovering the bourgeoisie—nothing new save perhaps in Serbia. I do not claim credit for the innovation. I will, of course, accept it." Moynihan to BBB, 27 January 1977.

2. Norman Podhoretz, "Between Nixon and the New Politics," *Commentary* (September 1972), and "Laureate of the New Class," *loc. cit.* (December, 1972).

3. Irving Kristol, "About Equality," *loc. cit.* (November 1972), reprinted in his *Two Cheers for Capitalism* (New York, 1978), pp. 171-77; "Business and 'The New Class,'" *Wall Street Journal* (19 May 1975), reprinted in *Two Cheers*, pp. 25-31; also see ibid., pp. 14-17, 111, 145.

4. Most notably by Kristol's protege, the political scientist Paul H. Weaver, who synthesizes Kristol, Podhoretz, and Moynihan in "On Adversary Government and the Liberal Audience," in *The Politics of Planning*, ed. A.L. Chickering (San Francisco, 1976); and "Regulation, Social Policy, and Class Conflict," *The Public Interest* (Winter 1978); also the symposium in *Commentary* (July 1975), and B. Bruce-Briggs, "Prospect of a Planned America," in Chickering, *op. cit.*

5. B. Bruce-Briggs, "The New Class: The Intellectuals and American Democracy," (typescript, November 1976). A negotiation to perform the study at the Hudson Institute was abortive; nevertheless, the text of the proposal has been used as the basis for Hudson Institute documents.

6. Michael Novak, "Needing Niebuhr Again," *Commentary* (September 1972); David T. Bazelon, *Power in America: The Politics of the New Class* (New York, 1967). An edited chapter was published in *Commentary* in 1966 and reprinted in Bazelon's *Nothing But a Fine Tooth Comb* (New York, 1967) where he also comments acidly on reactions to his thesis. For his 1970 views see the preface to the paperback edition of *Power in America*. For Harrington's reception see "The New Middle Class: Whose Camp Is It In?," *Village Voice* (1 June 1967), an abbreviated version of which appears in his *Toward a Democratic Left* (New York, 1968), chapter 10, the paperback edition of which has a 1969 afterword.

7. J.K. Galbraith, *The Affluent Society* (Boston, 1958), chapter 14. ("The New Class" first appears late in a book written Summer 1955-March 1958; Djilas' *New Class* appeared in English in mid-1957); *The New Industrial State* (New York, 1967), especially chapters 6 and 25.

8. Berle's memoir in the Columbia Oral History Collection; R.H. Tawney, *The Acquisitive Society* (New York, 1920), chapters 17 and 20.

9. It has, of course, had critics, e.g., F.A. Hayek, *The Counterrevolution of Science* (Glencoe, Ill., 1952); Michael Oakeshott, *Rationalism in Politics* (New York, 1962); James Gilbert, *Designing the Industrial State: The Intellectual Pursuit of Collectivism in America, 1880-1940* (Chicago, 1972).

10. On Machajski and Nomad, see Nomad's *Rebels and Renegades* (New York, 1932); "White Collars and Horny Hands," *Modern Quarterly* (Autumn 1932); *Aspects of Revolt* (New York, 1959); and *Dreamers, Dynamiters, and Demagogues* (New York, 1965). Fragments of Machajski's work are translated by Nomad in the *Modern Quarterly* essay and in *The Making of Society*, ed. V.L. Calverton (New York, 1937), pp. 427-36, from which the quotation is taken. For a Trotskyist response, see George Nowak, "Marx and the Intellectuals," *New International* (December 1935).

11. Max Nomad, "Masters Old and New" in Calverton, pp. 882-93.

12. While he has softened his analysis somewhat, Burnham sticks to the managerial thesis. See his 1959 introduction to the Indiana paperback edition of *Managerial Revolution* and "What New Class?," *National Review* (20 January 1978), apparently provoked by queries relating to this study.

13. Max Shachtman, "The Struggle for the New Course," (1943) in Leon Trotsky, *The New Course* (Ann Arbor paperback, 1965), pp. 219, 242. Shachtman lacks a biographer and the Shachtmanites a history, so my information on this subject is almost entirely from personal communications.

2

THE ADVERSARY CULTURE AND THE NEW CLASS

Norman Podhoretz

Among the many puzzles thrown up by the disruptions of the 1960s in the United States, none seemed more perplexing than the virulent hostility toward their own country which was evidently felt by some of the most privileged elements of American society. That blacks should resent or even be enraged by American society seemed entirely understandable and indeed proper. Having been victimized for so long by discrimination, poverty, and lack of opportunity, they had good reason to protest, to demonstrate, to disrupt. But what reason did undergraduates at Berkeley, Columbia, and Harvard have for feeling the same way and engaging in the same kind of behavior? Why should young people from prosperous families who had been given—as the saying used to go— "every advantage," who were enjoying what to all outward appearances was a life of luxury, indulgence, and ease, and who could look forward with relative assurance to positions of comparable status and reward in the years ahead, characterize themselves as "niggers"? ("The Student as Nigger" was actually the title of a widely circulated manifesto of the period.) In what intelligible sense could these young scions of the American upper classes be compared to a group at the bottom of the American heap?

Such talk of "the student as nigger" might have been dismissed as a particularly flamboyant form of adolescent self-dramatization if not for another perplexing fact: that it was ratified by very large numbers of people in the adult world, including as it sometimes seemed the entire membership of the academic and journalistic professions. Far from ridiculing the idea that the prosperous and privileged young of America in reality constituted an oppressed and downtrodden minority, sociologists and editorialists, foundation executives and columnists were busily at work generating arguments to prove that the contention was sound. These adult apologists, who kept telling us what the young people were "trying to tell us" (though their services in this respect often struck one as supererogatory), were moreover a privileged group themselves, occupying for the most part extremely well-paid positions to which great influence and considerable prestige were attached. Why should they be as hostile to America as the words they kept putting into the mouths of the "young" so clearly suggested they were?

Throughout the years roughly bounded by the end of the Civil War and the beginning of the Second World War, no one would have been surprised to find intellectuals* and aspiring intellectuals expressing hostility toward American society. With the rapid industrial expansion of the country in the decades after the Civil War, America more and more became the quintessential "business civilization"—a society in which tremendous power of every kind was vested in the business class. But as this power grew, and as the abuses flowing so abundantly from its exercise accumulated, resistance to it also developed. Antitrust laws, progressive income taxes, regulatory legislation, electoral reform, and the rise of organized labor—all were directed at diminishing or at least controlling the rampant economic and political power of the "robber barons," of "Wall Street," of the trusts and the monopolies. Efforts of this nature were supported by rival economic groups—farmers, small-town merchants, independent professionals, and manual workers—whose interests were threatened and often trampled upon by big business, and who attacked the new order of things in the name of values like free competition and equality of opportunity which big business itself of course also honored (if more in the breach than in the observance).

At the same time, however, a more radical assault on the new order was also being mounted which in the long run perhaps proved more decisive. It was an

---

*The term is of course notoriously difficult to define. I use it to mean people professionally, or anyway passionately, concerned with the study, propagation, and dissemination of ideas, attitudes, and ideologies. Usually such people have been exposed to a university education, but this is not a necessary condition. Sometimes they are very intelligent, but that is not a necessary condition either.

assault directed against the spiritual and cultural power of business—that is, against the very values which the populists and the Progressives and the labor movement shared with big business and to which they appealed in their own struggle for a greater share of political and economic power. In this cultural battle, the weapons used were not political, and progress was not measured in legislative victories. The relevant weapons were ideas and the object was to persuade and influence. Nor was the point to expose the injustices flowing from a business civilization (or a capitalist system, as some Americans later learned to call it); the emphasis here fell on spiritual rather than material considerations. Of course separating the spiritual from the material was not always possible or desirable. Nevertheless there did develop a critique of capitalist America which centered independently on what in our own day is known as the "quality of life." Indeed so vivid an autonomous existence did this critique achieve that it retained its plausibility even at a time when the strictly economic arguments against the system (the Marxist ones, among others) seemed to have been refuted by the spread of affluence to unprecedentedly large numbers of people.

This cultural critique consisted essentially of three related elements. First of all, it was said that a society in which business was the leading species of enterprise put a premium on selfishness while doing everything it could to dampen the altruistic potentialities of human nature. People were rewarded for being selfish and penalized for caring about others; they were encouraged to compete instead of to cooperate. The result was an erosion of communal attachments and loyalties, and the creation of a harsh, brutal, heartless society of isolated individuals connected one to the other by a "cash nexus" and nothing more lasting or binding.

In addition to encouraging the worst kind of "rugged individualism," a business civilization, it was charged, stimulated the basest of human passions—material greed. The lust for money and for the things money could buy became so ferocious that more elevated tastes were forced to go begging for satisfaction. People grew narrow and gross, incapable of appreciating anything whose value could not be counted in dollars. The arts were thus meaningless to them, or at best a showy adornment pressed into the service of an ostentatious vulgarity. And just as individuals living under such circumstances were related only by a "cash nexus," so their only religion was worship (in William James's phrase) of "the bitch-goddess SUCCESS."

These attacks on the individualism, materialism, and philistinism of a business civilization were rooted in Christianity and derived a good part of their effectiveness from the continuing strength, sometimes latent, sometimes active, of Christian belief in the United States. But there was a third element of the critique which was rooted in secular and even anti-Christian sources, and this was the attack on the puritanism of "bourgeois" or "middle-class" society. Such a society, it was said, while rewarding the lust for money, penalized all the healthier appetites. The only pleasures it sanctioned were whatever pleasures might be connected with work, ambition, the sense of having "made it" or won out in a brutal competitive struggle. All other pleasures, whether of the mind or of the body, were frowned upon as wicked or as debilitating or as a waste of precious time. A life lived under the rule of these values was stern, joyless, desiccated, prissy, provincial, repressed.

In elaborating this critique, intellectuals—and especially intellectuals primarily interested in the arts—quite naturally played the leading role. For the very act of becoming an intellectual or an artist in America* came to mean that one was in effect joining the party of opposition—placing oneself (to use the term made famous by Lionel Trilling in *Beyond Culture*) in an "adversary" relation to the business civilization and all its works. To be sure, some of these "works" to which most American partisans of the adversary culture were opposed (though there were prominent exceptions such as William Faulkner) included values like religious piety, patriotism, and the martial virtues that derived not from capitalism but from precapitalist roots: the ethos of the rural community and the small town. But as was evident from the term "booboisie" invented by H.L. Mencken to suggest an identification between the "hick" of the hinterland and the businessman (wherever he might live and however large or small his business), the two tended to flow together in the adversary American mind into a single enemy.

Nor did membership in the adversary culture merely involve subscribing to abstract doctrines critical of bourgeois society; it also involved matters of style and sensibility. Thus the "modernist" movement which began sweeping through all the arts around the turn of the century and which was characterized above all else by an unremitting impulse toward formal experimentation—Ezra Pound's "Make it new!" was the great slogan—represented something more than an effort to escape from played-out aesthetic conventions and to find fresher forms of expression and interpretation. There was in this movement a powerful will to *épater le bourgeois*, to provoke and outrage the middle-class audience by upsetting its normal expectations and offending its sense of intelligibility, fitness, and order. While very often attacking or ridiculing the bourgeois world in substantive terms (through, for example, unflattering por-

---

*This is not to imply that the attitudes of the adversary culture were indigenous or peculiar to America. Similar stories could be told of all the industrial countries. But there were important differences between Europe and America in this as in so many other areas. For example, in Europe opposition to the rising power of industrial capitalism came (at least until 1945) from the Right as well as the Left, taking the form of facism and of literally reactionary political movements which advocated the restoration of monarchy or of an essentially feudal social organization. Although major American writers living in Europe like T.S. Eliot and Ezra Pound were among the sympathizers of these movements, nothing really comparable materialized in the United States, possibly because this country had no feudal past.

traits and characterizations), the modernist movement was simultaneously mounting an assault on the very structure of its sensibility. Indeed, Edmund Wilson in his book on the Symbolists, *Axel's Castle*, went so far as to suggest that the modernist revolution in the arts was analogous both in purpose and significance to the Russian revolution: as the one represented a challenge to the rule of the bourgeoisie in the world of politics, the other represented a challenge to its rule in the world of imagination and ideas.

That modernist or avant-garde artists and their critical partisans should stand in an adversary relation to bourgeois society was to be expected almost by definition. But in America even artists and intellectuals like Theodore Dreiser or Van Wyck Brooks who were opposed on aesthetic grounds to modernism shared fully in its attitude toward the business civilization. Until, that is, the Second World War and its aftermath. While business as such continued to be treated with contempt throughout the 1940s and 1950s—this was the period of books like *The Organization Man* and *The Man in the Grey Flannel Suit* which amounted to nothing more than updated and popularized versions of the cultural critique—a new and more positive attitude toward American society itself, and even toward the capitalist system, began to emerge among artists and intellectuals. Those who participated in and applauded this surprising phenomenon said that as compared with the alternatives of Nazi Germany on the one side and Soviet Russia on the other, America looked very good to them—especially since "countervailing forces," as John Kenneth Galbraith called them, had by now cut into the power of big business and made for a more pluralistic cultural climate and one more hospitable to values other than those of commerce. Those who deplored this development said that the intellectuals were simply "selling out" for good jobs and a better social position, and that we were faced with the onset of a new "age of conformity."

Such worries, as we now know, were misplaced. The first postwar decade turned out to be not the beginning of a new "age of conformity"—that is, of amity between the intellectuals and American society—but a temporary aberration, destined to be corrected, and with a vengeance, in the decade ahead. To journalists and popular sociologists with short historical memories, this correction looked like a novel development. It was not; it was a return to the traditional stance of the intellectual community in relation to American society.

There was, however, one truly novel element in the situation of the 1960s: the vastly enlarged numbers of people who now either belonged to the intellectual community or were under its direct influence. In the past intellectuals had constituted a tiny minority of the population, but with the tremendous expansion of higher education in the period after World War II, millions upon millions of young people began to be exposed to—one might even say indoctrinated in—the adversary culture of the intellectuals. To be sure, very few of these young people actually became intellectuals in any real sense, but a great many were deeply influenced by ideas which had once been confined pretty much to the intellectual community itself. Thus what had formerly been the attitudes of a minuscule group on the margins of American society now began assuming the proportions of a veritable mass movement. And since so many of these young people eventually wound up working in the mass media, such attitudes acquired a new ability to penetrate into previously inaccessible areas of American culture.

But if this history helps to explain why so much hostility to American society was to be found in the 1960s among intellectuals and their students, and in the mass media, it does not tell us why the adversary culture should have returned with so great a force precisely at a time when intellectuals not only had less personal reason than ever before to resent American society, but also when the doctrines of the adversary culture itself had become less plausible as a description of American society than ever before.

After all, in the heyday of bourgeois self-confidence—during the "Gilded Age" of the 1870s and 1880s, or even during the boom of the 1920s—when people who had "never met a payroll" were held in contempt, when artists and intellectuals were often unable to earn a living, when works of the mind and spirit were either ridiculed or ignored, when originality or experimentation in the arts were derided and even persecuted—under these circumstances it would have been amazing if artists and intellectuals had responded with anything but an answering bitterness and hostility.

But conditions were very different by the 1960s. If in the past artists and intellectuals had been despised as compared with businessmen, they were now more and more being held in generally high esteem. They were honored, they were consulted, they were even envied for doing more important work and living more interesting lives than people engaged in the pursuit of material gain. If in the past it had been difficult or even impossible for artists and intellectuals to support themselves by writing or painting or composing, an increasing number were now finding new ways of managing. There were jobs—relatively well-paying jobs—at universities, there were grants to be had from foundations, and most important of all there was a new and responsive public growing up ready to listen to the things they had to say, and to buy (often at huge prices) the things they had to sell. And if in the past originality and experimentation in art and thought had encountered tremendous resistance, they were by now being welcomed as fervently as they had once been rejected. Stories and articles by "highbrow" writers were printed in mass magazines while books which had once been considered virtually unpublishable were appearing on best-seller lists. Paperback reprints of difficult modernist works which only yesterday had been regarded as beyond the pale were enjoying huge sales and were being taught as classics in schools and colleges. And there were similar developments in the worlds of painting, sculpture, music, theater, and dance, where the avant-garde became so powerful and so fashionable that all other styles were either deprived of cultural respectability or were altogether driven out. Despite its continuing sense of itself as engaged in a heroic battle against the philistine bourgeois world, the avant-garde, Hilton Kramer said in his definitive study, *The Age of the Avant-Garde*, had become *the* establishment, the country's most powerful cultural force.

Given this new situation, one might have expected the adversary culture to lose its bite or perhaps even to disappear—killed, as it were, by kindness. And yet exactly the opposite occurred. Beginning in the late 1950s, what one sympathetic observer has called "a second wave of modernism" began gathering force which was, if anything, even more virulent in its hatred of bourgeois or middle-class society than the first one had been. Listening to these latter-day epigoni of the modernist revolution, one might have thought that nothing had changed except for the worse. America, they said, and in the most strident tones, was still dominated by business and its values, and those values were still as grounded in materialism, philistinism, and puritanism as they had been in the past. Life in the "establishment" (in this usage a category which came to include virtually anyone who worked for a living, but never the speaker himself, no matter how successful in the worldly sense he might be) was a "rat race"; the only purpose of such a life was the consumption of material goods which grew even tackier and more useless; it was a boring life, a sterile "air-conditioned nightmare" lacking in vitality, spontaneity, or the capacity for sexual satisfaction. One of the first of the new modernists, Jack Kerouac, summed it all up in his novel *On the Road* as "millions and millions, hustling forever for a buck among themselves... grabbing, taking, giving, sighing, dying."

Yet the very success which writers who took this point of view began to enjoy in the late 1950s belied their claim that nothing had changed and that America was still dominated by business and its values. For paradoxically nothing was better calculated to win the applause of the "establishment" than denunciations of it. The publication of *On the Road* itself, for example, was hailed by a reviewer in *The New York Times* (then still in its old incarnation and still called "the good grey *Times*") as "a historic occasion," and Kerouac became a nationwide celebrity. So did many other writers associated with him in the Beat Generation, especially Allen Ginsberg who declared in his poem "Howl" that the "best minds" of his generation had literally been driven mad by life in middle-class America. And so, ultimately, did dozens upon dozens of their followers and successors—novelists, poets, playwrights, film-makers, social critics, journalists, and rock and pop musicians—who were rewarded with riches, fame, and adulation for heaping contempt and ridicule on the society around them.

The reason, then, that the adversary culture was not killed by kindness is that it was encouraged by kindness. Tocqueville points out that the French Revolution—the revolution of the bourgeoisie against the aristocracy—erupted out of an improving rather than a worsening situation. As the power and confidence of the middle class increased, so did its appetite and hence also its animosity toward the *ancien regime*. Is it too fanciful to apply the same analysis to the intellectual class in America in the 1960s? Certainly it did not seem too fanciful to many of the intellectuals themselves. During the 1960s, a theory began to circulate to the effect that a "New Class" was maturing in America made up of persons whose "capital" consisted not of money or property but of education, brains, and technical expertise—intellectuals, in the broadest sense—and that in an advanced stage of capitalist development such as the United States was now reaching this New Class would eventually replace the old owners and entrepreneurs—that is, the bourgeoisie—as the ruling elite.

In this "liberal" variant of the theory (propounded by writers as diverse as Daniel Bell, David T. Bazelon, and John Kenneth Galbraith) the intellectuals were seen as the beneficiaries of an orderly transfer of power destined to take place as the byproduct of structural changes in the economic organization of the system. But there was another variant—a radical or neo-Marxist one (whose most prominent proponent was probably C. Wright Mills). In that version the intellectuals were seen as the agents of revolution, replacing the proletariat, the class which Marx had cast in this role but which had evidently traded its historic birthright for a mess of affluent pottage.

Whether in its liberal or its neo-Marxist version, the dream of power seems to have acted upon the intellectuals as Tocqueville says the same dream acted upon the bourgeoisie in prerevolutionary France: it sharpened the appetite and exacerbated hostility to the tottering and doddering ruling class of the old regime which so stubbornly insisted on postponing the inevitable with one stratagem after another. Thus if in an earlier period bourgeois society was hated because it ignored and despised the intellectuals, now it was hated because, despite all the concessions it had made, it still refused to be *ruled* by the intellectuals.

Only once before in the post-Civil War period had American intellectuals seriously entertained so ambitious a vision for themselves, and that was in the early years of the Great Depression. Up until that time, the practical strategy followed by the adversary culture was generally to withdraw entirely from political activity. For the grip of the business class seemed so firm that one was reduced to railing from the sidelines in the manner of Henry Adams—who conducted a species of ideological guerrilla warfare against the new political order in America—or turning one's back in self-destructive despair. Of the young patricians of his father's generation, Edmund Wilson wrote:

> The period after the Civil War—both banal in a bourgeois way and fantastic with gigantic fortunes—was a difficult one for Americans

brought up in the old tradition . . . . They had been educated at Exeter and
Andover and at an eighteenth-century Princeton, and had afterwards been
trained . . . for what had once been called the learned professions; but they
had then to deal with a world in which this kind of education and the kind
of ideals it served no longer really counted for much . . . . Of my father's
close friends at college, but a single one was left by the time he was in his
thirties; all the rest were dead—some had committed suicide . . . . My
father had in his youth aimed at public life . . . . But he could not . . . be
induced to take part in the kind of political life that he knew at the end of
the century.*

There did, however, emerge an alternative to the course followed by Henry
Adams on the one side and the elder Wilson and his friends on the other, which
Edmund Wilson himself and many of his own friends adopted: emigration,
either literally to Paris or London where the atmosphere seemed more congenial
and more hospitable, or figuratively to a "bohemian" community in which the
values of the adversary culture were turned into the prevailing norm. In such
communities—the most famous sprang up in the early years of the century in
New York's Greenwich Village—it was the artistic vocation and the life of the
mind to which everyone aspired, and business that everyone despised; in such
communities there was (at least in theory) mutual encouragement and solidarity
instead of ruthless competition; and in such communities puritanism and its
institutional embodiments—chastity, monogamy, the family—were laughed at
and everyone believed in freedom, spontaneity, self-expression, and the pleasures of the flesh.

In such communities, in short, those who were "alienated" from the
spiritual "wasteland" into which the business class allegedly had turned their
country—those who had metaphorically been left homeless and driven into
internal exile—could find a haven and a new home. It went without saying that
in such communities everyone was more or less a socialist, or an anarchist, or a
pacifist, or even (though more rarely) a monarchist or a fascist—anything but a
Republican or a Democrat. But it also went without saying that these political
sentiments carried with them very little expectation of being translated into
actual political power. Some day, but certainly not now, things would change
out there in America, but certainly not yet.

Then came the crash of 1929 and the Great Depression, and suddenly the
opportunity for carrying the fight against the power of business directly into the

---

*The pathos here is a little exaggerated, since the elder Wilson *was* "induced to take part" in public
life to the extent of serving a term as attorney general of New Jersey in the administration of
Governor Woodrow Wilson (no relation). Throughout the past century, patricians (with a few
glaring exceptions like the two Roosevelts) have characteristically been much less successful at
getting elected to public office than at being appointed to it.

political arena looked amazingly good. Thus Edmund Wilson, who had in any case been growing disturbed throughout the 1920s by the thought that withdrawal from contemporary political struggles by intellectuals amounted to a complacent acquiescence in the rule of the business class, joined with Sherwood Anderson, John Dos Passos, Granville Hicks, Malcolm Cowley, and other important literary figures in an appeal to their fellow writers to vote for the Communist ticket in the 1932 Presidential elections, specifically on the ground that the Depression offered the first good chance since the Gilded Age to take the country away from the businessman. In order to do this the intellectuals would of course have to forge an alliance with the working class, which Wilson and his colleagues still imagined to be represented by the Communist party. But the end result would be a society in which "the power of the spirit" would at last prevail against the gilt of all Gilded Ages. It would be a society, in other words, run or managed by intellectuals.

No doubt it was as much with this vision in their eyes as with the passion for justice toward others in their hearts that so many American writers, artists, and intellectuals joined the Communist party in the early 1930s, or at least lent it their moral support. (Conversely, it was the discovery by some, like the group associated with the magazine *Partisan Review*, that the Communists were contemptuous of aesthetic values and of any kind of intellectual independence which led them to break with the party and to invest their revolutionary hopes for a time in the anti-Stalinist Trotskyist movement.) My contention is that it was a similar vision of power—clearly seen by a few, only intuitively or unconsciously sensed by others—which brought about the radicalization and politicization of the intellectuals in the 1960s. What the prosperous young intellectuals who compared themselves to "niggers" were really "trying to tell us" was that they were being denied their "fair share" not of the middle-class security and comfort with which they were already so obviously and plentifully supplied, but of the political power which they believed should rightly be theirs. (Naturally they never doubted for a moment that they would exercise it in the best interests of all, and especially the downtrodden.) This is why the issue of "participating in the decisions which affect our lives" became so important to the radicals of the 1960s and later to their milder liberal progeny.

Within the radical New Left it was believed that power would have to be wrested by force, and it was also believed—*sincerely* believed—that this was possible because the United States was in a "revolutionary situation." As in the Depression, the failures of the system—its inability to eradicate poverty and racism—were providing revolutionary fuel. But now, in contrast to the Depression, even the successes of the system—the spread of affluence to the great majority of the populace—were creating radical discontent. The "best" of the young were refusing to join the "establishment"; they were dropping out and developing a "counterculture" of their own based on the rejection of the

"Puritan ethic" and indeed of all middle-class values: work, ambition, discipline, monogamy, and the family. Clearly, then, the system was no longer viable; clearly it was being destroyed by "internal contradictions" which, if not precisely those foreseen by Marx (for the working class was being subjected to embourgeoisement rather than pauperization and could therefore no longer be depended upon to serve as the vanguard of the revolution), were nevertheless deep enough to tear everything apart and bring the entire structure down.

This analysis was developed long before American combat troops were sent to Vietnam and long before the first riot broke out in the black ghettos of the North. But it obviously gained in credibility as the war became a more and more burning issue, especially on the campuses, and as the civil-rights movement with its tactics of litigation and nonviolence gave way to a "Black Power" movement based on violence and threats of violence. For with every collapse of the authorities in the face of an aggressive challenge—violent demonstrations, the seizure and occupation of buildings, "nonnegotiable demands"—more and more evidence was provided for the idea that the system was falling apart and that a revolution was about to break out.

The 1960s ended, however, not with a revolution but with the election of Richard Nixon: Richard Nixon, who better than any single figure in American public life seemed to epitomize everything in opposition to which the adversary culture had always defined itself. But the response to this defeat was not a new withdrawal. It was, on the contrary, a new determination to mount an effective political challenge, this time "working within the system" to get rid of the usurper who had seized the throne and to place political power at long last into the proper hands. This effort, which called itself the New Politics, sought to forge a coalition of two disparate elements: those who were, or felt themselves to be, deprived of the full benefits of middle-class comfort and security (the blacks and the poor) and those who were, or felt themselves to be, deprived of the full benefits of political power (the New Class). Operating through the candidacy of George McGovern for president, the New Politics came infinitely closer to actual power than any political movement associated with the adversary culture had ever done before, and though it suffered a humiliating defeat at the hands of Richard Nixon in 1972, it participated centrally in the successful campaign to drive him from the White House in 1974. Two years later, the presidential candidate backed by the New Politics, Morris Udall, lost out to an ambiguous figure named Jimmy Carter who then went on as president to staff his administration with veterans of the New Politics and more recent converts to its point of view. Full political power, then, had not been achieved, but obviously great progress had been made.

Yet so far as the adversary culture in particular was concerned, much greater progress had been made in the world of ideas and attitudes than in the political realm. By the end of the 1960s the values of the business class were no longer dominant in America—or even, it sometimes seemed from the readiness with which it assented to attacks on its own position, within the business class itself. In one sense, for example, individualism had grown rampant in America, but not at all in the sense once prized by the business world. The ascendant ethic preached in the public schools, in the mass media, and even in comic books and pornographic magazines now seemed to be that nothing—not wives, not husbands, not children, and certainly not the state—must stand in the way of the individual's right to self-fulfillment and self-expression in the realm of morals, sex, and personal relations (which was, of course, the adversary culture's traditional version of individualism as well as its answer to middle-class or bourgeois values). But where economic enterprise was concerned, the opposite view prevailed: there everything must be put in the way of "rugged individualism" and the more state control the better. And a similar fate had overtaken the old materialism of the business class. Profits were now "obscene"; economic growth was now a "threat to the environment"; prosperity was now "waste" and the criminal squandering of putatively scarce natural resources.

Obviously the progress of the adversary culture in the war of ideas served the political interests of the New Class. For the more the economic life of the country shifted from private to state-controlled enterprise, the less power would accrue to businessmen and the more power would accrue to the professional and technical intelligentsia. But toward the end of the 1960s, a new and complicating element began to enter the picture. Repelled by the sight which the 1960s had vouchsafed of what the adversary culture looked like in action, and therefore of what it might look like in power, a group of dissident intellectuals, mostly but not exclusively associated with magazines like *Commentary* and *The Public Interest*, appeared on the scene to defend middle-class values as the indispensable basis of liberty, democracy, widespread material prosperity, and a whole range of private human decencies. One member of the group, Hilton Kramer, harking back to Joseph Schumpeter (who influenced other members of the group as well) even argued that the adversary culture itself owed its existence to these values, both in the sense that they had provided it with the freedom to develop—a freedom the "socialist" countries had never been willing to grant—and in the deeper sense that its commitment to experimentation and novelty were a reflection in aesthetic terms of the general bourgeois commitment to constant technological innovation and continuous social change.

These intellectual adversaries of the adversary culture were often called "neo-conservatives," a designation happily accepted by some (like Irving Kristol) but rejected by most others, who continued to think of themselves as liberals. "Neo-liberal" would perhaps have been a more accurate label for the entire group than neo-conservative, except for the fact that its liberalism was old and not new—that is, it derived from the New Deal and not from the New

Politics. The New Politics liberalism of the 1960s and 1970s, in the judgment of the dissidents, was not entitled to be called liberal at all, and was indeed antiliberal in many crucial respects. Thus, for example, the new "liberals," in direct violation of traditional liberal principles, supported quota systems rather than individual merit—or equality of result rather than equality of opportunity—as the road to social justice. But this brand of egalitarianism was not simply antiliberal; it also contributed to the undermining of middle-class values by making rewards contingent upon membership in a group favored for one reason or another by government rather than upon individual effort and achievement. It could be understood, then, as an extension into concrete social policy of the adversary culture's assault on the "Protestant ethic."*

In thus challenging the adversary culture, the new dissidents did not go quite so far as William F. Buckley on their right who once said that he would rather be ruled by the first two thousand names in the Boston telephone book than by the combined faculties of Harvard and MIT. But the new dissidents (several of whom were themselves distinguished Harvard professors) went far enough in expressing doubt over the desirability of a society ruled by their own kind to suggest the possibility of a deepening schism within the intellectual community.

Certainly these intellectual adversaries of the adversary culture were exerting a marked influence by the mid-1970s. Their writings were being read and discussed in many circles, and one of their number, Daniel P. Moynihan, was even elected to the United States Senate. To be sure, they still represented a minority within the intellectual community but no smaller perhaps than the adversary culture itself had once been within the world out of which it had dialectically emerged a hundred years before. The effect the new dissidents might have on the future course of events was difficult to predict. But as the first—and last?—century of the era of business domination in America drew to a close, the very existence of a significant party of intellectuals to whom the defense of middle-class values seemed necessary to the preservation of liberty, democracy, and even civilization itself, was already casting an anxious shadow over the otherwise cheerful prospects of the adversary culture in the realm of ideas and attitudes, and of the New Class in the arena of economic and political power.

---

*Of course there was a conflict between radical egalitarianism and the idea of a society run by intellectuals. But destroying middle-class values was more important for the moment than worrying about how the values that would replace them could be squared with those in the name of which the revolution was being fought. Needless to say, the New Class was not the first insurgent class in history to have faced this problem, and if its dreams of political rule were ever to come true, it would no doubt resolve the contradiction in the manner of all past revolutionaries: through ideological fiat backed by the coercive power of the state.

3

POLITICS AND THE NEW CLASS

Jeane J. Kirkpatrick

Other contributors to this volume have explored the history of the concept of the new class. I will simply stipulate that, for the purposes of this essay, the term "new class" will be used for a group with two characteristic political concerns: the control of the symbolic environment and the relationship between the ideal and the real. Though most new-class members have relatively high levels of education and income and are found in professions requiring verbal and communications skills, the new class can be recognized not by its socioeconomic characteristics but by its relation to culture: to the meanings that constitute a culture and to the symbols through which those meanings are expressed.

Though the political influence of the new class has increased significantly, its representatives are found less often at the apex of government and politics than among the more populous second-level stratum surrounding, sustaining, and conditioning the highest officeholders. The importance of this second-level stratum of the political elite should never be underestimated. Under conditions of political freedom, it can shape debate, determine agendas, define standards, and propose and evaluate policies.

I believe it is demonstrable that new-class power has increased in the last decade or so, and that the most important consequences of this increase have been the decline of consensus, the progressive involvement of broader cultural forces in politics (this was especially obvious in the presidential races of 1964, 1968, and 1972), and in the ever-increasing use of government power and organizations to achieve "rationalist" goals. The rise of the new class has also had a significant impact on the composition of the ruling elite and the standards and processes through which its members are recruited.

When politics is a voluntary activity, as in this society, political activity depends on a "fit" between personal predispositions and skills on the one hand, and role perceptions and opportunities on the other. Various types of politics feature distinctive preoccupations and styles that are attractive to different kinds of people. A "marketplace" politics dominated by economic interests and concerned with issues more or less in the here and now is very different from a politics dominated by intellectual questions and concerned with matters of justice and injustice in history. Since half a loaf *is* better than none, compromising over goods is relatively easy. But it is never easy to compromise the kind of moral and ideological questions preferred by political intellectuals, because compromise is tantamount to sellout and error. So people attracted to the one style of politics are likely to be bored and quite possibly offended by people attracted to the other.

In periods of rapid social change, political institutions also change, as new kinds of people perceive previously unnoticed opportunities for achieving personal and political goals. If enough of them become active in a political institution, they may "tilt" it from, say, a politics chiefly concerned with the distribution of goods to a politics concerned with morals. Such a process of institutional reorientation has been underway in American politics and government for some time, and has resulted in the increasing number and influence of new-class representatives and the declining role of business and labor in the polity.

The presence of the new class in the ruling elite was signaled by the changing educational and occupational characteristics of its members. The declining numbers of farmers and self-employed businessmen and the rising numbers of teachers, clergymen, and journalists not only reflect general occupational trends within the society but also testify to the increased prestige of "symbol skills" in politics.

Today, businessmen rarely seek public office and are not inclined to take part in the great debates surrounding politics. The repeated efforts of corporations to persuade their managers and executives to "get involved" in the political arena have come to little. When a captain of industry ventures into politics, he is likely to say something inept, which is then repeated and ridiculed by the guardians of the symbolic environment, who regard their own ability to communicate effectively as the *sine qua non* for respect and power. A single verbal *faux pas* can wreck political prospects: the presidential campaigns of George Romney, Edmund Muskie, and Gerald Ford provide instructive examples.

It will be (and often is) said that the manner in which a candidate expresses himself is important not merely as a measure of his verbal competence but for the insights it provides into the "true" man. And there is the proverbial grain of truth in this assertion: from Romney's confession that he had been "brain-washed" about Vietnam we learned that he was given to overstatement, from Ford's remarks on Poland we learned something about his tendency to defend a mistake once it was made, and so forth. These bits of information about the men who seek to rule us are useful—about as useful as knowing whether they have ever met a payroll. But it is unlikely that these insights will be better predictors of presidential performance than Harry Truman's business failure was. (That we were so much less concerned about Carter's business record than about his Baptist convictions is just one more example of the pervasive influence of the new class on political standards.)

I do not think that intellectuals emphasize verbal skills out of a crass desire to drive up the price of their talents (though the emphasis, in fact, has that effect). Businessmen do not simply have a "vested interest" in the capacity to "deliver" a district on election day; communications specialists do not simply have a "vested interest" in the ability to analyze arguments and state propositions clearly. More important, each is most sensitive to the aspects of the environment to which his predispositions and skills are most relevant. This is why the new class values verbal skills in politicians and other new standards of fitness. The new class has achieved increased influence in politics because many of its members conceive of public policies as relevant to their private destinies and see themselves as having the public mission of criticizing (and, more recently, defending) the dominant political culture; because they possess the skills (analyzing, criticizing, moralizing, and persuading) and other resources (the mass media and the educational institutions) needed to communicate that sense of mission; and because they have an audience today, the product of mass higher education, which is at least potentially attentive and responsive to their claims and critiques. What wealth is to the capitalist, what organization is to the old-style political boss, what manpower is to the trade unionists, words are to the new class. This is another way of saying that the new class comprises intellectuals and semiintellectuals (other specialists in communications, like clergymen and public-relations men); as Schumpeter, wrestling with similar problems of definition, observed, "intellectuals are in fact people who wield the power of the spoken and the written word." Harold D. Lasswell called this group "symbol specialists" and emphasized that their potential functions extend to the whole symbolic environment—including the definition of reality, purpose, morality, and obligation.[1]

In democratic politics, mass support is necessary to achieve political power. The existence of a large and continually growing educated class facilitates the rise of the new class, but is not a prerequisite to its accession to political power. The new class has recently achieved greater importance because of the profound cultural dislocations, involving challenges to the most basic beliefs, assumptions, values, and standards of contemporary society. Intellectuals pose questions about these matters, and intellectuals try to answer them. In traditional societies, habit underpins authority, obedience is customary, and doctrines of legitimacy are self-evident. But in periods of rapid change, moralists and wordsmiths become indispensable to rulers who need continuous legitimation of their power. The new class specializes in questions of legitimacy.

It is almost impossible to exaggerate the importance of political culture to the conduct of government and politics. Political culture locates the individual in the political world—the ethnic, religious, regional, racial, national, and other collectivities in terms of which politics is conducted. It states expectations about what government can do and should do, about the rights and duties of rulers and citizens and the relations between the two, and about the terms and limits of acceptable behavior in the pursuit and exercise of power.

The cultural hegemony of Marxism has tended to obscure the fundamental importance of political culture to our contemporary political system. But the relation between the two was no secret to earlier ages. Plato understood well the dependence of a regime on its political culture and emphasized the creation and/or protection of the central myths and values of the polity. In *The Republic* he proposed a myth to link the structure of the polity to divine purpose and to reinforce the distribution of social roles and the authority of the ruling class, which was to be the product of a most careful education in a most carefully controlled symbolic environment. By the time he wrote *The Laws*, Plato was less sanguine about the possibilities of creating an ideal state, but no less certain that an appropriate political culture was required to sustain a polity. And, like Rousseau, Plato proposed the death penalty for atheists—not because he valued piety for its own sake, but because he was convinced that religion provided necessary reinforcement for the authority and legitimacy of the state. Meanwhile, in Plato's Athens, a new class was actively analyzing the bases of law and the state, demythologizing religion and authority, and debating at length the obligations and limits of citizenship. Despite the execution of Socrates, their discussions continued.

Plato, Aristotle, and the Sophists were all engaged in the political activities for which intellectuals are best suited and to which they are most attracted: the demoralization and remoralization of politics and society. Demoralization makes explicit beliefs and loyalties that hold a society together and submits them to a comprehensive critique in the light of abstract, rationalist assumptions; remoralization provides new myths and new authorities. Both processes proceed by investing small questions with large meaning, by finding previously unsuspected moral significance in routine practices. Both offer the opportunity to define reality, to determine social stations and duties, and to reinforce personal visions and preferences with political power. The chance for all this presents itself only in times of rapid change and unusual freedom—like our own times, in places like the United States and Western Europe.

In any vital society, the initial attack on political authority (mounted by intellectuals) provokes a response and results in an intensified ideological struggle leading inexorably to the enhanced role of the new class. The greater the role of the new class in politics, the more ideological politics becomes; the more ideological politics becomes, the more important the new class becomes. Their critical skills are required to analyze the moral inadequacies of the existing society, their verbal skills to dramatize them. But other members of the new class are then needed to criticize the critics, to defend the symbols of legitimacy, to state the case for the values and beliefs embodied in the existing political culture and institutions.

As the above comments imply, *members of the new class do not necessarily share the same political views and values; they may be found across our multidimensional political spectrum*. The tendency to liberalism is strong, but the problems of welfare states, command economies, and Marxist-Leninist Leviathans have stimulated critiques of liberalism. And in the United States today, the new class includes such politically diverse types as the contributors to this volume, many of the nation's journalists, many of the clergy, the professoriate, some of the bureaucrats (especially those at upper levels), and others.

There will always be exceptions, but some reasonably accurate generalizations are possible. Members of the new class tend to share some orientations that transcend their differences over policy. The most important common characteristic is a marked tendency to a rationalistic, moralistic, and reformist approach to politics. Among these, the most basic is the tendency toward rationalism and the belief that reality will and should reflect a conception of history. Hegel's expectation that the ideal would be realized at the end of history lives on—not only among Marxists, who have explicitly incorporated it into their "laws of history," but among the new class, which uses historical criteria to judge political processes and institutions. Institutions are quite literally expected to *embody* ideas. Political parties, campaigns, and administrations are expected to stand for ideas; when they turn out to be multifunctional and ideologically impure (as they always do), new-class purists of Right and Left react with disappointment, disaffection, and, not infrequently, determination to reform them. The goal of the new-class reformer—whether of Left or Right—is to bring the real into conformity with the ideal (that is, with an *idea* of reality).

This goal explains the intellectuals' perennial enthusiasm for programmatic political parties, an enthusiasm found at all points of the political spectrum. It is not enough that political parties should have somewhat different clienteles and orientations; they must define their identity and mission in terms of programs. In this view, the function of candidates is to present a program and quite literally to stand for it; the function of activists is to win the election on behalf of the program.

The desire that parties, candidates, and governments stand for programs not only reflects the intellectual's fascination with policy, but also manifests a broader belief that social institutions can and should conform to and serve abstract principles. The most serious problems with this rationalist approach were recognized by Aristotle, who criticized Plato's blueprint for the ideal state. Plato believed that an individual's moral quality derived from his membership in a just society in which everyone accepted his assigned station and duties and voluntarily and consistently subordinated personal to collective goals. Aristotle argued that his teacher overestimated human malleability and underestimated the tenacity of organic ties and human wickedness. Aristotle also argued that experience and law were better guides than reason alone to the good society and that Plato's proposal would sacrifice real goods to illusory ideals.

Roughly the same criticisms were made for the next 2,000 years, to this day. As Aristotle perceived, rationalism in politics is closely associated with both extremism and utopianism. Its habit of confounding the realm of abstraction with that of experience invariably results in the oversimplification of social processes, because principles are never as complex or intractable as experiences. Rationalism also tends to utopianism and extremism, because it ignores the distinction between the possible and the probable and encourages optimism about the accomplishment of the highly improbable. The great danger of rationalist politics is that the complexity and multifunctionality of political institutions will be overlooked and that schemes designed to maximize one value will destroy the social tissue that supports many others.

Concentration on the manipulation of ideas and words (like concentration on the manipulation of paints or musical tones) probably induces an exaggerated notion of the world's plasticity and also of human powers, since the only limits on artistic or intellectual creation are those imposed by imagination, creativity, and skill. But even the slightest effort at manipulating the social world involves man in psychological problems and social relations of incredible and invariably unforeseen complexity. The unspeakable complexity of actual human societies creates obstacles to realizing ideas, and the difference between abstract principles and actual social systems makes principle and ideology a poor blueprint for political action. But the contemporary American new class has a great interest in ideology and little interest in the more useful study of history. New-class members also rarely have practical experience with the institutions that are the objects of their attention. Describing the class of which he was part (as I am), Schumpeter noted, with more cogency than kindness, ''One of the touches that distinguish [intellectuals] from other people who do the same [sorts of things] is the absence of direct responsibility for practical affairs. This touch in general accounts for another—the absence of firsthand knowledge—which only actual experience can give.''[2]

Contemporary politics is dominated by a rhetoric or dissatisfaction born from the new-class vision of possibility. Of course, the new class' generally negative orientation toward the status quo has other roots—in the businessman's concern for the practical and the material, and his underestimation of the importance of culture and the ''impractical'' people who specialize in the manipulation of meaning, and perhaps in the relatively low income and status of intellectuals in capitalist, democratic societies (as compared to their much greater power in contemporary revolutionary regimes). But I suspect that the most important source of the adversary culture is the intellectual's habit of measuring institutions and practices against abstract standards—reality is invariably found unsatisfactory. It seems almost certain that the rationalist orientation creates disenchantment with concrete people, places, and practices. When today's housing, health care, or income levels are compared with those of the last decade or those of other societies, the society may look progressive and reasonably successful. But when society is measured against an abstract conception of a just order, it will be seen to have failed.

It is also easy to understand why the new class is more often liberal than conservative. (See Table 3-1). The habit of measuring existing practices against abstract principles inevitably leads to discontent with the status quo, and the belief that reality can be brought into conformity with principles creates a predisposition to act to remedy unsatisfactory situations. Rationalism, optimism, and activism have been and still are the source of liberal and radical political action. They are also characteristics of the politics of the new class.

The tendency to find reality wanting is compounded by an equally marked proclivity for moralistic politics. It is not entirely clear why new-class activists of both Right and Left should invest politics with so much moral meaning, but the habit is strong. The Goldwater campaign and antiwar movement were both propelled on waves of moral indignation. In the mid-1950s, Daniel Bell, Richard Hofstadter, and others regularly ascribed moralistic politics to the ''radical right'' and linked it to evangelical Protestantism and the search for respectability. It now appears that moralism is linked to the decline of religion, but not in the expected way. Today, the relationship between secularism and moralism is especially clear on the Left, where absence of religious affiliation and faith is frequently associated with moralistic politics. (See Tables 3-2 and 3-3.) George McGovern's habit of lapsing into the fervent rhetoric of his

Table 3-1
Occupation and Ideology among Delegates to the 1972 Political Conventions[3]

	Symbol Specialists *	Lawyers	Material * Specialists	Housewives	Students	Clerical and Sales	Public Employees	Salaried Managers	Health Personnel	Other Professionals	Others
Self-Classification											
Radical	11	2	2	4	23	5	3	6	6	6	3
Very liberal	48	19	16	28	40	25	17	16	27	43	37
Somewhat liberal	22	31	17	22	20	32	28	13	8	17	34
Moderate	9	25	21	20	8	22	42	24	6	17	14
Somewhat conservative	9	18	32	19	9	13	11	33	44	12	11
Very conservative	1	4	11	7	0	4	0	9	8	6	2
Weighted N =	305	273	271	391	90	282	180	174	48	164	197
Political Culture Index											
Very liberal 1	47	21	9	31	54	31	11	12	26	33	17
2	32	33	24	23	35	31	41	19	4	33	48
3	14	37	31	29	11	27	42	46	22	23	28
Very conservative 4	6	9	36	18	0	12	6	24	48	11	7
Weighted N =	259	217	193	337	74	249	136	140	46	141	146

*"Symbol Specialists" include authors, clergy and religious workers, public relations and advertising, academics, editors and reporters, social scientists, and teachers. "Material Specialists" include self-employed workers, blue-collar and the low-status professions. Note also that Symbol Specialists were approximately two-and-one-half times as large a portion of Democratic as Republican delegates.

Table 3-2
Occupation and Religion among 1972 Convention Delegates[4]

	Protestant	Catholic	Jewish	Atheist-Agnostic
Symbol specialists*	10%	13%	13%	25%
Lawyers	12	14	15	10
Material specialists*	15	12	15	3
Housewives	15	10	18	15
Students	3	4	5	7
Clerical and sales	11	11	8	11
Public employees	9	13	6	7
Salaried managers	8	6	5	7
Health personnel	3	0	4	1
Other professionals	7	9	4	11
Others	9	8	8	3
	100	100	100	100

*Same categories as Table 3-1.

Methodist past illustrates the affinity on the Left between religious and political revivalism. The rhetoric of the ideological Right and Left alike shows how readily political contests may be conceived as ongoing battles between the forces of light and darkness. The higher the moral content of politics, the more interested the new class becomes; predictably, the more interested the new class becomes, the more the political universe is likely to be moralized.

Table 3-3
Ideology and Religion among 1972 Convention Delegates[5]

	Protestant	Catholic	Jewish	Atheist-Agnostic
Ideological Self-Classification				
Radical	2%	4%	6%	16%
Very liberal	15	25	54	56
Somewhat liberal	21	29	30	16
Moderate	25	25	7	7
Somewhat conservative	28	13	3	5
Very conservative	8	4	0	1
Political Culture				
Very liberal 1	18	27	37	67
2	27	32	52	28
3	36	27	10	6
Very conservative 4	19	13	1	0

New-class perspectives have been a regular feature of the American political scene since World War II. Recall the response to Harry Truman's nasal twang and down-home rhetoric, the disdain for Dwight Eisenhower's convoluted syntax and Lyndon Johnson's cornpone style, and the celebration of Adlai Stevenson's eloquence and John Kennedy's verbal grace. But the new class has been decisive in only a few political events of our times: the conflict over McCarthyism, the intensification of cultural conflict in politics, and the bureaucratization of almost everything.

Even today, two-and-a-half decades later, the set of events called McCarthyism resonates across the barriers of generation and time. The curious disproportion between the actual events and the emotions they have evoked in the political folklore of the century signifies that the controversy—like a fairy tale—raised perennial anxieties and provided a meaningful and reassuring resolution. The putative stakes in the struggle were the right of Communists and their sympathizers to hold jobs in government and in government-related enterprises. The actual prize was jurisdiction over the symbolic environment. Government was increasingly trying to reinforce with sanctions the demand for loyalty, and there was also a more generalized demand for conformity. Again and again, McCarthy and those associated with his crusade confused Communists with nonconformists, loyalty toward the regime with attitudes toward public ownership, religion, and even football. And McCarthy's foes, understanding as well as he did that the stakes were higher than stated, not only attacked his procedures and the impulse to social conformity, but also rejected the notion that government had any jurisdiction over the attitudes of its citizens.

McCarthy served then and now as a symbol of the demand that intellectuals support the values and beliefs of the society, revere what the society defines as sacred, and respect whomever the society defines as authorities and whatever it defines as authoritative. The extent to which McCarthy became a symbol for the demands of what was then termed the "radical right" is clear in the rhetoric and analyses contemporary with the events. Richard Hofstadter identified McCarthyism as a variant of status politics, emphasized McCarthy's demand for generalized conformity, and suggested that the "pseudoconservatives" of the radical right, of whom McCarthy was the prototype, had as their true targets "liberals, critics and nonconformists of various sorts as well as Communists and suspected Communists."[6] Garry Wills recently went even further, suggesting that McCarthyism should be equated with anti-Communism of all varieties. "It is unfortunate," he asserted in a paean to Lillian Hellman, "that McCarthyism was named teleologically for its most perfect product, rather than genetically—which would give us Trumanism."

The struggle against McCarthy, which now has the character of an epic, quickly came to stand for the demand of the new class for autonomy in the realms of truth and values, for jurisdiction over culture. The intellectuals won, and their victory was a precondition of the rise of the counterculture in the 1960s. And the fear of McCarthyism still continues because their authority never seems as secure or as complete as it might. It is challenged from time to time by parents or elected officials demanding control over textbooks, or by a prosecutor with an indictment for conspiracy to incite draft evasion or violence. The intensity of the intellectuals' opposition to Barry Goldwater's presidential campaign was guaranteed by his offensive against their cultural dominance. The mutual hostility of the new class and Richard Nixon was rooted in the conviction that he was still a censor at heart, who, if the opportunity presented itself, would turn the control of culture back to the Yahoos of the radical right. The Hiss case, too, I suspect, has been from the beginning part of the struggle for the control of culture. The reluctance of some intellectuals to accept Hiss' guilt (or Chambers' charges) is rooted in their prior reluctance to accept the notion that a government can legitimately demand loyalty from its citizens. The legitimization of disloyalty is, after all, only the next step (the last?) in a long process of emancipating the individual from ascriptive identifications. Our national progress down this particular slippery slope is already far advanced: from Private Slovik to "fragging" in Vietnam, from vigilante justice for draft "dodgers" to amnesty for war resisters, from Ezra Pound's incarceration to antiwar parades featuring Viet Cong flags and U.S. Senators, from the execution of spies to the prosecution of counterspies. Once the claims of the collectivity to the loyalty of its members are abandoned, and membership is made a matter of individual decision, the concept of treason is void, and rehabilitation is granted to "principled" spies.

While Joseph McCarthy symbolized the threatening demand for conformity, in the early 1950s the urbane and articulate Stevenson symbolized the promise of power to come and served as a catalyst for a new political generation. The appearance of significant numbers of college-educated, socially mobile, issue-oriented voters in urban and suburban reform clubs was noted by political observers in New York, California, Wisconsin, Missouri, and elsewhere.[7]

The new middle-class activists brought distinctive goals, standards, and styles into the political arena. Their ideal was almost invariably "reform," defined as wresting power from traditional leaders and organizations and transferring it to themselves and their political factions. Their new standards required that politics be conducted by articulate volunteers rather than political professionals who spoke like Richard Daley. The new style was issue-oriented, moralistic, and reformist.

The politics of the early 1950s provide the model for new-class concerns. McCarthy and Stevenson symbolized the issues and candidates with the continuing capacity to mobilize large portions of the new class. The Vietnam War and the Kennedys generated similar levels of antagonism and admiration in the

1960s. Like the struggle against McCarthyism, the antiwar movement pitted relatively educated, high-status nonconformists against traditionalists. That the peace marchers were far more aggressive in their defiance of traditional taboos than the timid victims of Joe McCarthy had been reflected the distance that the cultural revolution had proceeded. That the Kennedys were able to reap larger political profits from their personal elegance than Stevenson reflected the growing tendency to judge politics by standards previously reserved for entertainment. Both changes were at least in part a consequence of the enhanced influence of the new class in politics.

Since the struggle over McCarthyism, the involvement of basic cultural symbols in the political arena has become a regular feature of our politics. As *avant garde* culture spread through rising college enrollments, the electronic media, and mass-circulation magazines, antibourgeois attitudes previously limited to a few became the bases of the antiestablishment politics of the 1960s—with the "establishment" defined as nothing less than the entire social order. The presidential politics of 1968 and 1972 featured a full-scale challenge to the legitimacy of most of the society's major institutions—family, schools, trade unions, business, and especially government.* By 1968, significant portions of the nation's elite had responded empathetically to new-class critiques of traditional authority, obedience, discipline, law and order, force, and other key values of the political culture. There first began a dramatic and continued decline of popular confidence in political parties, politicians, government, courts, business, labor, and even the media, and a sharp increase in popular cynicism. Second, within the new class a backlash developed among intellectuals who found the counterculture and the New Politics less compelling and more dangerous than the traditional culture (especially the traditional political culture), which in turn stimulated a challenge within the intellectual community to the political doctrine and influence of the adversary culture. (The neo-conservative movement, the Coalition for a Democratic Majority, *Commentary, The Public Interest, The American Spectator*, and some of the New Right are the agents of this challenge.) Third, the intensified assault on traditional values and institutions precipitated the disintegration of traditional liberalism and conservatism. Eugene McCarthy, George McGovern, George Wallace, and Richard Nixon were both agents and beneficiaries of this process. Lyndon Johnson and Hubert Humphrey were among its principal casualties.

The election of 1972 nicely illustrated the politics of cultural polarization. In that election, issues achieved a salience unique in modern presidential politics. The issues that preempted voter attention were not the bread-and-butter questions that had structured the electorate since the New Deal, but cultural and

---

*It is doubtless significant that the media and the universities were simultaneously assaulted from the Right.

social questions that created new cleavages and coalitions pitting supporters of traditional notions of work and welfare, war and peace, law and legitimacy against supporters of the counterculture. Antiwar demonstrations celebrated new lifestyles and articulated new demands (including the right to support an enemy with whom the nation was actually if not legally at war). Welfare policy became involved in conflicting views of the work ethic, and day-care programs with the debate over women's liberation. Environmental protection was enmeshed in a generalized assault on technology, and law-enforcement policy entangled with broader judgements concerning the legitimacy of the social order. Cultural politics are especially intense because they involve values anchored in egocentrism.

The introduction of cultural conflict into American politics dramatizes the developing cleavages in the society and their social bases. It is now clear that the assault on the traditional culture was mounted by young and not-so-young representatives of the relatively privileged classes, while the basic institutions of the society were defended by less-prosperous, less-educated, lower-status citizens. A byproduct of these developments was a redefinition of the concept of liberalism (one version of which became the ideology of the privileged) and conservatism (a version of which is now the position of the less privileged); a partial realignment of the social bases of the two parties (with the Democrats acquiring the upper-income devotees of cultural liberalism and losing the loyalties and votes of a significant portion of the white working class); and growing distance between the political elite, which was heavily influenced by new-class liberalism, and the rank-and-file voters, who remained traditionalist in their cultural perspectives.

Cultural conflict played a much smaller role in the politics of 1976, doubtless because both parties were led by men who cultivated traditional virtues in their personal lives and avoided inflamatory rhetoric in their public lives. Since no candidate symbolized a challenge to the traditional political culture, there was only limited interest in its defense (though nearly enough to make Ronald Reagan the Republican nominee). However, it would be premature to assume that consensus has been restored to American politics. Most of the disagreements of the previous decade remain; most of the issues of the previous decade are still debated within the new class, where arguments are ready and waiting for the candidates and issues to dramatize them.

An equally important consequence of the increased political influence of the new class on American government is the expansion of what has come to be known as "the public sector." Although the expansion of government in this century is sometimes considered a defining characteristic of modernity, it is not really clear that government growth was an inevitable consequence of industrialization or modernization.

What is certain is that government's functions have both expanded and changed as conceptions of the purposes of government have changed. Theories of government change before governments change. Adam Smith made the case for a market economy before mercantilism was dismantled; Marx made the case for state ownership before the Bolshevik revolution; various socialists, neo-idealists, and communitarians made the case against minimal government and for expansion of government's role in the economy and society decades before governments began to assume these functions.

The New Deal brought significant numbers of intellectuals and semiintellec-tuals into government for the first time, to solve pressing problems that eluded other solutions. In fact, the perceptions that poverty and joblessness were intolerable and that government could and should do something about them preceded the New Deal and shaped its programs.

Historical conceptions of problems and appropriate responses vary along with other aspects of the culture.* As the contemporary culture specialists, the new class has a large and, I believe, decisive influence that in recent decades has been exercised to shift responsibility for the quality of social life from the individual, family, and other private groups to government. Two arguments were made to justify this shift: first, widely acknowledged ills were not being met satisfactorily, and second, transfers would promote social justice. These two motives frequently lead to quite different kinds of programs, although the differences are denied or glossed over. For example, it is sometimes argued that mandated busing is "merely" a logical extension of *Brown v. Board of Education*, or that racial or sexual quotas are "only" a logical extension of outlawing discrimination, or that regulations stipulating the size of toilet seats for employees are "only" a logical extension of the same concern for work safety involved in mine inspection. But there are important differences among these uses of government that are central to the current agenda of the new class and to the debates that have developed within it.

Until sometime in the mid-1960s, reform proceeded in reponse to some concrete evil. Since then, more and more reforms have been stimulated by the goals of reformers, rather than the desires of the affected groups. It is almost impossible to overstate the importance of the distinction between government programs that are desired by their beneficiaries, promulgated by elected offi-cials, and carried out with the consent of the affected communities and pro-grams that are undertaken because of a bureaucratic or judicial conception of the good of the putative beneficiaries, promulgated by judges and bureaucrats

---

*As I write, there are in the street below my office five Washington policemen with walkie-talkies, at least two police vehicles, and God knows how many "support personnel" busily defending passersby from a swarm of bees that has inexplicably invaded this urban sanctuary. Grateful though I am to have avoided stings, I cannot help wondering when protecting the populace against beestings was added to the list of government's purposes.

who are not politically accountable, and imposed by force on resisting communities. The difference is nothing less than the distinction between democratic government and the revolutionary dictatorship of a coercive elite. The fundamental premise of self-government is that ordinary people are better able to judge their own interests than any ruler is. The basic premise of dictatorship is that, by virtue of its superior wisdom, a vanguard is best able to judge the interests of everyone—since almost all are too blinded by "false consciousness" to know what they need or even what they "really" want.

No universal abstract principle can mechanically distinguish between caring that sustains and caring that coerces. There are only endless specific judgments about when and where the cumbersome and coercive machinery of government will reinforce autonomy and when it will subvert it. The peculiar predilection of intellectuals to a rationalist approach which pushes principles and policies toward their "logical" conclusion makes these distinctions especially troublesome. Harold D. Lasswell noted, in his *World Revolutionary Elites*, that revolutions of the "post bourgeois" era had brought symbol specialists to power in Fascist Italy, Nazi Germany, the Soviet Union, and China, as part of "the major transformation [of our times which] is the decline of business and of earlier social formations and the rise of intellectuals and semi-intellectuals to effective power." Lasswell's collaborator, Daniel Lerner, called these "new men with new ideas" "coercive ideologues" and noted that "each totalitarian regime began with its variant of 'intelligentsia' at or near the apex of the new elite." Supplementing Aristotle's observation that men do not become tyrants in order to avoid exposure to the cold, Lasswell and Lerner suggested that in our times men become tyrants because they believe they can use political power to bring society, culture, and personality into conformity with their vision of what they should be.

The political temptation of the new class lies in believing that their intelligence and exemplary motives equip them to reorder the institutions, the lives, and even the characters of almost everyone—this is the totalitarian temptation. This is also the reason that a politics featuring large roles for intellectuals is especially dangerous to human liberty.

Obviously, a free society cannot eliminate the new class from politics, any more than it can eliminate businessmen or truck drivers. But a society that cherishes liberty will do well to protect itself from the excesses of the new class. As surely as a monopoly of power or wealth is dangerous to the rest of us, a new-class monopoly on meaning and purpose is incompatible with the common weal.

NOTES

1. Harold D. Lasswell and Daniel Lerner (eds.), *World Revolutionary Elites* (Cambridge, Mass., 1965).

2. J.A. Schumpeter, *Capitalism, Socialism, and Democracy* (New York, 1950), p. 147.

3. Jeane J. Kirkpatrick, *The New Presidential Elite* (New York, 1976), p. 248.

4. Ibid., p. 274.

5. Ibid., p. 261.

6. In Daniel Bell (ed.), *The New American Right* (New York, 1955).

7. The type has been described for nearly two decades: Frank J. Sorauf, "Extra-Legal Political Parties in Wisconsin," *American Political Science Review* 48 (1954): 692-704; James Q. Wilson, *The Amateur Democrat* (Chicago, 1962); Francis Carney, *The Rise of Democratic Clubs in California* (New York, 1958); Stephen A. Mitchell, *Elm Street Politics* (New York, 1959); Robert S. Hirshfield et al., "A Profile of Political Activists in Manhattan," *Western Political Quarterly* 15 (1962): 489-507; Robert H. Salisbury, "The Urban Party Organization Member," *Public Opinion Quarterly* 29 (1965-66): 550-64; Dennis S. Ippolito, "Motivational Reorientation and Change among Party Activists," *Journal of Politics* 31 (1969): 1098-1101; Leon D. Epstein, *Political Parties in Western Democracies* (New York, 1967), pp. 122-26; Donald C. Blaisdel, *The Riverside Democrats* (New Brunswick, 1960).

4

THE WORLDVIEW OF THE
NEW CLASS:
Secularity and Its
Discontents

Peter L. Berger

The New Class first publicly manifested itself as an ideological novelty. Only later was the question raised of its roots in the social structure. This is not surprising: The glittering symbolism of the "superstructure" is more easily perceived than the vested interests, ambitions, and resentments of the "substructure." Nor is it surprising that this ideological innovation, like so many others before it, has been greeted in both extravagant and sharply contradictory fashion. To some, the New Class heralds the moral renascence of Western civilization; to others, it is the embodiment of decadence. Neither judgment is very helpful in gaining an objective understanding of the phenomenon, but the vehemence of both suggests that it touches upon passions that, throughout history, have been religious in character. The relation of the New Class to religion is therefore of some importance—indeed, of the utmost importance, to the point that the New Class cannot be adequately understood without grasping its religious dimension.

The New Class is an international phenomenon, at least throughout the advanced industrial societies of the West. I will focus, however, only on American society. Luckily, there does exist a considerable body of empirical data concerning the relationship of religion and class in America. Unfortunately, these data reveal little if anything about the New Class, since they do not differentiate between the New Class and other groups, such as the older strata of the upper-middle class, within larger categories of income and socioeconomic status. One of the main findings over the years has been that religious affiliation rises along with class. Higher-income Americans go to church more often than lower-income Americans, as do the better-educated when compared with those with less education. Andrew Greeley has used such findings to argue that the secularization of the American elite has been exaggerated. His interpretation is probably valid for the period leading up to the appearance of the New Class. But the evidence available so far suggests that the New Class has quite a different relation to religion.

In what follows, I will try to conceptualize the relationship between New Class ideology and religion, and to hypothesize about the roots of this relationship in the social structure. I must stress that my arguments are based on a relative paucity of controlled data and are, in principle, subject to modification as more data appear. One hypothesis, already indicated by the title of my piece, is that the New Class is indeed a highly secularized part of the American population, so that the old data about the relationship of class to religiosity do not apply. This hypothesis, however, is advanced on empirical rather than theoretical grounds. It is based on (admittedly impressionistic) social experience of New Class milieus, but also on the available ideological output of New Class spokesmen.

For the purposes of analysis, it is always a good idea to use terminology that is recognizable and perhaps even palatable to the group in question. The term "secular humanism" probably meets this requirement. "Secular" means the exclusion of transcendent or divine dimensions of reality. "Humanism" denotes a moral and perhaps even emotional orientation—compassion for and identification with the victims of social injustice, and a conviction that man is the measure of all things, that there are no standards other than humanly created ones.

To what extent the ideas and values of the New Class can be called "humanistic" is, at least in part, a matter of ethics rather than social science. Members of the New Class do commonly pride themselves on their humanitarian sensitivities, particularly their finely honed sense of compassion. During the movement against American involvement in the Indochina war, this class (though, of course, it was never called that) supposedly made up the new "constituency of conscience." Be this as it may, the New Class is a sector of the American population in which moral discourse is of a particularly intense quality. Moral exhortation has become the routine style of its spokesmen; one would have to go into hard-core areas of the Bible Belt to find anything comparable today.

But what about the secularism of the New Class? Much of its ideology, one may readily agree, could be held—and is held today—by religious as well as nonreligious people. Indeed, there is what may be called a powerful New Class lobby in the major religious denominations in America (a topic that cannot be dealt with here), and there have also been religious resurgences within the New Class. Still, my assumption is that the New Class, in the main, is a highly secularized group.

If this assumption is valid, the ideology of the New Class functions as a secular theodicy. The term "theodicy" is to be understood in the sense given it by Max Weber: any coherent explanation of suffering and evil. Throughout human history, religion supplied this crucial social and individual explanation—not necessarily through a belief in an afterlife (many religious traditions had no such belief) or by justifying existing social inequities (Marx's "opium of the people"), but always by *attributing meaning* to the human experiences of pain, sorrow, and moral injury. The meanings supplied by religion decrease or disappear altogether as secularization progresses. How, then, can suffering and evil be made meaningful? The struggle for a better world is one answer to this question. The ideology of the new class *locates* the painful realities in specific social processes; the political and/or therapeutic programs advocated by the New Class then supply the inspiration (so to speak) that makes the perception of suffering and evil emotionally tolerable. Some years ago the late Ernest Becker, in a brilliant and much-neglected book,[1] argued that all modern social science was motivated by the urge to construct a secular theodicy. The same argument applies even more to aspects of modern social thought that are geared to programs of political or individual melioration—and, above all, to leftist programs. The quasireligious function of modern revolutionary ideologies—to provide a secular substitute for the Judaeo-Christian eschatology—has often been analyzed; this analysis need not be repeated here. Suffice it to say that the secularism of the New Class insures its continuing susceptibility to revolutionary ideology.

In the absence of a reliable symbolic universe of meanings, the ideology of the New Class also supplies meanings for both the larger institutions of society and personal existence. (Emile Durkheim, somewhat ambiguously, called this "religion," but he meant by this all sorts of beliefs that would not ordinarily be called religious.) Modernization gravely threatens this universe of meanings, especially through the process of secularization. The symbolic universe becomes remote, uncertain, unreliable, imposing a quite new and deeply disturbing burden on the individual. The order of meanings, previously provided by his social milieu, must now be painfully and continually constructed by himself. Willy-nilly, every individual must become a world-builder. Since the task of constructing and then maintaining a coherent view of reality is impossibly difficult for most individuals, modern society has created a market in which world-maintenance kits, so to speak, are available in packaged form. Every modern ideology is such a package (except where the state has a monopoly on the ideological market). The ideology of the New Class has been a very successful package, by appealing to class needs, both social and psychic. When "purchased," such an ideology provides a more or less cohesive set of meanings that help organize the public involvements and private problems of individuals.[2]

The imperfections of the world, and most of all the ultimate imperfections of human mortality, have always been painful. The pain becomes excessively sharp in the wake of secularization, as the world is divested of all transcendent meanings. In this century, Albert Camus was perhaps the most eloquent voice describing the intolerable cha.   ter of this condition of loss and the irresistible urge to rebellion that it engenders. The quest for perfection, and perhaps implicitly for immortality, becomes very intense, taking on a quality of messianic urgency. Does this rebellious refusal to accept the existing world eventually lead to a denial of reality, especially the reality of human finitude and death? This question is one of philosophy rather than social science. My question is more modest: What are some of the structural causes for the secular humanism of the New Class?

This question belongs to the sociology of knowledge; it can only be answered hypothetically. Three relevant hypotheses may be offered. First, secular humanism results from the weakening, and in many instances the destroying, of the relatively small and isolated communities in which human beings lived through most of history. Modernity means living with a great variety of people and divergent, often contradictory, meanings and values. So certainty is hard to achieve. Its loss is especially noticeable in the areas of morality and religion, because coherent and continual social reinforcement is especially important. Modernity constantly forces one god to rub shoulders with all other gods, thus eroding the individuality of each. This in turn promotes tolerance: To the degree that all gods become interchangeable, religion becomes a matter of "preference." So secularism is linked with "humanism"—if a broad tolerance of every conceivable "preference" is to be defined as humanistic.

The plurality of values and meanings has been a mark of modernization since its inception; contemporary effects can be seen most dramatically in the Third World. Western societies, and American society more than any other, are highly pluralistic. The New Class, however, embodies perhaps the highest degree of pluralism. Members of the New Class move easily in and out of widely divergent sociocultural milieus; many of them have decisively moved out of the milieu of their birth. Their education has exposed them to precisely the sort of "critical" thought by which modernity has tried to cope with the blurring of former certainties—that is, the "modern scientific worldview," which animates higher education in modern societies. And the affluence of the New Class means that its members can "purchase" freely from the market of available ideologies—and thus "purchase" the packages that are most congenial to their individual and collective needs.

Second, secular humanism arises from the occupational roots of the New Class in the production and distribution of knowledge and in the agencies of planning and administration, where power derives from the manipulation of symbols rather than things. This line of argument is "Marxian"; it most directly links ideology to the socioeconomic interests of its adherents. There is a hard political side to this link: The ideology of the New Class, at least as it impinges on public concerns, enhances the power and the privileges of the New Class. This argument has recently been developed by the German sociologist Helmut Schelsky, in an analysis of the West German leftist intelligentsia.[3] Irving Kristol has similarly analyzed the current "class struggle" in America between the New Class and the business class. Such analyses help explain that the New Class adheres to left-liberal causes because its interest is to do so. The "humanism" of the New Class, especially in its intense moralism, may then be seen in essentially Marxian (or, even better, Nietzschean) terms—as a weapon in a struggle for power. The class interests of the New Class are masked by appeals to compassion and by the claim that they contribute to the welfare of the downtrodden. But whatever benefits the poor may have gained from the "war against poverty," there is little doubt about the benefits garnished by New Class professionals and bureaucrats administering the poverty programs. Schelsky has summed up these New Class interests in a neat formula: *"Belehrung, Betreuung, Beplanung"*—indoctrinating, caring, and planning, all justified as promoting the welfare of the general population.

Moreover, the highly abstract character of occupations in the "knowledge industry" socializes individuals into "critical" habits of thought that permit them, more than other people (such as businessmen or engineers, for instance, not to mention the lower-middle-class and working-class people), to handle the complex demands imposed by secularization. Put more simply, members of the New Class are more likely to have the theoretical tools necessary to cope with a world of moral and religious uncertainty—indeed, they are likely to have been taught that such uncertainty is a positive good.

Third, secular humanism results from the conditions under which most members of the New Class undergo primary socialization—the "new childhood," with its historically unprecedented physical health and psychic protectiveness. As the French historian Philippe Ariès has described in his classic work, the rising bourgeoisie of Europe "invented" childhood.[4] But it can be maintained that the "new childhood" has been greatly intensified, even "radicalized," by the American upper-middle class since about the 1930s. To say that child-rearing is now "permissive" may be correct, but this characterization is by no means exhaustive. More important than moral "permissiveness" is *cognitive* "permissiveness"—encouraging the child, from early on, to engage in the business of constructing his own symbolic universe. Because permissiveness is balanced by protectiveness, the child's universe will be a rather pleasant and "humanistic" one. The subsequent encounter with the harsher realities of social life are then likely to be very shocking. Both the sensitized compassion and moral outrage of the New Class may be explained by this shock.

Moreover, the new childhood also means that the pluralism of modernity is experienced by the individual at a very early age. Secularization is an expectable result when an individual has been exposed from early childhood to an array of relative systems of meaning. In this respect, the New Class shares some of the features of childhood with the broader upper-middle classes. However, the New Class has further institutionalized the "new childhood" and justified it with readily available psychological theories. Its children, in consequence, are peculiarly susceptible to both "humanism" and secularism.

These three arguments based on the sociology of knowledge rest on the master hypothesis of this article: that the New Class suffers greatly from the cognitive dislocations of modernity. The New Class in America is probably the most modernized group of people in the world today, not just in its social circumstance but also in the constitution of its consciousness. In the latter sense, the New Class is indeed a "vanguard."

The ideology of the New Class may depend not so much on developments in the realm of ideas as on the external social forces, especially the outcome of what Kristol has called the current "class struggle." Built-in tensions (a Marxist would say "contradictions") within the New Class consciousness are already pressing for resolution. The encounter of New Class morality with the hard realities of the real world may lead to disillusion, cynicism, or even a "neo-conservative" reaction; it might also lead to fanatical retrenchments. And the secularism of the New Class suffers from the weaknesses of any secular worldview in providing meanings and values to live by. The most serious of these are the unsatisfactory character of secular theodicies and the frustration of the apparently recurring quest for transcendence. The resurgences of religion within the New Class may be understandable reactions to its "repressive" secularism. If so, drugs, mysticism, meditation, and the revivalist movements of the "Age of Aquarius" would be much more than passing fashions.

NOTES

1. Ernest Becker, *The Structure of Evil* (New York, 1963).

2. For a general analysis of the relation of modernity to meaning see Peter Berger, Brigitte Berger, and Hansfried Kellner, *The Homeless Mind* (New York, 1973), and Peter Berger, *Facing Up To Modernity* (New York, 1977).

3. Helmut Schelsky, *Die Arbeit tun die anderen* (Oplanden, DBR, 1975).

4. Philippe Ariès, *Centuries of Childhood* (New York, 1962).

5

BUSINESS AND THE NEW CLASS

Robert L. Bartley

Although its intellectual roots can of course be found earlier, the concept of the New Class crystalized for me, and I suspect for many contributors to this volume, during the wave of student activism that began in 1965 with the Free Speech Movement at Berkeley and crested in 1970 with the tragedy at Kent State. The conventional wisdom is that the "campus revolts" arose from the moral revulsion against the Vietnam War. No doubt, protest was also partly fueled by the guilt of middle-class students at receiving college deferments while working-class youths were being drafted to fight and sometimes to die. But this has never been a wholly satisfactory explanation. The Free Speech Movement, for example, came before Vietnam was an overriding concern. And the student rebellion quickly spread to universities in Europe, where no one was in danger of dying in Southeast Asia. Besides, the rhetoric of "the counterculture" reached far beyond the draft and the war, suggesting a fundamental change in not only the structure but the values of the entire society.

A more satisfying explanation would take account of two immediately apparent facts. First, the revolt came from an especially large, and thus ultimately influential and important, age cohort. The college graduates of 1968 were born in 1947 at the crest of the postwar "baby boom." Second and even more obvious, the revolts took place in colleges, especially at the most prestigious universities. They drew considerable support and, with a few exceptions, only cowardly opposition from the university faculties, even though they often challenged values, like freedom of speech, that are fundamental to the academic pursuit of knowledge.

These two facts rapidly prompted an investigation of the subculture of the intellectuals. Lionel Trilling's observations about "the adversary culture" took on a new relevance during this period. Trilling observed that the intellectuals' calling made them natural critics of society; as a class, they reinforced and intensified this adversary stance by natural peer pressures. Although the members of "the counterculture" were not exactly intellectuals—one of my less charitable friends christened them "intellectualoids"—they clearly were close enough to be influenced by the impulses Trilling had described.

Trilling's elegant explanation had a special relevance to the plight of business in the 1960s. The most prominent private institutions of the society under attack were, of course, the large corporations. Significantly, Joseph A. Schumpeter, very likely the greatest economist of our century, had warned that the inability to control the critical impulses of intellectuals would prove the ultimate undoing of the capitalist system. When the class of 1968 began tearing up the nation's campuses, it was easy to imagine Schumpeter's prediction coming true almost overnight, and to envision "the counterculture" and its sympathizers sweeping into positions of power and influence in the immediate future.

Ten years later, society is indeed much different—but not necessarily in the expected ways. Southeast Asia lies in the grip of Communist dictatorships, with grizzly stories of atrocities emerging steadily from once-gentle Cambodia. The universities are facing a student shortage and are probably declining in influence. Members of the class of 1968 are ten years older, and many of them are turning out to be members of the "establishment." Indeed, some of the brightest have joined the counterreformation, the intellectual movement—often called "neo-conservative," for want of a better term—broadly represented in this volume. The society pages report that marriage is more popular than ever, and the Harvard class of 1978 stood in the rain to cheer Alexander Solzhenitsyn for telling them that they and their kind are cowards. It would seem that we underestimated the resilience of society, and that Schumpeter's forecast will be delayed, at least for a while. Indeed, the outcome of the struggle over capitalism may even be in doubt.

Yet the last ten years have actually witnessed something that looks suspiciously like a concerted attack on business, by something that looks suspiciously like the New Class. A whole new industry of "public-interest advocates" has sprung up to bedevil business over issues like pollution, safety, "questionable" payments abroad, executive perquisites, and so on. And this adversary agenda has been adopted by a new breed of powerful government regulatory agencies: EPA, OSHA, EEOC, and the like.

Much of this agenda is in principle commendable; not even businessmen oppose protecting the environment, equal opportunity, safety, and honesty. The problem is that these ends are pursued with little regard for other goals and values, particularly providing jobs and a higher material standard of living. Businesses that can eliminate 90 percent of pollution cheaply are asked to eliminate 99 percent at a possibly prohibitive cost. Businesses are in jeopardy of denying "equal opportunity" unless their workforce exactly reflects the racial and sexual composition of the population—a patently impossible goal, given the realities of history and biology. Laws are proposed to outlaw "political contributions" by businesses abroad, even in nations, like Canada, that encourage them as a public duty. Laws have been passed that stop a nearly complete $100-million dam in a dispute over a three-inch minnow that was discovered as a species long after the dam was started. A similar dispute stopped Consolidated Edison's Storm King pumped-storage power station, which almost surely would have turned the 1977 New York blackout into a trivial incident. Regulatory or "public-interest" advocates attack each alternative power project on different grounds until none can go forward.

In the midst of this kind of zealotry, it is not hard to locate the interests of the New Class, whose members populate, draw economic support from, and above all wield power in the name of the "public-interest" groups and regulatory agencies. Indeed, when activists advocate a "no-growth economy," one in which the power of the business class would necessarily fall, and anyone with an upper-middle class income would be secure from the threat of social mobility, their intentions are quite clear: a society in which rewards would no longer be distributed in wealth, but in power and status, to be won by precisely those skills (abstraction, moralistic rhetoric, manipulation of symbols) in which the highly educated New Class excels.

There is no better embodiment of this adversary agenda than Mr. Public Citizen—Ralph Nader, Inc. Nader was originally put into business by the multiple blunders of General Motors, which coughed up $400,000 and a public apology for sending a private detective to investigate him, supposedly on the suspicion that his impending book, *Unsafe at Any Speed*, which attacked GM's Corvair, was connected with lawsuits making similar claims.

Nader has skillfully parlayed this initial stake into ownership (in effect) of the Center for Study of Responsive Law, Public Citizen, the Public Interest Research Group, the Center for Women Policy Studies, the Small Claims Study Group, the Tax Reform Research Study Group, the Retired Professionals Action Group, Public Citizen Litigation Group, Health Research Group, Citizen Action Group, Aviation Consumer Action Project, Capitol Hill News Service, the Center for Auto Safety, the Center for Concerned Engineering,

Clearinghouse for Professional Responsibility, Corporate Responsibility Research Group, Fisherman's Clear Water Action Group, Professional Drivers, Professionals for Auto Safety, the Public Citizen Visitors Center, and Congress Watch.

As head of this largely tax-exempt conglomerate, Nader has carefully cultivated the image of a financial and sexual ascetic, telling reporters that he takes only $5,000 of his income annually for his personal expenditures, and that his sex life is a private matter. Every man is entitled to his own tastes in personal images, of course, but Nader's selection has served the purpose of stressing his single-minded devotion to "the public interest."

His image was clouded somewhat, though, when David Sanford, the *New Republic* writer who had originally discovered the GM detective following Nader, decided to air his growing doubts about the folk hero in his 1976 book *Me and Ralph*. While Nader claims to live in an $85-a-month apartment, for example, Sanford found neighbors to testify that he actually lives in an $80,000 home (1971 prices) owned by his brother Shakeef.

Sanford's investigations into the financial side of the Nader empire are even more interesting. He repeats the standard estimate that Nader personally earns $250,000 a year from speaking and writing. He is said to plough most of this back into his organizations, no doubt giving him the benefit of deductions for charitable contributions (though Sanford says that Nader's personal contributions are often to his nonexempt lobbying investigations). Nader has persistently refused to discuss his finances in detail or to release tax returns. Surely he is too shrewd to end up on the IRS list of persons with high gross incomes but no tax liability. But just as surely many $250,000-a-year executives wish they could find as many tax shelters for using their income to finance their individual infatuations.

Nader's personal earnings, of course, are only the tip of the iceberg. Public Citizen has taken in more than $1 million in contributions during a single year. There are also large foundation grants to his various organizations—for example, $316,000 from the Carnegie Foundation to the Consumer Complaint Research Center. There is also a large imputed income from his ability to attract volunteers and employees to work at low salaries (the image of an ascetic certainly helps in this regard). The contributors, foundation executives, and volunteers, of course, tend to be archetypal members of the New Class.

These points are worth belaboring, not out of any animus to Nader, who is obviously a highly intelligent entrepreneur, but to show how a successful career can be built by attacking business. As Sanford notes, Nader has been the prime mover behind some thirty-five books and reports, and has been widely credited with passage of legislation like the National Traffic and Vehicle Safety Act, the Highway Safety Act, the Wholesome Meat Act, the Natural Gas Pipeline Safety Act, and the Comprehensive Occupational Health and Safety Act.

All this is of course only partly an individual accomplishment. Like other entrepreneurs before him, Nader's genius was in identifying a hitherto unexploited market. His consumers—the contributors, the volunteers, the foundation supporters—are chiefly people who fit the definition of the New Class, with a class interest in derogating the opposing business class. They have been able to bestow on him celebrity, personal security, and control of very considerable financial resources. They have made him a person of power in American society.

Predictably, Nader has inspired a host of imitators, founding not only his own conglomerate but an entire industry. "Public-interest" law firms, in particular, support an increasing number of young attorneys. The largest law firm in the environmental movement, The Natural Resources Defense Council, has a budget of $2 million a year. Its board of trustees includes such people as Barbara Ward, Nobel Prize winner Joshua Lederberg, Yale's Sterling Professor of Law, Boris I. Bittker, and actor Robert Redford. It has been active in supporting litigation to get New York City to enforce an impossible traffic control plan, for example, and in suits delaying the exploration of oil off the East Coast. The NRDC is particularly interesting because it is practically a creature of the Ford Foundation. It was founded in 1970 with an initial grant of $100,000; subsequent Ford grants included $765,000 in 1972, $800,000 in 1974, and $340,000 in 1976.

Many of the great fortunes built from business empires have now been captured by intellectuals, and are now being used in effect to attack business and advance the New Class. The frustration that businessmen feel at this was never more poignantly expressed than when Henry Ford II resigned from the Ford Foundation Board of Trustees, severing the last link between the foundation and the family that founded it. Ford wrote:

> The Foundation exists and thrives on the fruits of our economic system. The dividends of competitive enterprise make it all possible. A significant portion of the abundance created by U.S. business enables the Foundation and like institutions to carry on their work. In effect, the Foundation is a creature of capitalism—a statement that, I'm sure, would be shocking to many professional staff people in the field of philanthropy. It is hard to discern recognition of this fact in anything the Foundation does. It is even more difficult to find any understanding of this in many of the institutions, particularly the universities, that are the beneficiaries of the Foundation's grant programs.

> I'm not playing the role of the hard-headed tycoon who thinks all philanthropoids are socialists and all university professors are communists. I'm just suggesting to the Trustees and the staff that the system

that makes the Foundation possible very probably is worth preserving. Perhaps it is time for the Trustees and staff to examine the question of our obligations to our economic system and to consider how the Foundation, as one of the system's most prominent offspring, might act most wisely to strengthen and improve its progenitor.

New Class attitudes and interests are troublesome enough within the foundations and the "public-interest" movement. But the real trouble comes when these attitudes carry over into government, particularly into the regulatory agencies. Most young lawyers who are willing to pass up promising careers in the private sector, for example, are likely to carry a large overlay of New Class attitudes. Even a conservative federal administration thus finds it difficult to avoid this cast in staffing its regulatory agencies.

When the Carter administration took office, the "public-interest" movement became one of its chief recruiting grounds. Juan Cameron of *Fortune* wrote, "Nader's Invaders are Inside the Gates." He was able to find about sixty strategically placed administration officials who had come from one or another "public-interest" organization—fourteen on the White House staff, for example. In the Department of Justice, to take another example, Assistant Attorneys General came from the D.C. Public Defender Service, the NAACP Legal Defense and Education Fund, the Sierra Club, and the Mental Health Law Project.

Often these appointments involved significant personal advancement. Joan Claybrook, who earned $12,000 a year as head of Nader's Congress Watch, landed a $52,000-a-year job as head of the National Highway Traffic Safety Administration. She promptly pressed through auto-safety standards intended to mandate the long-controversial air bag, though evidence about its effectiveness was rapidly becoming more doubtful. (Auto makers may yet avoid this device, at least in some models, by developing seat belts that fasten automatically.)

Costly and excessive regulation of business can often come from established agencies. Soon after Michael Pertschuk took over the Federal Trade Commission, it considered a program to require cereal companies to pay for counteradvertising about the relationship between sugar and tooth decay. The Securities and Exchange Commission, established to protect investors, found itself policing corporate ethics by requiring disclosure of "questionable payments"—of very doubtful relevance to stock values but of great use in discrediting the business class.

The recent regulatory surge has also succeeded in creating new regulatory bodies, the most notable of which is the Occupational Safety and Health Administration. Founded in 1971, OSHA promptly set about decreeing the proper heights of fire extinguishers, worrying about the placement of exit signs, requiring coat hooks in toilet stalls, and issuing booklets warning farmers that manure is slippery and may cause falls. OSHA's inspections were so burdensome, especially for small businessmen, that a case was actually taken to the Supreme Court, which ruled that the agency needed warrants but did not need to show probable cause of violations. Various reforms have been promised, but OSHA now proposes to increase the number of workplace inspections from 200,000 in fiscal 1977 to 220,000 in fiscal 1979.

Meanwhile, it has been exceedingly difficult to trace any impact of OSHA on the accident statistics. On-the-job death rates in manufacturing in 1977 were almost identical with those in 1960. Deaths in nonmanufacturing jobs fell between 1971 and 1977, following a trend reaching back to 1937. The Department of Labor's own statistics on injuries show that, per 100 workers, accidents were responsible for 55.3 lost workdays in 1973, 54.6 in 1974, and 56.0 in 1975. How this compares with pre-OSHA years is impossible to tell, since one of the agency's first actions was to abolish the old statistical series. However, for the businesses reporting to the National Safety Council—that is, the most safety-conscious businesses—the injury rate steadily increased between 1970 and 1975, the last year of comparable NSC statistics.

In fiscal 1979, OSHA—excluding the Mine Safety and Health Administration—was scheduled for a budget increase of 19 percent, to $162.7 million.

Cui bono?

Among others, John Froines. Froines first came to national attention as a member of the Chicago Seven, tried for and eventually acquitted of charges of conspiring to incite violence at the 1968 Chicago Democratic Party Convention. A Yale Ph.D., Froines dropped full-time antiwar activities to teach chemistry at Goddard College in Vermont in 1972. In 1974, he became director of occupational health in the Vermont Health Department. In 1977, he joined OSHA as director of its Office of Toxic Substances, a GS-15 position.

"After the trial," Froines told James W. Singer of *National Journal*, "I felt committed to the antiwar movement and I didn't feel I could coexist as a scientist in a university. I felt I had separate identities. Doing this kind of work, I feel I'm able to bring together my social commitment and my scientific training."

Now there is no reason to doubt that in talking of "social commitment," Froines is thinking of saving lives. Nor is there cause to doubt that Claybrook actually thinks the air bag will work, or that the NRDC staff believes everyone's lot would be improved by banning the automobile from Manhattan Island. Least of all is there any reason to doubt that Nader sincerely believes in his own righteousness. Yet none of this precludes the usefulness of looking at class interest. The good burgher does not think of the interests of the bourgeoisie when he talks of the necessity to turn an honest profit. And while class interest surely does not explain all of his actions, it does explain a great deal.

And it certainly does seem that Froines, Claybrook, Nader, and at times even members of the Ford Foundation staff *define* their social commitment in terms of curbing the sins of the "establishment" in general and the depredations of business in particular. They see "the public interest" as opposing "the vested interest," or in other words, as attacking the business class. Surely it is worthy of note that they and their kind would gain in status and power from the kind of society they seem to want to create. And while it may be a slight oversimplification, it is hardly far-fetched to think of this agenda as a struggle between the business class and the New Class.

A few words need to be said about the other side. How well is business defending its own class interests? It does win some battles. Despite his past successes, or perhaps because of them, the birth of Nader's Consumer Protection Agency has repeatedly been thwarted. Even in the Department of Transportation, the Claybrook proposal for a network of 600 government stations for before-and-after evaluations of auto repairs was greeted with laughter. Yet the pressure remains, and in defending itself business suffers certain handicaps.

One is a "go-along" attitude, which has its roots in the knowledge that costs will be passed along to the consumer. If OSHA wants toilet coat hooks even in factories where no one wears coats, the simple thing to do is go buy some coat hooks anyway. If the government sets a quota for left-handed paper hangers, what real choice does business have except to hire, train, and promote left-handed people for paper hanging?

In any event, destroying business through this process is very slow work. You can raise costs: Dow Chemical estimates that its costs of complying with government regulation in 1976 were $186 million, up 27 percent from the previous year, and equivalent to 5.5 cents on every dollar of sales. Of these costs, Dow rated $83 million in regulatory costs as "excessive" or "questionable." The sheer paperwork, according to Dow, cost $20 million. But as long as people want the products business produces, it is very hard to prevent the corporation from passing these costs along in the price of the product.

In a specific business, the regulatory process starts to bite only when it prices the product out of the market. This seems to have happened with nuclear power plants. After winning safety standards that drove the investment costs through the roof, environmentalists are now starting to argue against nuclear power on economic grounds. The same thing may yet happen with the automobile. Rapidly mandated price increases for safety and fuel economy have not yet dramatically slowed sales, but perhaps only because consumers feel they should buy now because they know even more onerous standards are on the way. If auto sales collapse, the general economy will suffer, but with their skills and capital flows, Ford and GM will find something else to sell. Of course they will fight, but at some point they will exercise the option of "go-along."

Another handicap is a certain infiltration of business by the New Class itself. When business finds it has problems in the regulatory or public arena, its instinctive response is to seek out "the experts." Predictably enough, the experts—in public relations, advertising, law, etc.—have the skills of the New Class, and are thus the people most likely to share its outlooks, interests, and agendas. Their advice aggravates the natural tendency of business to look to short-term solutions—in other words, to capitulate.

The third and in my view the most important handicap is business' inability to unite in defending its class interests. Macy's does not think it is locked in competition with the New Class—it thinks the enemy is Gimbels. And if some regulatory ruling would add to Gimbels' problems faster than it will add to Macy's, the latter may very well be willing to pay the price.

Thus the air bag comes to us courtesy of not only Joan Claybrook but also the insurance industry. The economics of an insurance company are particularly difficult to calculate, since its earnings come from both underwriting and investment. If autos become more expensive to repair, the insurance companies may lose temporarily on underwriting income; but as those costs are passed along through higher premiums, the companies will have a larger cash flow for investment.

Similarly, the catalytic converter, an expensive device that may or may not produce cleaner air, comes to us courtesy of General Motors. GM switched its lobbying efforts at a crucial point in the debate over the converter, since its investments in the technology were by then made. The alternative technologies, which might have been better for the air in the long run if standards had been slightly lowered in the short run, belonged to Chrysler and Ford.

And of course, regulatory excess works inherently to the advantage of "industry leaders," the biggest and best-financed concerns. They have more resources to devote to dealing with regulators; in this struggle, they can outlast the competition. The big bureaucratic corporations are far more equivocal champions of free enterprise than the small individual entrepreneurs. The New Class regulator can divide and conquer.

For all of these reasons, individual corporations can defend themselves far more effectively than business can defend itself as a class. It may be to the advantage of some concern to go along with the coat hooks, or to drop its lobbying against some dubious safety device. But every time it does, it helps cement the notion that business is careless, that the public needs the protection of the New Class.

The ultimate class danger is that the regulatory (and tax) load will drive up prices, drive down profit opportunities, and eat up investment capital to the point where capitalism will be unable to deliver on its basic promise of a progressively higher standard of living for those less fortunate than most members of the New Class. When capitalism loses the ability to increase production, the New Class will win. Come to think of it, this is pretty much what Schumpeter predicted.

To conclude on a less gloomy note, business has a fourth handicap in any public battle. Its motives are perceived to be materialistic, even if the often different motives of competing corporations go unrecognized. This assumption has allowed the New Class to arrogate the term "public interest." If it is more widely recognized that the New Class has its own materialistic and power agenda, this disparity will be greatly diminished. It will then be easier to understand that business is sometimes right, and Ralph Nader and Friends are sometimes wrong—and even that the public interest may often be served by more careful attention to a balance between benefits and costs.

6

THE NEW CLASS AND THE PROFESSORIATE

Seymour Martin Lipset

Almost all the Western writers who have identified the emergence of the New Class—a socially liberal or radical, highly critical intelligentsia—locate its principal base in the academy, particularly among creative scholars and intellectuals. But this conception runs against the assumption of Marxist and other functionalist analyses that those who formulate the ideas and values legitimating the basic structures of society must serve the established interest. And throughout history, most intellectuals, most professors and purveyors of the written or spoken word, have largely accepted the prevailing values and institutions.[1]

Yet, since the Renaissance, both contemporary commentators and later historians have attributed a major role to the intellectuals in undermining the legitimacy of existing orders and in providing the vision of a new social system. The literati played an important role in the events leading up to the French Revolution; in 1798, President John Adams, who felt that the revolutionary turmoil stemmed from the academy, asked his Secretary of State to try to prevent a visit by a party of French savants. In 1873, Whitelaw Reid, the editor of *The New York Tribune*, expressed a similar view:

> Exceptional influences eliminated, the scholar is pretty sure to be opposed to the established. The universities of Germany contain the deadliest foes to the absolute authority of the Kaiser. The scholars of France prepared the way for the first Revolution, and were the most dangerous enemies of the imperial adventurer who betrayed the second.[2]

About the same time, Arinori Mori, the first Minister of Education in Meiji Japan, emphasized the need for an excellent educational system but noted that the universities could not be expected to accomplish their task without freedom of inquiry, which would inevitably produce dangerous thoughts: "what was taught in Tokyo University should not be conveyed to the masses...."[3]

Opposition to the established is compatible with a conservative or right-wing position as well as a liberal or left-wing one. In many countries, at different times, intellectual opposition to the status quo has frequently taken the form of a reactionary critique of democracy for creating a mass society in which the vulgar tastes of the populace destroyed creative culture, or in which demagogues or "alien" elements subverted national values. In nineteenth century America, the segment of the intellectual world linked to the elites of New England and the South tended to oppose egalitarianism and capitalist materialism. Similar attitudes also appeared in Europe and Latin America, and helped to undermine support for democracy in several countries. Wilhelm Ropke described the situation under the Weimar Republic:

> In Germany ... where the university professor has always had exceptional standing ... it was from the universities that most of the other intellectuals drew the disintegrating poison that they then distributed .... Naturally the faculties of social science provided a special opportunity for practicing intellectual treachery and preparing the way for Nazism.... [I]t is mainly the names of jurists and philosophers that could here be given.[4]

THE AMERICAN HISTORICAL RECORD

American academics and intellectuals are distinctive for their adversary role. Richard Hofstadter noted that "it has been the tradition of American intellectuals of all kinds and stamps to find themselves at odds with American society. This, I think, to a degree that is unusual elsewhere." D.P. Moynihan has stressed that since "about 1840, the cultural elite have pretty generally rejected the values and activities of the larger society. It has been said of America the culture [the intellectual elite] will not approve that which the polity strives to provide." Whitelaw Reid told graduating classes in 1873 that American academics were in the center of "radical" criticism of social institutions and that their political role was to be that of critic of the "established." In the next decade, James Bryce noted in *The American Commonwealth* that the college teachers "are at present among the most potent forces making for progress." Their influence

> tells primarily on their pupils and indirectly on the circles to which those pupils belong, or in which they work when they have left college. One is amused by the bitterness—affected scorn trying to disguise real fear— with which "college professors" are denounced by the professional politicians as unpractical, visionary, pharisaical, "kid-gloved," "high-toned," "un-American."

During the 1890s, according to the historian Laurence Veysey, "faculty opposition to imperialism . . . was observed as general all over the country." Leading academics continued to engage in antiwar agitation during the Spanish-American War and opposed suppression of the Filipino insurrection. According to a turn-of-the-century article in *The Atlantic Monthly*, college professors had acquired a reputation for taking obstructionist political positions and were being denounced as "traitors," and their utterances were credited as being "largely responsible for the assassination of President McKinley." In 1901, Whitelaw Reid noted that it was unfortunate for the country that college "instructors are out of sympathy with its history, with its development, and with the men who made the one and are guiding the other."[5]

Comparable, sometimes more extreme, evaluations of the political orientation of American faculty have been made in the twentieth century. They basically support Richard Hofstadter's estimate that "at least from the Progressive era onward, the political commitment of the majority of the intellectual leadership in the United States has been to causes that might be variously described as liberal (in the American sense of the word), progressive or radical."[6] According to Laurence Veysey, in the late nineteenth and early twentieth century

> academic mugwumpery [opposition to the established party system] symbolized the professor's relationship to all institutions, including his own: uneasy discontent, yet an unwillingness to "throw his vote away." He far preferred to purify one of the major parties . . . . and (commonly though not always) [he] adopted some form of Progressivism after 1900.

During the early 1920s, the visible discontent on the campuses led many in business and politics, including Calvin Coolidge, to denounce the radicalism of college faculties.[7]

Even during the period of McCarthyism, Paul F. Lazarsfeld and Wagner Thielens, Jr. concluded from survey data that social scientists, living within a predominantly left-of-center community, were relatively unintimidated, and that it was more dangerous for an academic to be a public supporter of McCarthy than to be a bitter opponent. And, more recently, John Kenneth Galbraith boasted in 1971 that

> it was the universities—not the trade unions, not the free-lance intellectuals, nor the press, nor the businessmen . . . which led the opposition to the Vietnam war, which forced the retirement of the President, which are forcing the pace of our present withdrawal from Vietnam, which are leading the battle against the great corporations on the issues of pollution, and which at the last Congressional elections retired a score or more of the more egregious time-servers, military sycophants and hawks.[8]

Lest it be thought that the intellectuals' opposition to the "polity" has been limited in modern times to periods when Republicans have been in office, or when there were very exceptional circumstances (as, for example, under Lyndon Johnson), it should be noted that James Reston of *The New York Times* felt moved to write in October 1961 of the intellectuals' discontent with John F. Kennedy—also the subject of a *Harper's* article by Joseph Kraft, published just before the assassination. Reston noted that the Kennedy government was being described as "the third Eisenhower administration," and that the intellectuals were "disenchanted by the absence of new policies, the preoccupation with political results, the compromises over education and the techniques of appointing conservatives to put over liberal policies and liberals to carry out conservative policies." Reston reminded his readers of an earlier liberal Democratic president who sought to appeal to the intellectuals and had comparable difficulties with them—Woodrow Wilson, who saw an inherent "perennial misunderstanding" between "the men who act . . . [and] the men who write." Long before he took office as Richard Nixon's foreign policy adviser, Henry Kissinger reiterated Wilson's complaint: "For intellectuals outside the administrative machines . . . protest has too often become an end in itself. Whether they have withdrawn by choice or because of the nature of their society, many intellectuals have confused the issues by simplifying them too greatly." The novelist Saul Bellow has acknowledged the validity of the complaint of the political leaders:

> American intellectuals don't enter government service very willingly, and they look upon government as a cold-blooded monster. They're

separatist and radical by education, and they feel they're serving higher ideals—to resist, to stand aside. States are distrusted, establishments attacked.[9]

This repeated characterization of a left-leaning, politically influential faculty fostering social change in America has been sharply challenged in the past decade by a variety of leftist critics, such as Noam Chomsky, Alvin Gouldner, Louis Kampf, Staughton Lynd, and Alan Wolfe, supported by assorted "radical caucuses" in different disciplines. They perceive a preponderantly establishment-oriented academe, at best apolitical and impervious to social injustice, and at worst collaborating with the powers that be. The radical critics have pointed to prominent scientists who played leading roles in producing weaponry and to social scientists who supported "conservative" foreign, military, and domestic policies or seemingly defended the status quo. Gouldner charged that academic sociology "is disposed to place itself and its technical skills at the service of the status quo, and to help maintain it in all the practical ways sociology can."[10]

Table 6-1
Political Self-Identification[11]

Faculty					U. S. Public	
Carnegie			Ladd-Lipset		N.O.R.C.	
	1969	1975		1977	1977	
Left	4%	5%	Far Left	3%	Extreme Liberal	2%
Liberal	37	36	Very Liberal	12	Liberal	11
			Somewhat Liberal	30	Slightly Liberal	14
Middle of Road	29	28	Moderate	20	Moderate	37
Moderately Conservative	27	28	Somewhat Conservative	25	Slightly Conservative	16
Strongly Conservative	3	3	Very Conservative	5	Conservative	12
			Far Right	0.2	Extremely Conservative	3
			None of those	5	Don't like categories	5

The image of a conservative or divided academe may also be sustained by recent opinion data indicating that professors, though clearly more liberal and Democratic than other strata, are not a radical, left, or even liberal group, if such descriptions mean that they are overwhelmingly on one side of the ideological spectrum on all issues. When asked in various opinion surveys in the late 1960s and 1970s to identify themselves as left, liberal, middle-of-the-road, or conservative, slightly less than half the professors described themselves as left or liberal. By a small majority, they described themselves as middle-of-the-road or conservative. The overall pattern of faculty political self-identification has changed little between the highly politicized late 1960s and the calm mid-1970s. Two polls taken by the Carnegie Commission on Higher Education in 1969 and 1975, which used the same question format, found practically identical distributions in both periods (Table 6-1).

In a 1977 survey conducted by Everett Carll Ladd and myself, which offered faculty respondents seven "overall political inclinations," from "far left" to "far right," 45 percent located themselves on the liberal or left side of the spectrum, 30 percent called themselves conservative or right, while 20 percent chose the "moderate" option. (Various surveys of the general population find more self-identified conservatives than liberals.) In 1972, 43 percent of the faculty voted for Richard Nixon, and in 1976 32 percent preferred Gerald Ford to Jimmy Carter. Two decades earlier, the presumed hero of the "eggheads," Adlai Stevenson, was opposed by 44 percent of academe.

The professoriate has also been divided on various domestic issues. The 1969 Carnegie poll found that slightly more than half of the professors opposed busing to achieve "racial integration of the public elementary schools," and a 1975 Ladd-Lipset survey found no change. Recent attitudes toward capital punishment and pornography also reveal a divided academy. In 1975, almost half the professoriate supported capital punishment and favored laws "forbidding the distribution of pornography."[12]

Even more conservative faculty orientations on economic issues are evident in the results of the 1977 Ladd-Lipset survey. Businessmen who regard the campus as a bastion of hostility to the free-enterprise system may be surprised to learn that 81 percent of the faculty agreed with this statement: "The private business system in the United States, for all its flaws, works better than any other system devised for advanced industrial society." Similarly, 69 percent endorsed the view that "the growth of government in the United States now poses a threat to the freedom and opportunity for individual initiative of the citizenry." A much smaller majority, 54 percent, endorsed the proposition that "economic growth, not redistribution, should be the primary objective of American economic policy." Perhaps more telling of the "conservative" views of the most liberal stratum is that two-thirds evaluated "the private business system" positively, while only 52 percent were satisfied with the "judicial system," and a bare quarter with "religious values."

Questions about how much confidence faculty had in "the people running" fourteen different institutions found that the faculty gave the highest approval to their own leaders—82 percent had "a great deal" or "a fair amount" of confidence in them. But the second highest vote of "confidence," 65 percent, went to "banks and financial institutions." Negative judgments, however, outweighed positive views about those "running major companies," by 53 to 47 percent. By contrast, the leaders of "organized labor" were disapproved of much more strongly, 79 to 21 percent.

If American academe is in fact sharply divided in its political views and if many, often a majority, support the conservative position on many of the major issues of the day and 45 percent voted for the Republican presidential candidate instead of Democratic nominees closely identified with campus support, such as Adlai Stevenson and George McGovern, why have both sophisticated intellectual commentators and conservative political and business leaders repeatedly identified the professoriate with the American Left and academe as the heart of the New Class?

The answer is simple and lies in two further facts about the politics of academe. First, in most forms of political behavior and attitudes, professors have been *more* liberal or radical than all other strata. Since 1972, professors have given a higher percentage of their vote to Democratic and/or left-wing third-party candidates than other identifiable occupational groups (Table 6-2). They are also more inclined to describe their politics as liberal or left than are other groups.

Table 6-2
Democratic and Left Third Party Vote, 1952-76[13]

	1952	1956*	1964	1968	1972	1976
All Voters	44%	42%	61%	43%	39%	52%
Occupational Groups						
PROFESSORS	56	62	78	61	57	66
Professional/						
Managerial	36	32	54	34	31	42
Clerical/Sales	40	37	57	41	36	50
Manual	55	50	71	50	43	58
Education						
College	34	31	52	37	37	42
High School	45	42	62	42	34	54
Grade School	52	50	66	52	49	58

*No 1960 data on professors available

Faculty liberalism relative to other groups is also evident by comparing the responses of professors with those of the leaders of a number of institutions and activist groups to questions dealing with "equality of results" of income. The 1977 Ladd-Lipset survey included two questions from a poll conducted by the

Washington Post and the Harvard Center for International Affairs. Professors were much more sympathetic to the view that "there should be a top limit on incomes so that no one can earn very much more than others" than were leaders of feminist groups, black civil rights organizations, farm associations, the media, business associations, and students in major universities. The proportion of the leadership groups who "strongly disagreed" with a top limit on incomes ranged from 63 percent of the feminist leaders through 77 percent of the black spokespersons to 97 percent of the business leaders. Only 37 percent of the faculty "strongly disagreed," although a majority voiced some disagreement. Similarly, when asked to locate their own views on a seven-point scale ranging from belief in competitive "equality of opportunity" at one end to "equality of results" at the other, three-fifths or more of the other leadership groups, compared to only a third of the professors, took the most extreme procompetition position and rejected equality of results.

The second reason for the widespread characterization of the professoriate as "left" is that the most liberal academics are in the most prestigious and politically influential positions. Specifically, left-wing views, actions, and voting behavior are most prevalent among the more productive professors at the most prestigious universities, among those at the center of the research-graduate training establishment, and among social scientists, whose academic concerns are often directly relevant to key issues of public policy.

The earliest large-scale opinion study of academe, dealing with religion in 1913, found that academics as a group were more likely than nonacademics to disdain religion, and that academic eminence was associated with religious disbelief within the professoriate. Although religious and political beliefs are clearly separate, a variety of studies, including some of faculty opinions in the last two decades, indicate a high correlation between religious and political outlooks. Irreligious people are much more likely to have liberal and left-wing views than believers. Some indication that the relationship between academic prestige and leftist views existed before World War I is found in the impressionistic comments of a young socialist intellectual, Randolph Bourne, and a conservative English visitor, Alexander Francis. The faculty in "the advanced universities" (Bourne) and in "colleges and universities which have received large pecuniary gifts from millionaires" (Francis) were the most likely to have radical or "socialistic" views.[14]

Four decades later, Lazarsfeld and Thielens, in their survey of a national sample of social scientists, reported a comparable relationship between academic achievement and attitudes toward civil liberties for unpopular political groups as well as voting behavior in the 1952 elections. A 1966 National Opinion Research Center survey found that

> roughly four out of five faculty members from high quality schools consider themselves liberal as compared to only forty-five percent of

those at low quality schools. On the other hand . . . only sixteen percent of the individuals from high quality schools . . . claim to be conservative, but forty percent from low quality schools say they are conservative.

The Ladd-Lipset analyses of the huge 1969 Carnegie survey and the two faculty surveys conducted in the mid-1970s reiterated these findings. In the spring of 1969, for example, 49 percent of faculty at lower tier (less prestigious) institutions either still supported Nixon's Vietnam policies or favored escalation, as contrasted to only 26 percent at major universities.[15]

These findings, representative of results from a myriad of questions bearing on an immense variety of issues over many decades, demonstrate that opinions in academe differ greatly from opinions in society generally and within most other occupational groups, where conservative views and Republican sympathies are correlated with higher status and income. In academe, liberal-to-left, socially critical orientations are linked to professional success and to recognition for creative scholarship. These results attest to the validity of hypotheses advanced by such analysts as Thorstein Veblen, Joseph Schumpeter, C.P. Snow, and Paul Lazarsfeld, who suggested that the emphasis on creativity and innovation, central to the concept of modern scholarship, is related to the rejection of the established, the traditional, and the conventional in society at large. Veblen noted in 1919:

> The first requisite for constructive work in modern science, and indeed for any work of inquiry that shall bring enduring results, is a skeptical frame of mind. The enterprising skeptic alone can be counted on to further the increase of knowledge in any skeptical fashion . . . . [T]he skepticism that goes to make him an effectual factor in the increase and diffusion of knowledge among men involves a loss of that peace of mind that is the birthright of the safe and sane quietist. He becomes a disturber of the intellectual peace.[16]

Academic discipline also separates the conservative from the liberal. This point is well known to all who inhabit the university, and I will not belabor it here, other than to note its magnitude. In 1968, Richard Nixon received 20 percent of the vote among social scientists, 39 percent among the natural scientists, 55 percent among faculty in business schools, and 62 percent in agriculture schools. This distribution of sentiment was found on all opinion variables surveyed. A study of the signers of anti-Vietnam War ads in *The New York Times* found social scientists most highly represented in proportion to their numbers, with humanities professors second, followed by natural scientists, and professors in applied subjects far behind. The 1977 Ladd-Lipset survey indicated that almost three-fifths of those in the social sciences and humanities identified themselves as liberal or left, compared to 41 percent of natural scientists, 29 percent of the faculty of law and medical schools, 29 percent of the engineering and business school faculty, and 13 percent of professors in agriculture. Academic electoral behavior in 1976 followed along the same lines. Only a fifth of those in the social sciences and humanities voted for Gerald Ford, while he carried the business, engineering, law, medical, and agricultural schools (Table 6-3).[17]

Table 6-3
Politics, Ideology, and Voting by Discipline[18]

	Social Science	Humanities	Natural Science	Law & Medicine	Business & Engineering	Agriculture
Ideology						
Liberal	58%	58%	41%	29%	29%	13%
Moderate	18	22	20	19	20	22
Conservative	18	16	5	47	48	60
None of these	6	4	5	3	3	5
1976 Vote						
Carter	75%	76%	60%	45%	43%	39%
Ford	19	21	36	52	54	58
Confidence in People Running Major Companies						
A great deal	3%	4%	9%	20%	15%	17%
A fair amount	30	32	47	44	50	60
Only some	37	40	33	28	27	18
Hardly any	30	24	11	7	8	5

While it is possible to argue that academe as a whole does not contain a liberal majority, its most publicly visible segment, social science professors at major universities, is to the far left of a profession whose views are considerably more liberal than other segments of American society. Conversely, however, the academy includes many conservatives, who, however, are concentrated in the least visible part of the academy, the lower status colleges and the professional schools, the least politically involved group. These differences were shown in the 1975 survey (Table 6-4).

The differences between social scientists in high-status institutions, the most liberal of all, and applied professionals in the lowest-status schools, the most conservative of all, are of a magnitude rarely found in opinion research. The range of difference between the two groups runs from 40 to 56 percentage points on various questions.

Related to these variations are differences in occupational self-image. In 1977, academics were asked to identify themselves as intellectuals, scholars, scientists, teachers, or professionals. Those choosing "intellectuals" were the most liberal on all of the issue questions, followed in order of declining

Table 6-4
Selected Attitudes of Faculty at Different Level Institutions[19]
(percentage in agreement)

	Major Universities		Lower Status Colleges		All Faculty
	Social Sciences	All Faculty	All Faculty	Applied Subjects	
Income differences should be reduced	78%	65%	52%	33%	58%
Favor busing for integration of elementary schools	63	55	40	18	47
Favor capital punishment	32	47	69	88	57
U.S. spending too much on welfare	25	31	47	65	37

liberalism by "scholars," "scientists," "teachers," and "professionals." The first two groups, "intellectuals" and "scholars," were most likely to be the self-descriptions of those in the social sciences or humanities. Those who saw themselves primarily as "teachers" (found, of course, in all disciplines) were invariably relatively more conservative, in this as in previous studies. "Professionals," located primarily in the professional schools, were even more right-wing in their views.

Replies to the question, "Do your interests lie primarily in research or in teaching?" also correlated with political orientation. In 1977, of those who reported themselves "very heavily in teaching," 38 percent identified themselves as conservatives—twice as large a proportion as that of those "very heavily in research." "Teachers" were also much more likely to have voted for Ford (38 percent) than "researchers" (21 percent) (See Table 6-5).

Commitment to teaching is seemingly more conducive to a conservative outlook than is interest in research, or intellectual creativity and commentary. It may be that teaching involves the transmission of received culture or knowledge while research and intellectual creativity emphasize the need to improve, change, innovate, or critically evaluate what exists or is known, and hence, to reject elements of the status quo.

THE POWER AND INFLUENCE OF INTELLECTUALS

A number of variables mentioned here as determinants of an adversary stance by intellectuals, whether academics or not, have also been specified by various writers as creating a political class consciousness. Although there are parallels between an adversary intelligentsia and the fully conscious working class

Table 6-5
Scholarly Emphasis and Political Orientation[20]

	Very heavily in research	In both, but leaning to research	In both, but leaning to teaching	Very heavily in teaching
Political Identity				
Liberal	53%	53%	42%	41%
Moderate	16	17	25	17
Conservative	19	24	29	38
None of these	13	7	4	4
1976 Vote				
Carter	77	74	58	58
Ford	21	23	38	38

described by Marx, the differences are significant. Whereas the proletariat engages in material production, the intellectual is employed in the production of nonmaterial objects and the creation and elaboration of ideas and symbolic forms. The industrial working class has been thought to have revolutionary potential because its members are exploited, share a common low status, and are deprived of effective political power. In contrast, though growing at a rapid rate, the intellectual stratum is much smaller and is relatively "well-to-do," if not privileged, in income and prestige.

Yet, to the extent that intellectuals constitute a critical intelligentsia, they have great potential for inducing social, political, and cultural change. This point was emphatically argued by C. Wright Mills, among others. In "The Decline of the Left" (1959), Mills wrote:

> No other group of men is as free [as are intellectuals to make political decisions about their work]; no other group, just now, is as strategically placed for possible innovation as those whose work joins them to the cultural apparatus; to the means of information and knowledge; to the means by which realities are defined, by which programs and politics are elaborated and presented to publics . . . .

> Intellectuals have created standards and pointed out goals. Then, always, they have looked around for other groups, other circles, other strata to realize them. It is time, now, for us in America to try to realize them ourselves—in our lives, in our own direct action, in the immediate context of our own work.

> As intellectuals, we should conduct a continuing, uncompromising criticism of this established culture from the standpoint of—what so-called

> practical men of affairs call—utopian ideals . . . . If we as intellectuals, do
> not define and redefine reality, who will?[21]

In his article "The New Left," published the following year, Mills expressed
even more forthrightly his conviction that intellectuals should be regarded as
the revolutionary class by the nascent left-wing movement. Distinguishing
himself from contemporary Marxists who regarded the working class as the
historic agency of radical change, Mills pointed to "the really impressive
historical evidence that now stands against this expectation" and characterized
the belief as a "labor metaphysic," "a legacy from Victorian Marxism that is
now quite unrealistic." He proposed that those on the Left direct their attention
to "the cultural apparatus, the intellectuals—as a possible, immediate, radical
agency of change." [22]

To appreciate the intellectuals' potential for social change, it is necessary to
consider their functions and their relationships to other social elites and to the
body politic generally. A key function of intellectuals is to provide symbolic
formulations for the cultural construction of reality. Hence, they can "restruc-
ture" man's conception of himself and his society. Beyond that, they may be
able to motivate others to act toward their favored ends through the threat of
withholding needed services, the influence derived from their high prestige,
and the values generated by their elaboration of ideology.

It is clear that intellectuals, creative scholars, scientists, artists, and writers
supply services vitally needed by various social groups and their elites. At the
same time, they depend on others for resources, particularly financial support in
the form of remuneration or grants. Because of this interdependence, the extent
to which they can exercise power depends on the degree to which their services
are needed, the degree to which they control the market, and the degree to
which they depend upon services or resources that others supply. Although
government relies on intellectuals for skills and expertise in many areas,
including military research and development, there are, for the most part, many
separate suppliers rather than a single monopolistic force. For that reason, the
intellectuals' power over government has been obscured by the more manifest
power of the political authorities over them. The relationship, however, is not
constant and may not always be so asymmetrical. Intellectuals, particularly
when organized, may exercise considerable leverage over other elite groups,
including political leaders.

The growing significance of science and other branches of knowledge has
contributed to the increased political importance of intellectuals. The rapid
expansion of occupational groups engaged in knowledge production and the
growth of the "service" sector have led some to posit the beginning of a new
social era. As elsewhere in this volume, Daniel Bell speaks of the centrality of
theoretical knowledge in "post-industrial" society. In a similar vein, Zbigniew

Brzezinski speaks of a "technetronic" age, in which technology and especially electronics increasingly become the principal determinants of social change, altering social structure, values, mores, and the global outlook of society.[23]

Coinciding with the scientific-technological revolution are major changes in the occupational structure. The "disparity between the scientific and technological revolution and industrialization" was stressed by a group of Czech scholars. In the late 1960s, they pointed "to a relative *decline* in the amount of labour absorbed by *industry* and associated activities" and the prospect that the tertiary sector will encompass 40 to 60 percent of the national labor force in industrial countries in the coming decades, as was already the case in the United States. They particularly emphasized the rapid expansion of the labor force engaged in science, research, and development: until recently a fraction of 1 percent, these experts now constitute about 2 percent in the technologically advanced countries; by the end of the century they may account for 10 percent, and in the first half of the next century 20 percent or more.[24] More recently, Daniel Bell, in various writings on "post-industrial" society, including his chapter in this volume, has documented these trends in American society.

Not only have the knowledge workers been increasing in number at a phenomenal rate, but they have also become more conscious of their social role and more widely valued by the general population. It is important to realize that though the scientist's or scholar's specialized knowledge may be comprehensible to only a relative few, his personal prestige is widely appreciated.

Some evidence of the social standing of the professoriate is found in two comprehensive surveys, conducted by the National Opinion Research Center in 1947 and 1963, of how Americans evaluate the relative prestige of occupations. "College professor" ranked close to the top among ninety occupations in both years, outranked only by physicians, some scientists, and major political jobs—Supreme Court justice, governor, and federal cabinet member. The job title, "professor," was evaluated more positively than "lawyer," "member of the board of directors of a large corporation," "mayor of a large city," "banker," and "owner of factory that employs about 100 people." There was little change in occupational rankings over the sixteen-year interval, but the evaluation of "college professor" improved slightly, and the categories that moved up most were the scientific occupations—including scientist, government scientist, chemist, nuclear physicist, psychologist, sociologist, biologist, economist. The increased prestige of the professoriate during the post-World War II period is also reflected in studies of undergraduate career choices at prestige schools during the 1950s and 1960s. The proportion of students with high-status background and high academic attainment who planned a scholarly career rose from the freshman to the senior year. Those drawn to business careers increasingly came from the academically least successful half of the graduating seniors.[25]

Significantly, the Czech scholars argued that it is even *more essential* under socialism than under capitalism for intellectuals to be accorded high prestige and allowed freedom of inquiry, since socialism seeks to limit material differences among occupational groups. Yet such conditions help promote a critical intelligentsia as an independent political force. The Czech scholars themselves seemed to be aware of, but by no means disturbed by, that possibility. Before the Russian invasion in 1968, they applauded the idea that the intellectually creative expert might become a social critic under these conditions of intellectual freedom:

> The expert is of service to socialist society when he points emphatically to the opportunities for advance and to the barriers, when he is fully informed about science, technology and cultural developments in other countries, when he breaks new ground with full confidence that what furthers socialism will find the recognition due to it. The expert who carries out instructions to the letter has no opinions of his own, avoids taking risks, or is timid, absorbed in his own worries and incapable of criticising superiors and subordinates when things need to be pushed ahead, is of no value to socialism. Today all types of society are facing a test of their ability to create the climate needed for free development and universal application of science.[26]

The greater international impact of intellectuals and the university community on the body politic is not a function simply of increased numbers, or the vital services provided, or even their increased social prestige. By certifying other elites as technically competent through their control of formal education and by helping to produce the intellectual and cultural resources that they need, the academics and intellectuals have come to exercise great influence over government, the churches, business, and the mass media. In the United States, the most prestigious groups within the intellectual world politically tend to be disproportionately to the left; they can influence the beliefs of less intellectually involved people, both within and outside the university, in the same direction. The opinions of the most visible and distinguished scholars and scientists are important to those who respect their intellectual accomplishment.[27]

In the West, the universities and the intellectuals generally contribute to the historic process of secularization. The Protestant and Roman Catholic churches currently suffer severe internal tensions as they seek to adjust their identity, theology, and ritual to contemporary conditions. Although the complex changes occurring in the churches have a variety of causes, a major source of change is the increasing tendency of church leaders—those concerned, above all, with theology and morals—to conceive of themselves as "intellectuals" and to seek the approval of leading secular intellectuals, especially around the universities. Numerous dilemmas confront churches seeking to maintain the belief in revelation and tradition, while also aligning themselves with the critical innovations of the universities. In general, the modernization of many religious denominations reflects the extent to which theology has become part of the broader intellectual life. Instead of being simply a conservative institution, organized religion is increasingly becoming an institution pressing for broad social reform, often of a radical nature. The changes in the churches surely have important consequences for the value system of the larger society.

The mass media are a second sphere of activity whose elite show strong signs of being affected by the intellectual and university world. In the United States and in other Western countries, journalists and broadcasters increasingly have the same values and political orientations as the critical intellectuals. A 1969 Harris survey of editors found that 40 percent described themselves as "liberals," and only 13 percent as "conservatives," which puts them far to the left of the public. Harris reported, moreover, that 63 percent of those in charge of major media in the major cities were liberal.[28] Similar patterns are indicated in three more recent surveys, as summarized by Stanley Rothman:

> According to Johnstone's [national survey] data 14.3 percent of the media elite classified themselves as "Far Left," and 55.8 percent classified themselves as "a little to the left," for a total of 70.1 percent in about 1970. In contrast 37.3 percent of the non-elite portion of Johnstone's sample classified themselves as "left" or "far left." Of course one question proves very little. However, the Bureau of Applied Social Research under Allen Barton asked a far wider range of questions of a somewhat broader group of media leaders from 30 relatively large cities [in 1970-71], with much the same results. The national media elite, as he defined it, is among the most liberal in the country, especially on cultural issues, but even on reform and economic redistribution issues, despite their relatively high salaries. A more recent study [1976] sponsored jointly by Harvard University and *The Washington Post*, reveals much of the same pattern among the Washington Press Corps. Approximately 61 percent of the group voted for McGovern in 1972 while only 22 percent supported Nixon. About 59 percent classify themselves as liberal or "radical."[29]

It may be argued that those who have risen to prominent positions in the mass media wish to be accepted as intellectuals and, like many contemporary theologians, regard the critical intelligentsia as a key reference group. Such people may identify prestige with success at an intellectual institution, not in the media business. Since many who work in the mass media identify with the intellectual world, the "working press" is often composed of individuals sympathetic to social change. Consequently, though the most influential American mass media—the Columbia Broadcasting System, National Broadcasting Company, *The Washington Post, The New York Times*, and the like—are big business establishments, they have presented an increasingly sympathetic view of those who seek to change society from the left.

A third elite group on which the intellectual community exerts growing influence is the government bureaucracy. Commenting on how the antibusiness values of the intellectuals were undermining the legitimacy of capitalism, Schumpeter stressed the

> direct relationship between the intellectual group and the bureaucracy . . . . Except for inhibitions due to professional training and experience, they are therefore open to conversion by the modern intellectual with whom, through a similar education, they have much in common, while the tinge of gentility that in many cases used to raise a barrier [particularly in Europe] has been fading away from the modern civil servant during the last decades. Moreover, in time of rapid expansion of the sphere of public administration, much of the additional personnel required has to be taken directly from the university.

The government bureaucracy, increasingly dependent on the expertise of the university, is now staffed, particularly at its upper levels, by men with close ties to the academy. Since many of them seek academic approbation, they appear responsive to the changing orientations and generally liberal-to-left dispositions of prominent figures in the academic world. In Barton's study of different groups of American leaders in the second year of the Nixon administration, top-level career civil servants (GS 17 and 18) with administrative responsibility for agencies and major programs were predominantly very liberal in their views on a variety of social and economic issues.[30]

A fourth group whose increasing liberalism has been linked to the impact of academic values is the judiciary. As Nathan Glazer argues,

> the judges follow the weight of judicial analysis and opinion . . . . But this entire process is guided by the weight of educated opinion. How is this educated opinion made? . . . Essentially it is formed by accepting the facts presented by professors and journalists in the mass media and believed by lawyers who, after all, come through the universities in which these facts are developed and diffused.[31]

In the United States, the leadership group most resistant to this trend is business management. One would expect business executives to support conservative values, since they manage the dominant economic institutions of the society. Yet Barton's study of leadership groups found that even they have been somewhat affected by the liberal consensus within the educated elite. Not surprisingly, they are more conservative than other leadership groups on most issues. Still, three-quarters of a sample of the owners or top executives of large corporations did not agree that "too much is done for the poor"; almost three-fifths agreed that "the federal government should support the creation of jobs in the public sector for those to whom the private sector does not provide employment"; almost three-quarters rejected the proposition that "in times of recession, government spending should be held down to avoid a deficit"; and slightly over three-fifths felt that "in the next five years . . . the real level of defense spending should be reduced."[32] Business and management are beginning to face problems from the growing functions and prestige of the university. Particularly in capitalist society, as was noted by Schumpeter and later by the radical sociologist J.P. Nettl, the business establishment finds it necessary to protect the right of intellectuals to undermine the system. Schumpeter argued:

> In capitalist society . . . any attack on the intellectuals must run up against the private fortresses of bourgeois business which, or some of which, will shelter the quarry. Moreover such an attack must proceed according to bourgeois principles of legislative and administrative practice which no doubt may be stretched and bent but will checkmate prosecution beyond a certain point. Lawless violence the bourgeois stratum may accept or even applaud when thoroughly roused or frightened, but only temporarily . . . because the freedom it disapproves cannot be crushed without also crushing the freedom it approves . . . .
>
> From this follows both the unwillingness and the inability of the capitalist order to control its intellectual sector effectively . . . the intellectual group cannot help nibbling . . . and criticism of persons and of current events will, in a situation in which nothing is sacrosanct, fatally issue in criticism of classes and institutions . . . .
>
> In defending the intellectuals as a group—not of course every individual—the bourgeoisie defends itself and its scheme of life. Only a government of a non-bourgeois creed—under modern circumstances only a socialist or fascist one—is strong enough to discipline them.[33]

One cannot preclude the possibility of a right-wing reaction to severe challenges from the intelligentsia, but in the United States, at least, as David Riesman has suggested, the top business executives are increasingly respectful of the "intellectual values" articulated in universities and significantly sensitive to criticism by the academy and the intellectual world.[34]

CONCLUSION

Professors and their apprentices, university students, have never been as numerous as they are today. Given the increased requirement of post-industrial society for university-trained workers and continuing high levels of innovative research, the university is needed more than ever before. While the society is becoming more dependent on intellectuals, it is also more influenced by them.

It may be argued that the growth of a critical intelligentsia disposed to support the "adversary culture" and reject the worth of dominant political and economic institutions is undermining the capacity of modern societies to maintain social equilibrium. Leadership itself is under question by intellectuals everywhere.

The critical intellectual denies the possibility of participating in government without risking a betrayal of his values. Faced with attacks on their legitimacy from intellectuals and students, many in the governing elites exhibit a "failure of nerve." They find it difficult to ignore or suppress groups whose values of scientific and intellectual progress they are committed to. The basic tensions within the system increasingly come from within the elite itself—from its own intellectual leaders supported by large segments of its student children. If, in Hegelian terms, the contradiction of capitalism was its dependence on an ever-growing working class brought together in large factories, the contradiction of post-industrial society may be its dependence on large numbers of intellectuals and students for research and innovation on great campuses and in a few intellectual centers of communication and influence.

Yet the more critical segment of the American intellectual community has not (yet?) adopted a radical stance toward the legitimacy of American society and its basic institutions; a large majority endorsed the free-enterprise system in a 1977 faculty opinion poll. The predominant political concern of intellectuals, at the moment, is the old progressive opposition to war, political corruption, and environmental pollution, which they still blame on the inherent greed of commercial civilization. In a larger sense, their relatively conservative or moderate outlook (by comparison with many European intellectuals) may reflect the fact that the American polity has remained fairly stable, unthreatened by mass radical movements; as a result, the leaders of the American intelligentsia do not know what they want for a new society, although they know what they dislike in the existing one. As Crane Brinton noted:

> [I]t is clear that the American intellectuals for the most part do not know the good arrangements, institutions, beliefs—not even the "ism"—they want in place of existing evil ones . . . .

> This lack of a firm positive program, even in politics, is surely a major reason why the alienation of American intellectuals today is not a "trans-

fer of allegiance,'' not a symptom of possible revolutionary action in our society . . . and this lack is also a major reason . . . why the state of mind of our intellectuals in 1932 was no sign of a coming revolution, a coming which was hardly threatened, or promised, in the slightest in our perhaps all-too-stable American society.[35]

NOTES

1. I do not suggest that all or most professors or others involved in scientific and professional work are intellectuals. For efforts to define the concept operationally, see S.M. Lipset and Richard Dobson, ''The Intellectual as Critic and Rebel,'' *Daedalus* (Summer 1972), pp. 137-38, and Lipset and Asoke Basu, ''Intellectual Types and Political Roles,'' in *The Idea of Social Structure*, ed. Lewis Coser (New York, 1975), pp. 433-34, 441-44. For an earlier effort to sum up analyses of the political attitudes and behavior of American academe, see Lipset, ''Academia and Politics in America,'' in *Imagination and Precision in the Social Sciences*, ed. T.J. Nossiter (London, 1972), pp. 211-89.

2. John Adams, *Works*, ed. C.F. Adams (Boston, 1853), III, 596; Whitelaw Reid, ''The Scholar in Politics,'' *Scribner's Monthly*, 6 (1873), pp. 613-14.

3. Michio Nagai, ''The Development of Intellectuals in the Meiji and Taisho Periods,'' *Journal of Social and Political Ideas in Japan* (April 1964), p. 29.

4. Wilhelm Ropke, ''National Socialism and Intellectuals,'' in *The Intellectuals*, ed. George B. de Huszar (New York, 1960), pp. 346-48.

5. Richard Hofstadter, ''Discussion,'' in A. Alverez, *Under Pressure* (Penguin paperback, 1965), pp. 111-12; ''Text of a Pre-Inauguration Memo from Moynihan on Problems Nixon Would Face,'' *New York Times*, 11 March 1970, p. 30; Reid, *loc. cit.*; James Bryce, *The American Commonwealth* (Toronto, 1891), II, 295-95; Laurence Veysey, ''The Emergence of the University,'' (Ph.D. thesis, University of California Berkeley, 1962), p. 160; ''B.P.,'' ''College Professors and the Public,'' *Atlantic Monthly* (March 1902), p. 286; Whitelaw Reid, *American and English Studies* (New York, 1913), I, 241-42.

6. Richard Hofstadter, *Anti-Intellectualism in American Life* (New York, 1963), p. 39.

7. Veysey, pp. 160-61; Robert W. Iverson, *The Communists and the Schools* (New York, 1959), p. 14. See also Laurence Veysey, *The Emergence of the American University* (Chicago, 1964).

8. P.F. Lazarsfeld and W. Thielens, Jr., *The Academic Mind* (Glencoe, Ill., 1958), pp. 95, 104; J.K. Galbraith, ''An Adult's Guide to New York, Washington and Other Exotic Places,'' *New York* (15 November 1972), p. 53.

9. *New York Times*, 1 December 1969, p. 43.

10. Alvin W. Gouldner, *The Coming Crisis of Western Sociology* (New York, 1970), p. 59. For a critical evaluation of this thesis, see S.M. Lipset and E.C. Ladd, ''The Politics of American Sociologists,'' *American Journal of Sociology* (July 1972), pp. 67-104.

11. 1969 and 1975 Carnegie Commission Faculty Surveys; 1977 Ladd-Lipset Faculty Survey; 1977 NORC Survey.

12. E.C. Ladd and S.M. Lipset, *The Divided Academy: Professors and Politics* (New York, 1975), p. 33; 1975 Ladd-Lipset Faculty Survey.

13. Data on the voting of professors for 1952 and 1956 are from a study by Lawrence Howard; for 1964-76 from surveys conducted by Ladd-Lipset. The findings for other strata are based on secondary analyses of cumulated Gallup surveys.

14. James H. Leuba, *The Belief in God and Immortality* (Chicago, 1921), pp. 219-87; Randolph Bourne, *Youth and Life* (Boston, 1913), p. 295; Alexander Francis, *Americans: An Impression* (London, 1909), pp. 228-29.

15. Edward Noll and Peter Rosse, *General Social and Economic Attitudes of College and University Faculty* (National Opinion Research Center private report, November 1966), p. 21; for other analyses of the relationship between academic achievement and social and political views, see Ladd and Lipset, pp. 125-48.

16. Thorstein Veblen, *Essays on Our Changing Order* (New York, 1934), pp. 226-27.

17. Ladd and Lipset, pp. 55-124; E.C. Ladd, "Professors and Political Petitions," *Science* (31 March 1969), pp. 1425-30.

18. 1975 Ladd-Lipset Faculty Survey.

19. Ibid. (Questions and responses abbreviated).

20. 1977 Ladd-Lipset Faculty Survey.

21. C. Wright Mills, *Power, Politics, and People*, ed. I.L. Horowitz (New York, 1963), pp. 231-33.

22. Ibid., p. 256.

23. Daniel Bell, "Technocracy and Politics," *Survey* (Winter 1971), pp. 1-24; "The Post-Industrial Society: The Evolution of an Idea," *Survey* (Spring 1971), pp. 102-68, and his works cited in this volume; Zbigniew Brzezinski, *Between Two Ages: America's Role in the Technetronic Era* (New York, 1971).

24. Radovan Richta et al., *Civilization at the Crossroads* (White Plains, N.Y., 1968), pp. 120-24.

25. Robert W. Hodge et al., "Occupational Prestige in the United States: 1925-1963," in *Class, Status, and Power*, ed. R. Bendix and S.M. Lipset (New York, 1966), pp. 322-34; Donald H. Akenson and Lawrence F. Stevens, *The Changing Uses of the Liberal Arts College* (New York, 1969), pp. 14-27, 86-110.

26. Richta, p. 233. "Many specialists will lack the incentives existing under capitalism—social distinctions cannot be unduly sharpened. The greater then the need for socialist countries to contrive and safeguard a suitable regime for creative work, leaving people as free as possible to do their special jobs; the more important it is to raise the prestige of working science and technology and, most important, to give the socialist expert a wide field for freely creative self-assertion." Ibid., p. 232.

27. See Lazarsfeld and Thielens, p. 250, for a discussion of this process within academe as it affects younger faculty and graduate students.

28. Louis Harris Survey, "Report on Study of Culture Critics and Editors," released by Church of Christ, 16 March 1970.

29. Stanley Rothman, "The Mass Media in Post-Industrial America," in *The Third Century: America as a Post-Industrial Society*, ed. S.M. Lipset (Stanford, forthcoming).

30. Joseph A. Schumpeter, *Capitalism, Socialism and Democracy* (Harper paperback, 1962), p. 155; Allen H. Barton, "Consensus and Conflict Among American Leaders," *Public Opinion Quarterly* (Winter 1974-75), pp. 508, 513-15.

31. Nathan Glazer, *Affirmative Discrimination* (New York, 1975), pp. 218-19.

32. Barton, pp. 513-15.

33. Schumpeter, pp. 150-51. "This explains the social effectiveness of intellectuals in bourgeois society (as well as their effectiveness in transforming it radically)." J.P. Nettl, "Ideal, Intellectuals, and Structures of Dissent," in *On Intellectuals*, ed. Philip Rieff (Garden City, N.Y., 1969), p. 57.

34. David Riesman, "The Spread of 'Collegiate' Values," in Huszar, pp. 506-07.

35. Crane Brinton, "Reflections on the Alienation of the Intellectuals," in *Generalizations in Historical Writing*, ed. Alexander Riasanovsky and Barnes Riznik (Philadelphia, 1963), p. 220.

7

LAWYERS AND THE NEW CLASS

Nathan Glazer

I had hoped, in analyzing a single occupational group that is generally regarded as a prominent element of the "new class," to escape the conceptual tangle with which many other contributors to this volume have manfully wrestled. After all, if the heart of the "new class" is found among the professional classes and the highly educated, and if the social forces that have helped create a "new class" include the increasingly larger scale of government, the expansion of regulation, and the increasing reach of rights and entitlements, would not lawyers be well qualified to be members of the "new class"? Could not one analyze their role to get a better grasp on the "new class" and what it means for society?* No such luck. The conceptual tangle around the "new class" persists when we try to get a fix on a single occupational stratum; it must be cleared

---

*In a review of Irving Kristol's *Two Cheers for Capitalism* in the June 1978 *Across the Board*, Albert J. Sommers notes that Kristol places lawyers second among the categories making up the "new class." But Kristol qualifies their inclusion by specifying lawyers who make their careers in "the expanding public sector" (pp. 15, 27). However, to the lawyer David T. Bazelon, lawyers epitomize the "new class."

away before we can relate lawyers to the "new class" and its values, views, and role.

Before considering the role that the "new class"—and lawyers among it—might play in producing them, let me first list the social developments that critics of the "new class" regard negatively: the expanding *size* of government; the animus, in parts of the media and among government administrators, against private business; the expanding regulation of business; the increasingly egalitarian taxing policies, particularly the policies limiting funds for investment and rewards for entreprenurial and investment success; the downgrading of entreprenurial and business roles as noncreative and useless for society; the bias against the market and in favor of government regulation as a form of control.

Now the problem with this list or any other that might be made up is that in our legal system, a lawyer is inevitably on either side of any dispute. This certainly cannot be said of any other member-category of the "new class." The legal system alone guarantees an occupational division on almost any issue, a situation that is not as likely among intellectuals, professors, government bureaucrats, scientists, social workers, planners, engineers, or what have you. This may explain the traditional antagonism to lawyers (in the old adage, one lawyer in a town will starve, while two will find a good living), but it does not explain why lawyers are uniformly included as members of the "new class."

Aside from this formal problem, more serious difficulties arise when we look at the distribution of lawyers on both sides of issues involving regulation of business and expansion of state power: many more lawyers are on the side of business than on the side of government, and only a tiny fraction are in those numerous but relatively small "public-interest" law firms whose aim is generally to badger government to become more restrictive of business. In a big case dealing with the environment, consumer interests, nondiscrimination or affirmative action in hiring, or some other characteristic issue in which government tries to control business, the resources expended on the side of private business—in legal fees, in numbers of lawyers and researchers employed—are far greater, one can assume, than the resources spent by small public-interest law firms or even by major government agencies. At times, government expenditures do match or exceed those of the private sector—when the target is a relatively small businessman. Generally, on any case regarded as vital to its interests, the big corporation can spend more than government can or will. One wonders whether business is really getting much more results by employing such expensive legal talent, but it is beyond dispute that business can and does spend more than government or public-interest firms.

At best, only a fraction of lawyers might be considered members of the "new class" because of their roles or attitudes. To begin with, a very substantial number are solo practitioners, about 40 percent and rising, according to the

American Bar Foundation.[1] The solo practitioner is the typical small businessman, clearly the antithesis of the "new class," however it may be characterized. He is antagonistic to what the "new class" has done through
government—its leveling taxes, its regulation and protection of employees, its
demands for ever more reports and forms, its large plans for urban renewal and
urban planning, which may wipe out his place of business. Not only is the solo
practitioner a small businessman, but his chief clients are other small businessmen. Another substantial chunk of lawyers is in partnerships and small firms,
equally small businesses. Another large group work in large firms employed by
larger businesses and corporations and wealthy individuals. Another group are
salaried lawyers for large business enterprises. We would certainly not include
any of these categories in the neo-conservative version of the "new class."

What then remains from the category of lawyers to be considered as part of
the "new class"? Two major groups, one quite large, one very small. The large
group consists of lawyers who work for government—twenty thousand for the
federal government alone.* Many more are employed by state and local
governments.† Perhaps 20 percent of the lawyers in the nation are employed by
government, and since they are engaged in defending its interests, writing its
regulations, and negotiating with and prosecuting those who do not comply,
and since much of their work does not deal with ordinary criminal activity
(which both the "new class" and the old classes agree should be a concern of
government), some government lawyers might be considered part of the "new
class."

But when people think of lawyers in the "new class," they have in mind
another group: the lawyers who work for nonprofit reform groups or in government and foundation-supported law firms to defend the rights and interests of
minorities, the poor, welfare recipients, public-housing tenants, environmentalists, consumers, prisoners, the mentally ill, the mentally retarded, and other
groups, and who have contributed mightily to a huge increase in litigation, the
expansion of rights, and the increasing requirements for reporting and monitor-

---

*"At last count, there were 20,000 lawyers in the federal government engaged in the lawyer-like
functions [excluding, I presume, employees with law degrees who do not practice law]. Only
approximately 4,000 of this group serve in the Department of Justice; the remainder are employed
by 28 other federal government units which have or excercise authority to conduct at least some of
their litigation."[2]

† The 1970 Census found 277,000 lawyers and judges, while the American Bar Association lists
432,000 in 1977, up from 355,000 in 1971.[3] Clearly, the number of members of the bar is larger
than those who identified themselves as lawyers and judges to the Census. The Census did break
down lawyers and judges by employer, and 19.2 percent worked for government—6.8 percent for
the federal government, and 5.4 percent for state and 6.9 percent for local governments. The
proportion of lawyers working for government has undoubtedly gone up since 1970.

ing that have accompanied the establishment of new rights. These "public-interest" lawyers are the ones naturally regarded as being part of the "new class." They are seen as being particularly antagonistic to big business and business in general, because their pursuit of the interests of minorities, the poor, consumers, and the environment often places them in opposition to business as well as government.*

The number of such lawyers, however, is remarkably small. There are 2,000 lawyers supported by the Legal Services Corporation, the heir of the poverty program. While these lawyers have played a substantial role in legal reform, the greater part of their activity is simply devoted to providing legal services to the poor for family, consumer, housing, and welfare problems. One-quarter of their time is devoted to "law reform" work, such as changing regulations, getting new judgments about rights generally, filing class actions and test cases—all the activities that involve not, or not simply, personal legal service but the intent to change the pattern of law and regulation.[4]

More important than these lawyers are the public-interest lawyers who spend just about all their time in law-reform work. Their major interest is not a client but a pattern of law, regulation, and judicial interpretation affecting the condition of a class of people or interests they have undertaken to represent. A recent study that attempted to find every lawyer employed full-time by such groups between 1969 and 1973 found only 450 lawyers.[5] Even if we double or triple this number—and missed organizations and expansion since 1973 might permit such a radical upward adjustment—the number of lawyers engaged full-time in public-interest law is less than 1 percent of the legal profession in the country.

This account omits the substantial number of lawyers who work full-time or part-time for legal-aid societies. But they are primarily engaged in defending people against criminal charges; to my mind, the part of the law dealing with

---

*I place quotation marks around "public interest" because one cannot take it as a matter of course that their activities are in *the* public interest, even though they have appropriated the term and are generally given the right to use it. But when such lawyers litigate to get more welfare, or to lower rents, or to stop a new development on environmental grounds, or to insist on large investments for safety, a variety of interests are in conflict, all of which have some claim to being considered *public* interests—the defendant is not only soulless corporations or unfeeling governments, but the taxpayers who may pay more in taxes, the workers who may lose jobs, the communities that may be left with a high rate of unemployment. But since no alternative term comes to mind, and an overabundant use of quotations interferes with readability, I will reluctantly drop the quotes.

Further muddying the term is the fact that a new group of public-interest law firms has been set up specifically to oppose the firms that grew out of the civil-rights, antipoverty, and environmental movements. These new firms are also supported by individual and foundation contributions, are nonprofit, have salaried lawyers, contest key cases, and operate principally at the appellate level—but they defend general business and private interests against the expanding reach of governmental regulation. Although they have an equal right to claim that they act in the public interest, I will omit them from my discussion.

ordinary criminal activity, whether prosecution or defense, is not very relevant to a consideration of lawyers as members of a "new class" engaged in shaping a new society. Crime, alas, is always with us, and while we could examine possible connections between the ideology of the "new class" and crime, they would have less significance for the history of the "new class" than the expanding role of government as the regulator, shaper, and defender of new rights.

This is one possible way of characterizing the legal profession: largely self-employed (53 percent, according to the 1970 Census) and overwhelmingly engaged in working for businessmen and the wealthy, with less than 20 percent employed by government, and less than 1 percent engaged in expanding the rights of minorities, the poor, and the unrepresented. This has been the point of view of most commentators on the legal profession, and has been for some time. Writing on "The Modern Legal Profession" in the 1933 *Encyclopedia of the Social Sciences*, A.A. Berle described the American bar as follows:

> The complete commercialization of the American Bar has stripped it of any social functions it might have performed for individuals without wealth. The great law office either does not care to or cannot profitably handle cases which, while of great importance to individuals, have only limited financial significance. The smaller offices and individual practitioners, especially if they are struggling for survival, will extract the maximum compensation from their clients, whether the service is worth it or not.

Forty-five years later, Roger Cramton, Dean of the Cornell Law School and chairman of the Legal Services Corporation, gave a similar characterization in a major address to the California State bar in 1976: "The most generous estimates indicate that less than 15 percent of the legal needs of the poor are being met today . . . . Less than 2,200 lawyers—only about one-half of 1 percent of the American Bar—are working full-time to meet the legal needs of one-sixth of the population."[6] And President Carter, in a widely reported speech on 3 May 1978, echoed the same complaint about the maldistributed resources of the American bar. Of New York City's 35,000 lawyers, he said, "only a handful are available for service to the city's one million poor—one for every 5,000." He urged the expansion of legal services to the poor, even though, as he pointed out in his talk, the United States already has more lawyers per capita than any nation but Israel. Carter advocated further expanding the resources available to the new interest groups that sprang up in the later 1960s and 1970s to gain new rights: "Overcoming procedural barriers means that groups with distinct interests to defend—in civil rights, economic questions, environmental causes and others—must be able to defend them fully. We are supporting efforts to broaden the use of class action and to expand the definitions of standing to sue.''

And so we have a paradox, or indeed two, if we consider lawyers as part of the ''new class.'' First, there are very few public-interest lawyers, and while there are considerably more lawyers in government who may be advancing the interests of the ''new class,'' the total number cannot be more than a few percent of the American bar. (As I suggested above, most lawyers in government are engaged in prosecuting criminals.) Moreover, most lawyers in public-interest firms see government itself as an enemy, indeed *the* enemy. In what sense, then, could government lawyers be representatives of the ''new class''?

Let us consider the second paradox first. The problem with the idea of a ''new class,'' as so many contributors to this volume have pointed out, is that so many elements are mixed up in it. Common to all elements, or almost all, is a rejection of the market as a means of allocating wealth, whether on grounds of justice or efficiency. But this does not mean a unified and favorable attitude to the expansion of governmental powers. This may be the dominant orientation of the elements we group under the ''new class,'' but it is obviously combined with a great suspicion of government, as well. Government should be expanded, the ''new class'' says, but it must also be watched closely and monitored from outside government, for even as it expands to regulate private business, it may be captured by private business. Even if not captured, government might be slack in its enforcement; the energy and enterprise that public-interest lawyers characteristically bring to their task (and that lawyers generally are socialized in law school to expend) might not be found in government servants, including the lawyers among them.

This fear leads to a sharp eye on government regulation. Much litigation undertaken by public-interest lawyers against government does not, of course, demonstrate a fundamental hostility to government expansion as such, since it is designed to increase the power of government, to force it to take on what it does not want to do, to undertake what law or regulation or constitutional interpretation says it should do with more energy and greater resources. If this is the attitude of public-interest law to government, then it basically has no argument against the expansion of governmental powers.

But there is another side to public-interest law that is indeed fundamentally hostile to government. A long tradition of public-interest law generally opposes some governmental action on the grounds that it restricts civil liberties. This branch of public-interest law does want government to do less, and so do many of the newer branches dealing with the schools, prisoners, the mentally ill, and the mentally retarded. They will argue that records should not be kept on students, that students should not be disciplined, expelled, or placed in special schools, or that special schools should not exist. Similar arguments are made on behalf of prisoners, or the mentally ill, or the mentally retarded. "Deinstitutionalization," a growing movement strongly assisted by public-interest law, asks government to do less and even promises that the cost of social services may be reduced if new approaches are adopted.

Of course, there is a certain selectivity in the defense of rights. Not all constitutionally protected rights are equally the concern of public-interest groups. For example, consider the right to bear arms, (the Second Amendment) or the right to be compensated for the "taking" of private property (the Fifth Amendment). But my main point is that the defense of rights, however selective, is often a defense against government doing something—and thus, at first glance, seems to be a bar to governmental expansion.

Another branch of public-interest law is critical of government in a different respect. It opposes the power of government-licensed professions and urges self-help for education, health, and other needs, and urges less dependence on the highly trained professional. Does this branch also warrant inclusion in the "new class"? It is part of the many-faceted revolution of the 1960s, which simultaneously expanded the rights of minorities (and the number of those to be considered minorities), expanded government regulation, and urged radical change in social services. If one branch of public-interest law calls for the expansion of government, and another calls for its withdrawal or its restriction, what happens to the relationship between public-interest law and the "new class"?

There is an answer to this paradox. Both aspects of public-interest law—that which expands governmental power and that which calls for its restriction—emphasize rights, primarily constitutional rights, but also rights grounded in statute and regulation. On the one hand, the right that is asserted requires government to do more; on the other, it requires government to do less. And in emphasizing rights, the two branches share other common elements: for example, the insistence that ever more lawyers are needed to defend and secure these rights. By operating through the courts, even the public-interest lawyers who apparently want government to do less are in effect asking that another branch of government, the courts, do more. The relationship of public-interest law to governmental expansion differs from the liberalism of the New Deal, which saw no problem in expanding government to deal with any problem. At least the legal branch of the "new class" does see problems with this approach, but its chosen solution is to expand another branch of government, the judiciary, to deal with them. Or, as D.P. Moynihan pointed out in the title of a recent address, "An Imperial Presidency leads to an Imperial Legislature leads to an Imperial Judiciary."[7]

Thus, as a result of a law suit charging deprivation of the constitutional rights of the inmates, the Willowbrook Developmental Center, a huge center for the retarded on Staten Island in New York City, is to be reduced in population from

5,300 to 250. Government, attacked by public-interest lawyers who were defending the right of patients to good treatment and not to be placed in an institution, was required to reduce one of its monster institutions. But the consent judgment resulting from the suit requires that government create hundreds of new mini-institutions to house the retarded and many programs in the community to provide them with work, education, therapy, and other needs; in doing so, it requires not only the expansion of state agencies creating such institutions and programs, but the creation by the judiciary of a new form of government, the Willowbrook Review Panel, to oversee the process. But all this is as nothing compared to the need for new lawyers that the Willowbrook decree causes by creating and specifying a vast array of new rights: the right to community placement, the right to six hours of program, the right to notice before being moved, the right to be fully informed of one's rights, the right to a process of appeal and adjudication if there is disagreement over one's rights. The Willowbrook judgment is enough to keep an army of lawyers busy for many years, and if the army were provided, there would have to be an appropriate increase in judges and court personnel to respond to their efforts.

The passion for rights now knows no bounds. Critical of government, it nevertheless causes an increase in the number of lawyers. "Deinstitutionalization" may reduce the number of those employed in institutions, but it certainly increases the number of lawyers. Lawyers in the field of "deinstitutionalization" are convinced that no benevolence can be expected from those who run institutions for the mentally retarded and the mentally ill. Ideally, each inmate should have a lawyer. The child must be protected not only against the state and the mental-health professionals, but also against his parents—a point of view that is now actually becoming law. A three-judge federal panel in Pennsylvania recently ruled that it was unconstitutional to commit mentally ill and mentally retarded children to institutions "without a hearing and without legal representation." As part of its ruling the court ordered that the 3,390 children now being held in Pennsylvania institutions, both public and private, must be released within the next six months or recommitted under the new procedures.[8]

One of the main arguments against the "new class" is that, seeking good, it finds ways of expanding its own numbers and its own power; despite the rather special role of lawyers within the "new class," in this respect they resemble government employees, social workers, city planners, and all the others who, whatever their differences, see more need for more people with their own training. This process is not cynical; the public-interest lawyers who have created a situation in which ever more of their kind will be needed do not rub their hands in sly delight at what they have wrought. Instead, they are wearied and overcome by what they see as the heaped-up problems around them, which even great victories cannot reduce and even seem to magnify. But it is undeniable to them that an increase in their numbers—whether they are ½, or 1, or 2 percent of the bar—is essential to any progress.

Even when it is critical of government, the public-interest bar generally feels that government should be forced to do more—more regulating, more enforcing, more monitoring.* And when it wants to limit government, it is in effect expanding another segment of government—the judiciary. In both cases, it is undoubtedly increasing the need for lawyers, within and without government.

But then we come to the first paradox mentioned above: as a proportion of all lawyers, the public-interest bar and the regulators and the authors of government regulations do not amount to much. Why then are lawyers regarded as *members* of the "new class" rather than *opponents*, considering their interest as small businessmen whose clients are other businessmen, small and large? Because the relatively small group of public-interest lawyers represents an essential thrust of the law itself, something even its opponents within the law grudgingly acknowledge. The law is a matter of due process and of rights, and if lawyers set themselves up to insure due process and to vindicate rights, the bar—whatever the interests of most of its members and most of its clients—will go along. The Bar Association, for example, supported the creation of legal services for the poor under the Office of Economic Opportunity.[10] Some established lawyers might have seen it as competition (though the poor do not provide much legal business); more might have seen it as threatening the interests of their clients—the landlords, employers, manufacturers, and retailers. But the ABA decided that government-supported legal services for the poor should be backed by the bar, regardless of the clash with certain interests, because the law itself incorporates as a key principle the right to representation and due process, which only lawyers can provide. It is interesting that, despite all the opposition that developed among governors, mayors, and others, legal services handily survived the demise of the Office of Economic Opportunity itself, was set up as a separate government corporation, and was able under a Republican administration both to protect itself from political hazards and to continue in very much the same line as it had started.

The bar presents the strange spectacle of having interests that should be quite critical of governmental expansion, of the extension of due process, of the creation and extension of new rights. After all, these harm lawyers as businessmen (but of course they have their own in-house talent to deal with such issues), and harm their clients, who employ them to struggle against the untoward effects of expanded regulations, rights, and due process. But as *lawyers* they see the compelling logic in these new entitlements. How can a lawyer, as a lawyer, resist the demand that everyone needs a lawyer—even if he sees a certain fantastic element in, for example, a case where all parties agree

---

*Indeed, members of this part of the public-interest bar find no problem passing over into the service of government. Those left behind may suspect a weakening in the commitment of their former colleagues, but the easy passage from the outside critical role to the inside regulating role shows the close connection.[9]

that institutionalization is the best course of action, and yet a lawyer is nevertheless required to certify their agreement?

And because this logic is built into the law itself, it is at its strongest in the
faculties of law schools, particularly elite law schools, where we find the most
refined elaborations of due process, the most extended implications of a right,
and all the various developments within American law that have emphasized its
role in reforming and restructuring society. The bar as a whole may be
conservative, and its interests suggest that lawyers—if we had polls—would
have conservative political opinions. But this is not true of law-school faculties.
While not as liberal as social scientists, they are considerably more liberal than
professors in general, and the high-status law schools are even more liberal.[11]
One can see why, despite the easy and jejune interpretations that simply assume
that law professors, linked to a conservative profession serving conservative
interests, will obviously be conservative. They are liberal because the nature of
the law itself emphasizes many themes that have become the essence of
liberalism: due process, a careful consideration of rights, a system of reasoning
by analogy, which permits moving from restricted conceptions of due process
to more extended ones. They are liberal, too, because law-school faculty are in
very substantial proportions, of Jewish ancestry (25 percent, as against 17
percent of social-science faculty, 9 percent of all faculty, and 3 percent of the
population), and Jews are liberal.[12] The more liberal law schools and the elite
law schools (the two categories overlap), which shape new approaches justifying a more interventionist profession (interventionist, that is, in favor of the
kinds of interests the educated elite espouse), attract students inclined toward
liberalism and toward creative legal intervention for the rights of such newly
defined minorities as prisoners, the mentally ill, and the mentally retarded, and
for the protection of the environment and the consumer.

It is true that there has been very little study of the political effect of law
school attendance. The overwhelming impression given by the literature,
popular and scholarly, is that law school makes law students conservative,
interested in making money by helping businessmen make money. After all,
their courses deal primarily with law affecting business, and they expect for the
most part to work for business. One interesting study of attitudes of law students
at one major university, contrasting their attitudes just before beginning their
studies in 1973 with their attitudes after almost two years of law school in 1975,
did show a modest drift toward a more conservative self-definition. Their
interest in doing public-interest law also declined. But the changes were only
modest, and could have been attributed to their professors (who, whatever their
liberal inclinations, might have been more conservative than their students), or
the changing temper of the times, or the fact that their self-image was changing
as they approached the time to begin looking for jobs, or the fact that they were
getting older, or some other possible cause. But on the evidence of this study,
law school prompts no strong shift to conservatism.[13]

Another key part of the bar diverges from the conservative inclinations of most lawyers: the federal judiciary. Federal judges are not by training or social background interventionist. But in recent decades they have supported the expansion of government powers, for varied and complex reasons—among them, the fact that Congress, the presidency, and the bureaucracy have also expanded governmental powers, and judges simply interpret law and regulations. But one reason for this development is that appellate judges depend in large measure for their legal reasoning on elite law-school faculty who analyze and interpret legal trends and point the way to further development, and on the best students of elite law schools, who serve as law clerks. As I wrote recently,

> the judges follow the weight of judicial analysis and opinion . . . . [I]n . . . complex cases, they must be guided by what is set before them in lengthy briefs and analyses of complex facts. These analyses are then digested by other lawyers for them, generally the brightest graduates of the law schools. But this entire process is guided by the weight of educated opinion, an educated opinion which is convinced that morality and progress lie on the side of the broadest possible measures of intervention to equalize the employment of minority groups in every sphere and level of employment, and to evenly distribute students and teachers and administrators [by race] through school districts . . . .[14]

Of course, there are other factors that explain judicial interventionism, among them the independence of the judiciary from the opinions of the general public—though not, as I have indicated, from educated public opinion. It is of course possible that a long line of conservative appointments to the Supreme Court and lower courts by a conservative president would moderate the interventionist orientation of the federal judiciary. But the tendency toward interventionism—whether the result of judicial insulation from the pressures of mass public opinion, of the influence of legal commentators or legal clerks, or of the steadily more expansive interpretation of due process and equal rights— is so strong that eight years of Eisenhower appointments did nothing to change it, and eight more years of Nixon and Ford appointments did little more.

At its peak—among elite law-school faculty, students in elite law schools, the federal judiciary—the law is quite different from what a random sample of legal practitioners would show, and much closer to the "new class" in its orientation to government and business. Despite their small numbers, interventionist lawyers—the public-interest lawyers, the government regulators—are not alone. The corporate body that represents the bar, as we have seen, will give them support, even if grudgingly. Distinguished law professors will mark out the path they should take, and justify it before they have entered upon it. Appellate judges will be influenced in various ways by elite law-school faculties. Lawyers are indeed important members of the "new class," if we consider that its essential character is to call for, to defend, and to benefit from the expansion of government.

Admittedly, there are other traditions within the law that might serve to moderate the expansion of government and the law itself. As neither a lawyer nor a philosopher of law, I would hesitate to say that traditions emphasizing restraint and a limited role for law rather than its endless expansion are any more authentic than traditions that have served the expansion of government and law. And it would take a different and more extended discussion to explain why it is that the legal traditions that serve the "new class" rather than those who might oppose it have become dominant—not in the law itself as a profession, but in the law schools, where it is forcefully carried into the courts, with great effects upon our society.

NOTES

1. *Wall Street Journal*, 2 June 1978, pp. 1, 33.

2. Assistant U.S. Attorney General Drew Days, III, Speech before the District of Columbia Chapter of the Federal Bar Association, 1 May 1978.

3. *Wall Street Journal, loc. cit.*

4. Joel F. Handler et al. *Lawyers and the Pursuit of Legal Rights* (New York, 1978), pp. 54-55.

5. Ibid., p. 197. This survey, which covered thirty groups, seems to have missed some groups and more have been established since 1973 (and undoubtedly some have gone out of business). The list of organizations does not include, in the field of mental retardation alone, which has grown rapidly since 1973, the Mental Health Law Project, the National Center for Law and the Handicapped, the Disability Law Resource Center, and the Mental Disability Legal Resource Center. The volume is generally valuable for its survey and analysis of the field of public-interest law.

6. These quotations are from a valuable syllabus for a course on "The Legal Profession" given by Richard Abel at the U.C.L.A. Law School.

7. Herbert J. Lehman Memorial lecture, 28 March 1978, reprinted as "Imperial Government," *Commentary* (June 1978).

8. *Philadelphia Inquirer*, 26 May 1978, p. 1.

9. Juan Cameron, "Nader's Raiders are Inside the Gates," *Fortune* (October 1977).

10. Handler, p. 32.

11. Seymour Martin Lipset and Jonathan S. Paris, "The Sociology of Law Professors," (unpublished manuscript, 1977).

12. Ibid.

13. Howard S. Erlanger and Douglas A. Klegon, "Socialization Effects of Professional School: The Law School Experience and Student Orientation to Public Interest Concerns," (Institute for Research on Poverty Discussion Paper, Madison, 1977).

14. Nathan Glazer, *Affirmative Discrimination* (New York, 1975), p. 218.

8

PURSUING THE NEW CLASS:
Social Theory and Survey Data

Everett Carll Ladd, Jr.

Before displaying survey data on the opinions and values of the "new class," some discussion of the conceptual frame imposed upon the inquiry is appropriate. How one looks at any complex topic naturally shapes to some significant degree what one finds. Several of the contributors to this volume have noted the many different concepts of a new class. Once the group has been identified and the changes in the social structure contributing to its development are specified, various assumptions about its outlook and values—its distinguishing ideological tendencies—readily evolve. Then we can use the enormous body of available survey research data to attempt to determine the extent to which the expected tendencies can actually be found.

In my view, the idea of a new class has appeared in recent years because the United States has entered a period of class conflict very different from the kind that became familiar during the New Deal era. From the 1930s to the mid-1960s, a middle class confronted a working class. The middle class was more inclined to conservatism—in the New Deal sense of that term—and regularly gave more support to the Republican party, while the working class was more inclined to liberalism and backed the Democrats. The conflict was muted, as it always has been in the United States, but it was real enough.[1]

Today, I argue, the primary form of class conflict pits a lower-middle class against an upper-middle class. This is profoundly confusing, because it departs so abruptly from what prevailed until recently, and is described in terms of an "embourgeoised" working class against an "intelligentsia." Neither group is "conservative" in the Barry Goldwater-*National Review* sense. Both take the "liberal" political economy of the New Deal for granted. But they occupy markedly different places in contemporary American society, with contrasting needs, goals, and values.

The intelligentsia* today adopts a political stance that is called liberalism, but clearly differs from the liberalism of the New Deal era—ergo, it is the "new liberalism." Working-class dissenters from this *new* liberalism must therefore express a *new* conservatism. As if all this terminological confusion were not enough, the ideologies of the contemporary class conflict do not separate primarily along party lines, as they did from 1935 to 1965; a schism exists *within* the Democratic party as well.

Two key developments in the social structure have set the stage for the new form of class conflict. First, the upper-middle class in the United States has increasingly become an intelligentsia rather than a business class. Entrepreneurial business is no longer a mass economic interest. Managerial business remains an important stratum, but it suffers internal divisions that could not have been contemplated in earlier periods. Large segments of the broad, new upper-middle classes, including the professional and managerial categories, who are the most affluent, secure, and closely associated with advanced culture and technology, increasingly cease to defend business values. They even cease to think of themselves as "business" in the historical sense and are now part of the rising new class—the intelligentsia, responding to intellectual rather than business values and orientation.

The extraordinary expansion of higher education in the post-World War II period is a key factor defining the intelligentsia as a new class. The number of students enrolled in degree-credit programs in colleges and universities—now about 10 million—has multiplied sevenfold since 1940: college students are

---

*Following Seymour Martin Lipset, I use "intelligentsia" to include those persons whose background and vocation associates them directly in the application of trained intelligence. It includes, that is, not only intellectuals—people involved in the creation of new ideas, new knowledge, new cultural forms—but also that larger mass whose training gives them some facility in handling abstract ideas or whose work requires them to manipulate ideas rather than things. College education, an experience shared by some 40 million Americans, defines the outer boundaries of the intelligentsia.

now nearly 5 percent of the total population, compared to just over 1 percent in 1940. Roughly 40 million Americans age 21 and older—30 percent of the adult population—have received some college training from the 600,000 faculty members at the nation's 3,000 colleges and universities. One of six Americans 21 years of age and older—about 21 million people—have completed at least four years of formal college training. The size of this college population has made it the decisive, controlling audience for an elaborate national communication structure.

This huge college-educated population is not a business class. About 60 percent of all college graduates have occupations classified as "professional, technical, and kindred" by the Census Bureau; only 17 percent hold "managerial or administrative" jobs.[2] As the American upper-middle class has been transformed into an intelligentsia, the working class, which up to World War II disproportionately included "have nots" who behaved accordingly, has become "embourgeoised," particularly the skilled manual workers and those in related blue-collar occupations. In a wonderfully American semantic contradiction, a large segment of the working class has become (lower) middle class.

A complex set of events is involved here, but one stands out: In the quarter century after 1947, the median *real* income (in 1972 dollars) of American families doubled, from $5,665 to $11,120. In 1947, America was already the richest nation in history, yet during the following generation the average family gained more purchasing power than in all preceding periods of American history combined. Most people moved a long way in their basic economic position through this momentous change; they might reasonably have been expected to become a conservative force.

But is there really a persisting conflict between a "bourgeois" working class and an upper-middle-class intelligentsia? What kind of ideological cleavage should have opened up? Has it? Using survey data, we can first try to determine how the two strata *should* position themselves ideologically and then see whether they have in fact done so.

The two broad strata *should* manifest significant differences in the way they feel about American society. There is no need to suggest total alienation on the one hand or complete support on the other. But an upper-middle-class intelligentsia, sharing in the critical orientation long associated with secular intellectuals, should be hostile to established society and culture. The embourgeoised working class, like its counterparts of earlier eras, should be conservative regarding domestic affairs as well as the world role of the United States. The college-educated, upper-middle class should be reducing its support, to an increasing degree, for traditional "bourgeois" values—an emphasis on work, thrift, the importance of material acquisitions, and the like—while the working class should uphold these middle-class values. The higher strata should be more inclined to reject traditional cultural norms and lifestyles together with older codes of behavior; the *new morality* should receive its strongest backing from college-educated professionals, and the *old morality* its greatest backing from the working class.

The two groups *should* have different attitudes toward economic growth and the relative importance of material as opposed to nonmaterial values. Because it is better situated economically and increasingly disdainful of business values, the upper stratum should emphasize the importance of continued high economic growth less than the aspiring working class. The new class should give more support to the environmentalist movement in its conflict with industry and favor the curtailment of energy use.

During the New Deal, the working class provided the main support for the growth of government, and it should continue supporting governmental intervention. But to the degree that it is embourgeoised, it can be expected to worry increasingly about inflation and the impact of new public spending programs on its economic position. The intelligentsia should be notably progovernment—indeed, it should be *the* progovernment class of contemporary America. Large segments of the college-educated, professional stratum—people in research and development, education, public bureaucracies, and the like—are directly dependent upon government for their income and for the support of their professions and institutions. Therefore, the upper-middle strata should be more likely to back new programs and public spending than the old working class.

The two strata *should* manifest distinctive differences in their allegiance to various interest groups—most notably unions, the font of American liberalism during the New Deal. Today, in an interesting historical twist, the embourgeoised working class, although committed to the "new conservatism," should be prounion. At the same time, the upper-middle class, which is more "liberal," should be suspicious of unions, not because of a traditional business aversion to labor but because unions are too "conservative."

LOOKING BACKWARD:
CLASS AND POLICY COMMITMENTS IN THE NEW DEAL ERA

Extensive analysis of available survey information indicates that high-socioeconomic-status groups in the United States, by whatever definition, were consistently more conservative than middle- and low-status groups during the 1930s, 1940s, and 1950s. The upper strata were more inclined to describe themselves as conservatives and to reject parties and causes labeled liberal, and were generally more opposed to New Deal programs. The upper strata were more internationalist and somewhat more sensitive to civil liberties, but their relative overall conservatism was clear.[3] The college educated consistently gave less support to New Deal social programs than did the high-school and grade-school educated. (See Table 8-1). In 1952, for example, Gallup asked a national sample of Americans whether they favored a national health insurance plan run by the government. Eighty-eight percent of college-educated Republicans opposed Medicare, compared to 74 percent of all Republicans; 52 percent of college-educated Democrats rejected Medicare, while only 39 percent of all Democrats took that position.[4]

Table 8-1
Public Opinion by Education, 1946-47[5]

Favor:*	High school or less	Some college	College grads	Everyone
government-owned electric power	30%	29%	15%	27%
government-owned telephone system	44	32	25	41
government-run health plan	46	44	27	43
vote for 18 year-olds	57	56	47	55
wages for housewives	30	25	27	29
federal equal-employment law	80	76	79	79
state equal-employment law	52	45	55	51
U.S. A-bomb manufacture	67	68	71	67
Truman going to left, following views of labor & other liberal groups	22	15	8	20

*In all tables, the proper display of the exact questions asked and responses offered has been abbreviated to improve clarity and conserve space. The abbreviated questions and answers correctly represent the originals; in any event, any misrepresentations would be irrelevant since the central concern here is the *relative* responses by specified sub-groups.

In the tables, these abbreviations are used for educational categories:
    "postgraduate"—five or more years of college
    "college grad"—four years of college or college, graduated
    "some college"—one to three years of college or college, incomplete
    "H.S. grad"—twelve years of school
    "less than H.S. grad"—less than twelve years of school.

Where no "postgraduate" figure is shown, none is available, so "college grad" includes postgraduate.

Tables 8-1, 8-3, 8-4, 8-5, 8-7, 8-8, 8-10 were prepared by B. Bruce-Briggs.

However, although the surveys of the immediate postwar years do not contain many "social issues," they do suggest a substantial uniformity of views cutting across education/class lines, with, if anything, a slight tendency for the lower strata to be more favorable toward changes of the sort we now associate with cultural liberalism. The lower socioeconomic cohorts were consistently more Democratic than their higher-status brethren. In 1947, a large survey of college-trained Americans showed clear Republican pluralities (Table 8-2). In the 1948 presidential election, college-educated Americans favored the Republican candidate by about 20 percentage points more than the American electorate at large.

Table 8-2
Party Identification, 1947[6]

	Republican	Democrat	Other; Independent; Undecided
All college graduates			
Doctoral/professional degree	40%	24%	37%
Master's	33	25	42
Bachelor's	39	27	34
College graduates under age 40			
Doctoral/professional degree	34	27	39
Master's	29	25	46
Bachelor's	35	29	36

THE NEW LIBERALISM AND THE NEW CONSERVATISM: THE CLASS BASE

These data support the conventional wisdom that the college cohorts and the upper-occupational groups of the New Deal era were mostly a business class and were thereby inclined to conservatism, while the high-school and grade-school educated and those in lower-status occupations were a (relatively) reformist working class. The data that follow, based on a rather elaborate examination of contemporary survey information, make sense only if the college and upper-professional cohorts are now a reformist intelligentsia, while the grade-school and high-school educated and the blue-collar work force have increasingly become a conservative class.[7]

In recent years, several research firms, most notably the National Opinion Research Center (NORC) and Yankelovich, Skelley, and White have conducted elaborate public-opinion polls on fundamental personal, social, and political values. The results, some of the most striking of which are summarized in Tables 8-3 and 8-4, exhibit a remarkable new class configuration and provide impressive documentation of the extent to which values associated with the traditional bourgeois culture now find greater support among the grade-school and high-school educated and among the blue-collar work force than within the ranks of college-educated professionals.

Table 8-3
Personal Values, 1976[8]

	Less than H.S.	H.S. grad	Some college	College grad	Post grad	Everyone
favor self-fulfillment over economic security & providing for family	17%	15%	17%	25%	42%	19%
do not consider "very important":						
work	31	35	38	48	45	37
money	55	64	77	80	81	67
saving money	36	49	58	58	66	50
financial security	34	43	54	50	56	44
not being in debt	31	38	41	51	61	40
success	55	63	67	73	61	63
welcome less emphasis on money	55	54	63	59	73	58
welcome parents making less sacrifices for children	38	39	36	36	45	38
disagree that country is changing too fast	20	35	48	52	N.A.	39

Nowhere are present-day differences between the upper- and lower-socioeconomic-status groups more striking than on attitudes toward the social, cultural, and lifestyle issues that have been thrust into prominence since the mid-1960s. For example, 70 percent of Americans with five years of college training or more believe that a pregnant woman should be able to get a legal abortion simply because she prefers not to give birth to the child; only 45 percent of high-school graduates and 33 percent of grade-school-educated Americans support abortions in this instance. A married person having sexual relations with someone other than the spouse is described as "always wrong" by 49 percent of those with five years of college or more but by 81 percent of those with less than a high-school education, and by 56 percent of the new class but by 78 percent of the working class.

Table 8-4
Social Issues, 1972-77[9]

	Less than H.S.	H.S. grad	Some college	College grad	Post grad	New* Class	Everyone
favor legal abortion on demand by married women	33%	45%	56%	63%	70%	64%	45%
homosexuality not always wrong	14	26	39	52	57	52	28
should be no laws against pornography for adults	51	58	67	64	77	69	59
adultery not always wrong	19	26	38	43	51	44	29
premarital sex not always wrong	57	69	75	80	80	78	67
women should not leave running the country to men	44	67	78	86	89	86	64
would vote for local equal housing law (whites only)	28	35	41	45	47	45	35
against antimiscegenation laws (whites only)	42	69	80	88	92	89	65

*This table and others that follow show figures for "New Class." This is not intended to define the new class, but is merely shorthand for those respondents who are college graduates or postgraduates and who hold occupations in the "professional, technical and kindred" and "managers and administrators" occupational categories that most survey research organizations have adapted from the U.S. Census Bureau.

The college educated are vastly more in support of changes in traditional sex roles and status than are the high-school educated and manual workers in the population. The statement that "women should take care of running homes and leave the running of the country up to men" seems outrageously absurd to most members of the intelligentsia, but it finds a high measure of approval within the working class.

There are also significant generational differences, with the young typically more in favor of newer values and the old more resistant. When age and class are combined, to distinguish between young members of the new class and the elder members of the working class, the differences become huge—for the public at large and within the ranks of the great American liberal party, the Democrats.

In the New Deal era, higher-status groups were dependably more resistant to public spending. This is no longer the case. NORC has examined public attitudes on a range of spending programs: improving the condition of black Americans, welfare, space exploration, environmental matters, health, urban problems, education, crime, drug addiction, defense, and the like. On most of these, college-educated Americans now support increased public spending more than their high-school and grade-school counterparts. The new class backs a higher level of public expenditures in most of these areas than does the working class, which increasingly acts like a traditional middle class, manifesting relatively great pocketbook concerns. To be sure, it is a *new* bourgeoisie; it displays no wholesale rejection of the New Deal state, but is less likely to favor increased levels of public expenditures. (See Table 8-5.)

Table 8-5
National Priorities, 1972-77[10]

	Less than H.S.	H.S. grad	Some college	College grad	Post grad	New Class	Everyone
This country spending "too little" on:							
space exploration	4%	7%	15%	16%	15%	16%	9%
improving/protecting environment	51	59	66	69	67	67	59
improving/protecting nation's health	61	63	66	65	66	66	63
solving problems of big cities	49	52	57	57	64	60	53
improving nation's education system	46	51	58	55	60	57	51
halting rising crime rate	69	73	67	67	64	66	70
dealing with drug addiction	67	64	62	56	54	55	59
This country spending "too much" on:							
military armaments, defense	23	28	41	50	53	24	32
improving condition of blacks	27	27	24	19	18	25	25
welfare	47	60	57	54	50	54	54

In only three spending areas covered by the survey did the middle to lower strata favor public expenditures more than the college-educated professionals and managers: to halt the rising crime rate, to respond to increasing drug addiction, and to provide for the national defense. In all of the other areas surveyed, the familiar New Deal relationship between class and support for public spending has been turned on its head.

Table 8-6
Distribution on the Index* of Public Spending, 1972-77[11]

	Quintile most supporting high public spending 1	2	3	4	Quintile least supporting public spending 5
Postgraduate	23	23	23	16	15
College graduate	23	19	22	18	18
Some college	21	19	23	18	18
High school graduate	16	21	26	20	18
Less than high school	18	19	22	18	23
Whites	13	18	24	20	26
Blacks	45	22	15	9	9

*The index was constructed from the eight domestic spending variables in Table X-5. The response that the U.S. is spending "too little" was given a value of three; "too much," zero; "about the right amount," one. Each respondent's "scores" on the eight variables were then added together. The totals, ranging from 0 to 24, were divided by the number of items that the respondent answered. All respondents were located in one of five quintiles—ranging from the 20 percent most inclined to high public spending to the 20 percent least supportive.

Either of the NORC questions on whether "too much money, too little money, or about the right amount" is being expended for public needs involve programs in the domestic arena. An "Index of Public Spending" was constructed to summarize the overall responses of the several social strata. Table 8-6 shows that by a modest but nonetheless clear margin, the most highly educated give the greatest support to public-sector spending, while the least educated (grade school only) are least favorable. This relationship holds *despite* the fact that blacks, a group notably committed to high public spending, are

Table 8-7
Energy, Economics, Environment, 1972-77[12]

	Less than H.S.	H.S. grad	Some college	College grad	Post grad	Everyone
country spending too little on protecting/ improving environment	51%	59%	66%	69%	67%	59%
favor government limitations on gasoline usage during an energy crisis	61	62	71	74	78	66
favor tax on gas-guzzling cars even at cost of unemployment	36	39	44	60	N.A.	45
favor higher gasoline tax, even at cost of inflation	26	25	26	40	N.A.	39
not very important for U.S. to be world leader in standard of living	27	30	41	47	52	34

disproportionately represented among those with the least formal schooling. Distributions by occupation follow the same general pattern; people in professional jobs are more favorable toward high public spending than are blue-collar workers.

The growth-environment-energy policy area also shows sharp and consistent class differences (Table 8-7). College-educated professionals, more than grade-school and high-school-educated manual workers, support environmental defense and energy consumption even at the cost of unemployment and inflation. A 1977 California survey showed that 37 percent of those with postgraduate education adhere to an "antigrowth" position, compared to just 24 percent of high-school graduates and 20 percent of those with less than a high-school education.[13]

In the New Deal era, the sharpest split over foreign affairs separating the upper strata from the lower involved the question of internationalism versus isolationism. The college educated and those in business and professional occupations were generally more favorable to an internationalist role by the United States. A very large class division still exists, but it bears little resemblance to the former alignment. The college-educated are more critical of the United States than are the high-school and grade-school educated. The new class is less of the opinion that the United States has any claim to international superiority. While hardly procommunist, the new class is markedly less hostile to communist regimes. Presumably because the upper strata are more critical of their country's international involvements, they are less likely to support military spending (Table 8-8).

Table 8-8
Foreign and Defense Policy, 1972-77[14]

	Less than H.S.	H.S. grad	Some college	College grad	Post grad	Everyone
U.S. not an unqualified force for good in foreign relations since WWII	30%	23%	28%	31%	35%	28%
hardly any confidence in military	10	11	20	20	27	14
U.S. should cut back defense spending:	33	28	39	44	60	35
even if it means U.S. strength falls behind U.S.S.R.*	18	19	38	61	58	33
even if it means unemployment*	32	36	59	75	66	49
not very important for U.S. to be world leader:						
in military strength	25	26	33	39	45	30
in moral values	30	34	42	46	40	37
communism not worst kind of government	40	46	60	69	74	50
not a threat to U.S. if the following became communist:						
Western European countries	15	18	25	34	42	21
Italy	30	39	47	62	65	42
Japan	18	21	28	46	42	25
African countries	31	37	45	57	61	41
Latin American countries	16	19	24	39	48	23
oppose U.S. defense of S. Korea	84	77	80	84	91	81
oppose U.S. military involvement if Arabs cut off oil to Europe	76	68	74	75	79	73
favor full diplomatic relations with Cuba	54	58	70	73	85	63

CIA should not work inside foreign countries to strengthen pro-American elements	35	30	40	46	61	38
do not fully agree that the American way of life is superior to other countries	32	32	38	41	N.A.	35

*Question asked only to those respondents who favored a cutback in defense spending.

The changing positions of the college and noncollege populations concerning foreign affairs and military policy parallels the shift in their responses to a wide range of national issues. But on the matter of support for trade unions and their place in American society, the relationship of the 1930s and 1940s still applies. While college-educated professionals are notably inclined to liberalism, they do not support unions. For example, NORC found that the proportion of high-school- and grade-school-trained manual workers expressing high confidence in trade-union leadership was more than three times the percentage of college-educated professional and managerial workers. Support for unions declines steadily as the level of education rises. The traditional bourgeoisie remains especially critical of unions. A full 45 percent of self-employed professional and business/managerial workers in the profit sector, for instance, stated in NORC interviews that they had "hardly any confidence at all" in labor leadership, while only 9 percent of this group professed high confidence.

The above will surprise few. The working class may be embourgeoised, but it is also unionized. The new class—with some notable exceptions among public employees—is not unionized and has reason to oppose many of the stands taken by the leadership of the American labor movement. These responses to organized labor are very important politically. The working class shows high support for the new conservatism without dropping its attachment to unionism. Neither the college-trained professionals who give primary backing to the new liberalism, nor self-employed businessmen who are the essential support of the remaining New Deal era conservatism and the Republican party, share this commitment to organized labor. And this is surely an important factor in the pursuit of electoral alliances.

THE ELECTORAL RESPONSE

Since the 1960s there has been a significant move toward an inversion of the familiar New Deal relationship between social status and partisan attachments, which had changed markedly by the time of the 1968 presidential contest. The more liberal Democratic nominee was supported by half the high-status whites under thirty years of age, but by only 39 percent of middle-status whites under thirty and by just 32 percent of low-status whites under thirty. In 1972, those with a college education voted Democratic more often than those who had not attended college, those in the professional and managerial categories voted Democratic more often than the semiskilled and unskilled work force, and so on. Among the young, Senator McGovern was backed by 45 percent of the college-educated young, but by only 30 percent of those with a high-school education or less.[15]

Table 8-9 provides further information on the extent to which historic voting patterns have shifted—although the 1972 presidential vote distributions admittedly represent an extreme case, because the Democratic presidential nominee unambiguously associated himself with the new liberalism. For the first time in modern electoral history (and probably for the first time ever), college-educated Americans voted more Democratic than their fellow citizens with a high-school or grade-school education.

Table 8-9
1972 Presidential Vote[16]

	Less than H.S.	H.S. grad	Some college	College grad	Post grad	New Class	Everyone
McGovern	42%*	33%	36%	40%	42%	39%	38%
Nixon	55	64	62	59	54	59	59
Other	3	3	2	1	3	2	3

*whites, 35%; blacks, 82%

However, in more typical elections in the 1970s, the college stratum has voted Democratic less often than the high-school or grade-school cohorts. But the Democratic position within the college-educated, professional stratum has been strengthened enormously since the New Deal era, in part because college-trained professionals have come to support the Democrats' liberal programs and policies.

NEW CLASSES:
THE MATTER OF DEFINITION

A good many terms have been swirling around here: new class, the intelligentsia, working class, the college educated, the high-school and grade-school educated, college-trained professionals, noncollege manual workers, etc. A

Table 8-10
Distributions of the New Liberalism Index,* By Selected Demographic Characteristics, 1972-77[17]

	Quintile most supporting the New Liberalism				Quintile least supporting the New Liberalism
	1	2	3	4	5
Everyone	17	24	20	18	22
White	15	22	21	20	24
Black	30	35	14	11	10
Male	17	22	20	18	24
Female	17	25	20	19	20
Education					
Postgraduate	31	23	15	14	17
College graduate	31	23	16	12	18
Some college	23	25	17	16	19
High school grad	13	22	22	20	23
Less than H.S.	11	24	21	20	24
Whites	8	21	21	22	27
Blacks	21	35	17	15	11
New Class					
Young (under 35)	36	27	13	12	12
Old (over 35)	20	19	20	16	25
All	29	23	16	14	18
Industry†					
Profit sector					
professionals	29	23	15	15	19
Nonprofit sector					
professionals	26	25	17	16	17
Occupation‡					
Professionals**	28	23	16	15	18
word workers	43	24	13	8	12
traditional					
professions	36	23	14	9	17
teachers	25	23	16	16	20
number workers	17	22	23	20	18
Businessmen and					
officials	13	23	18	19	27
White collar	18	22	20	18	21
Blue collar	14	23	21	19	22
Family income					
$25,000 and over	19	19	19	18	25
$20,000-$24,999	15	23	22	21	20
$15,000-$19,999	15	21	21	21	23
$10,000-$14,999	16	23	21	18	22
Under $10,000	18	26	19	17	20

Party identification					
Strong Democrat	19	28	18	16	19
Not very strong Democrat	17	24	21	19	19
Independent/close to Democrat	28	26	16	16	14
Independent	17	25	21	19	18
Independent/close to Republican	14	21	21	20	24
Not very strong Republican	9	19	21	21	30
Strong Republican	8	16	19	23	34
Age 35 and under by education					
Postgraduate	39	28	12	8	14
College graduate	42	28	13	10	8
Some college	33	27	16	14	10
H.S. graduate	19	27	24	18	12
Less than H.S.	19	28	21	18	14
Census region					
New England	23	27	16	17	17
Middle Atlantic	20	25	21	17	17
E. North Central	16	23	20	20	21
W. North Central	15	25	19	20	22
South Atlantic	14	24	20	18	25
E. South Central	11	19	18	24	28
W. South Central	15	21	21	18	26
Mountain	12	22	20	21	25
Pacific	20	27	19	16	21
College graduates by region					
New England	43	22	13	8	14
Middle Atlantic	36	21	19	12	13
E. North Central	30	27	14	13	16
W. North Central	23	27	17	13	21
South Atlantic	25	25	16	15	20
E. South Central	21	21	15	18	25
W. South Central	25	22	10	11	31
Mountain	25	18	11	23	23
Pacific	40	20	17	9	14
College graduates age 35 and under by region					
New England	58	21	9	6	6
Middle Atlantic	42	29	13	8	8
E. North Central	41	31	12	10	7
W. North Central	36	32	13	13	7
South Atlantic	30	27	15	13	15

E. South Central	26	26	11	15	22
W. South Central	32	25	7	11	25
Mountain	—insufficient data—				
Pacific	50	28	14	3	5

*The index has been constructed from six highly interrelated questions involving opinions or values representing several dimensions rather than a single dimension of the new liberalism:

A. Are we spending too much, too little, or about the right amount on improving and protecting the environment?

B. Are we spending too much, too little, or about the right amount on military, armaments, and defense?

C. Should divorce in this country be easier or more difficult to obtain than it is now?

D. Where would you place yourself on this scale: extremely liberal; liberal; slightly liberal; moderate; middle of the road; slightly conservative; conservative; extremely conservative?

E. In general, do you favor or oppose the busing of (Negro/black) and white school children from one school district to another?

F. Do you favor or oppose the death penalty for persons convicted of murder?

This index was computed much like the spending measure in Table 8-6. The "new liberal" response was given a value of three, the opposed response received a value of zero, and intermediate positions were assigned a value of one. Each respondent's "scores" on the six variables were then added together, the totals were divided by the number of items the respondent answered, and all respondents were located in one of five quintiles, from the highest new-liberal scores, to the lowest scores on this additive measure.

†Nonprofit sector—government administration, education, hospitals, and other Census Bureau industrial categories that are normally nonprofit. Profit sector is all others.

‡The conventional Census Bureau occupational categories have been reaggregated:
   professionals—"professional, technical and kindred" less technicians;
   businessmen and officials—"managers and administrators" plus "farmers" and
                           "salesworkers" less sales clerks;
   white collar—"clerical and kindred" plus technicians and sales clerks;
   blue collar—all others.
**Within the reaggregated professional classification these subgroups were created:
   word workers—clergy, social scientists, actors, editors and reporters, public
                   relations specialists, radio and television announcers, etc.;
   traditional professions—architects, lawyers, physicians, etc.;
   teachers—non-college teachers
   number workers—engineers, mathematicians, natural scientists, etc.

new ideological cleavage, which we have been discussing in terms of "the new liberalism" and "the new conservatism," has opened up in the contemporary period, and all of these groups are involved in this new division. But can we get somewhat more of an empirical handle on the relationship between social strata and the ideology?

The division of the New Deal era was between economic privilege and privation more than anything else. By contrast, although the new class or intelligentsia surely has economic interests, it is defined primarily not by its relative prosperity but by its high level of education. This definition is admittedly insufficient, but education is the clearest and most unambiguous index of the new ideological divide. In Table 8-10, a "new liberalism index" does not so much prove this point as summarize and illustrate it. There is an unusually strong relationship between higher education and support for the new liberalism. For example, 31 percent of those with five years of college or more are found in the most supportive quintile, compared to 23 percent of those with one to three years of college, 13 percent of high-school graduates, and just 11 percent of respondents with less than a high-school education. No other variable discriminates so strikingly.

There are also clear variations by occupation, roughly corresponding to the pattern predicted by various theoretical investigations of the occupational base of the new class and by other studies of the sociopolitical perspectives of groups within the intellectual stratum. Professionals are clearly more liberal than managers and (lower) white-collar workers. Professionals in the social sciences, journalism, and the literary world give much more support to the new liberalism than do engineers, natural scientists, and those in applied professions like medicine. Seymour Martin Lipset and I have repeatedly found that within the American professoriate, social science and humanities faculties are markedly more liberal than biological and physical scientists and professors of engineering.[18] And their attitudes presumably have the same sources, including the tendency of the various fields to attract people with disparate political orientations and the capacity of a discipline to define different subcultures reaching far beyond the political dimension but linked to sharply contrasting political stances.

On the whole, though, the data tend to question theories about the sources of the new class that emphasize occupation, sources of income, the profit versus nonprofit sector, and the like. The traditional differences separating the basic occupational categories—professional, managerial, white-collar, blue-collar—are more modest than the differences produced by education alone. The most applicable and narrowly defined occupational categories, such as "word workers," indicate about the same support for the new liberalism as does the simple indicator of postgraduate education.

The distinction between the "profit" and "nonprofit" sectors yields almost nothing. Contrary to expectations, professional men and women employed by profit-making industries are slightly but consistently more liberal (on social issues) than their counterparts in the nonprofit sector.

Even more telling, when education is held constant, the occupation-related differences disappear completely. College-graduate professionals, managers, and clerical/sales/blue-collar workers show almost identical distributions on the "new liberalism index" and on the entire range of specific issues I have been discussing. *By contrast, education-linked variations are sharp within each occupational category*. Employing education and occupation together does not discriminate more sharply between support for or opposition to the new liberalism. For example, 29 percent of those who are college educated and in professional, technical, managerial, administrative, and kindred jobs are in the most supportive quintile on the "new liberalism index," compared to 11 percent of the grade-school and high-school educated holding jobs—less of a differentiation than education alone yields. It is important to stress that these relationships hold all across the spectrum of policy questions—defense, foreign affairs, views of government, social and cultural issues, etc.

Table 8-10 shows that variations by family income are modest indeed. Nineteen percent of respondents with family incomes of $25,000 and higher are in the most supportive quintile, as against 18 percent of respondents with family incomes of $10,000 or less.

One would expect an emerging ideological position favoring new social values to find more support among younger members of the population, and youth *is* strongly associated with support for the new liberalism. But education-related differences are undiminished when age is held constant. Yet support for the new liberalism is notably high among the college-educated young. For example, 39 percent of all respondents with five years of college or more in the under-age-35 cohort are recorded in the most supportive quintile of the "new liberalism index."

Differences in support for the new liberalism by sex are nonexistent, and those by race are modest, especially when one notes that two of the questions asked deal specifically with the interests of black Americans. Regional differences are quite striking. Even when one controls for education (for example, looking only at college graduates), the differences are sharp between New England and the Pacific states (the areas most supportive of the new liberalism) on the one hand and the Southern and Mountain states (the areas least supportive) on the other. Not surprisingly, New England and the Pacific coastal states manifest those social-structural properties most associated with post-industrialism. Brought together, college training, age, and region have a powerful cumulative impact upon new-liberalism support: An extraordinary 58 percent of young (under 35) college graduates in New England and 50 percent of their counterparts in the Pacific states are recorded in the most supportive quintile of the new liberalism measure.

The new liberalism is not a Democratic or a Republican phenomenon. Those strongly adhering to the Democratic party and the strongest proponents of the GOP differ in the expected direction, but fairly modestly, in their allegiance to the new liberalism. This suggests a number of things, the most important of which is the capacity of the new liberalism/new conservatism division for partisan mischief. It bisects, rather than overlays, the Republican-Democratic cleavage that developed out of the New Deal partisan experience.

THE CASE OF THE PROFESSORS

I have been arguing that a large segment of the college-trained professional and managerial stratum has assumed the role of an intelligentsia in the social structure. It shares the policy commitments and concerns of the intellectual community—especially those who direct the contemporary university and its faculty. It is interesting to note that the college-educated segment of the general public has opinions that follow the direction of faculty views—without going quite as far. College-trained Americans are more (new) liberal than the rest of the populace; as Lipset and I have shown on a number of occasions, the professoriate is somewhat more liberal than the entire college cohort.[19] We see this relationship when we look at political self-description (Table 8-11). For example, 47 percent of professors locate themselves on the liberal-left end of the continuum, as do 43 percent of all Americans with postgraduate training and 39 percent of those with four years of college. By contrast, only about a quarter of the high-school- and grade-school-educated segments of the population identify themselves as liberals. Data on the professoriate are elaborated in Lipset's paper in this volume.

Table 8-11
Political Self-Description of Faculty and Educational Groups in the General Public[20]

	Liberal	Middle-of-the-road	Conservative
Professors			
at research universities	54%	21%	25%
all	47	21	32
Total population			
postgraduate	43	20	36
college graduate	39	25	37
some college	36	33	32
H.S. graduate	23	47	29
less than H.S.	28	43	29
all	29	40	31

SUMMARY

With basic changes in American social structure in the contemporary period—changes of the sort *post-industrialism* suggests—a new form of class conflict has appeared. This conflict is, in the American tradition, vague, often contradictory, always muted. But the phenomenon is nonetheless consistent and perceptible. An upper-middle-class-as-intelligentsia confronts an embourgeoised working class. These two strata bring different interests, values, and perceptions to a wide range of current issues. The new liberalism and the new conservatism appear as ideological tendencies distinguishing the strata.

What is especially striking in the survey data is the consistency of the inversion of the old New Deal relationship of class and ideology, and the range of this inversion.* Thus, the college cohorts are more "new liberal" than their high-school- and grade-school-trained counterparts, not only on the social, cultural, and lifestyle issues that are so often discussed, but on a broad assortment of public policy matters ranging from economic growth and environmentalism to foreign affairs and national defense. And behind the specific issues and the new relationship of the upper and lower social strata lie more diffuse differences in views of the society and of the state, in orientations toward social change, in social values.

It would be overstating things to claim that I have "proved" the emergence of a class conflict in which tensions between an intelligentsia and an embourgeoised working class are central. I *have* demonstrated the presence of consistent and persisting differences among social strata on a broad range of policy and value questions *that are exactly the differences one would expect to find if the intelligentsia/new-bourgeoisie conflict were emerging as hypothesized*.

Such broad and internally disparate groups in the general public as the college educated and the high-school educated can only display ideological tendencies. The real political payoff of the developments described must occur at the level of activism—as tendencies evident among mass publics sustain contending activists who refine the tendencies, give them coherence, form interest groups, and pursue their conflict in the various arena where American

---

*It should be noted that in the data analysis sections of this paper, I have purposely selected policy and value questions that emphasize the new liberal/new conservative change. It would be less than honest not to acknowledge that one can locate items where the divisions run in the opposite direction. We are dealing with often "mushy" survey data and with groups of extraordinary internal variety. But I am satisfied that the amount of change detected for the years from 1947 to the present—especially given the lack of precision of survey research and the vagaries of the analytic categories—are as dramatic as one could ever expect to find. We have as much data bearing on the reality of the tendencies as could be expected.

public policy disputes are carried on. It is hardly surprising that activists have already built upon the ideological tendencies identified here to alter dramatically the shape of contemporary American political life.

NOTES

1. Samuel Lubell has argued this case forcefully in *The Future of American Politics* (Garden City, 1956). Another thoughtful analysis making the same point is James L. Sundquist, *Dynamics of the Party System* (Washington, 1973).

2. These figures are derived from six large surveys of the American population conducted between 1972 and 1977 by the National Opinion Research Center of the University of Chicago (NORC). The composite file contains 9,120 cases.

3. For data on these relationships and analysis of the data, see my *Transformations of the American Party System* (New York, 1978), especially Chapter 4; and Ladd and Charles D. Hadley, *Political Parties and Political Issues: Patterns in Differentiation Since the New Deal* (Beverly Hills, 1973).

4. Gallup (AIPO) Poll number 504.

5. Gallup (AIPO) Poll numbers 369, 373, 392, 396, 400, 404, 408.

6. *Time* magazine survey of college graduates, 1947.

7. I have examined aspects of this elsewhere. See, in particular, "Liberalism Upside Down: The Inversion of the New Deal Order," *Political Science Quarterly* (Winter 1976-1977), pp. 577-600.

8. Yankelovich-General Mills Family Survey, 1976; Yankelovich-*Time* Polls, 1976.

9. NORC General Social Surveys, 1972-77.

10. Ibid.

11. Computations from NORC General Social Surveys.

12. NORC General Social Surveys; Center for Political Studies 1976 National Election Survey; Yankelovich-*Time* Poll, 1977; Harris-Chicago Council of Foreign Relations Survey, 1974.

13. The Field Poll, Report 77-044, 1977.

14. NORC General Social Surveys; Harris-Chicago Council of Foreign Relations Survey, 1974; Yankelovich-*Time* Polls, 1976.

15. Gallup (AIPO) Polls numbers 769, 770, 771, 773, 857, 858, 859, 860. For further elaboration of these data, see my "Liberalism Upside Down."

16. NORC General Social Surveys.

17. Computations from NORC General Social Surveys.

18. See in particular, E.C. Ladd and S.M. Lipset, *The Divided Academy: Professors and Politics* (New York, 1976), pp. 55-92.

19. Ibid., pp. 25-36; Ladd and Lipset, *Academics, Politics, and the 1972 Election* (Washington, 1973), pp. 14-18; "Academics: America's Most Politically Liberal Stratum," *The Chronicle of Higher Education* (20 October 1975); and "Professors, Politics, and Academe's 'Internal Logic'," *The Chronicle of Higher Education* (3 November 1975).

20. 1977 Ladd-Lipset Faculty Survey; NORC General Social Surveys, 1974-77. Slightly different choices were offered the two samples:

    faculty—far left, very liberal, somewhat liberal, moderate, somewhat conservative, far right, none of these.

    general public—extremely liberal, liberal, slightly liberal, middle-of-the-road, slightly conservative, conservative, extremely conservative.

9

THE NEW CLASS AND THE LEFT

Michael Harrington

Is there a new class that uses socialism as an ideology to mask its aspiration to become the ruler and exploiter of society?

That is a problematic question that cannot be answered easily—or perhaps at all. For one thing, the very concept of the new class is about as solid as jello (even though there is a significant residue of meaning to the term). But the difficulties of defining the new class are minor compared to the problem of reaching a general agreement about what "socialism" is. The dispute over the definition of "socialism" has been going on for more than a century, and the partisans of the various definitions have sometimes tried to annihilate one another. At this very moment, Arabs who call themselves socialists are trying to wipe out Israel, where socialists were, until quite recently, the political major-ity; bitter quarrels between democratic socialists and Communists have been going on since 1917; in Africa, socialists in the *maquis* are trying to overthrow socialists in the cities.

Note that I have only touched upon the differences among those who call themselves socialists. I have not added to the cacophony the various definitions of the antisocialists (who, interestingly enough, seem to overestimate socialist success because of a fuzzy notion of what it means). In any case, the reader is forewarned: The opening question will be dealt with speculatively, without any pretense of being definitive. But precisely because of the limitations of that question, I would ask a related question that can be confronted more empirically: What is the relation of the new class (or stratum) to the American Left today?

Responding to that requires generalizing about the nature of the various protest and activist movements of the recent past and trying to assess their impact upon American politics. Were, and are, those movements an expression of a new class? If so, have they helped create a genuine Left—or acted as a front for the emergence of a pseudo-Left providing a radical rationale for the ambitions of a new elite? Although there is no mass socialist movement here, these questions reveal the American aspects of the larger issue of the relationship between socialism and the new class. My analytic framework has already been presented at book length in *The Twilight of Capitalism*; I see no point in doing anything more than summarizing it in the first section of this article.

The entire world is inexorably moving toward collective forms of social life. The simplest way to describe that trend is to note that economic decisions are increasingly being made politically; in the not-too-distant future, the decisive choices in every nation on the planet will be made politically.

Of course, history is not moving in a neat and linear fashion. The bureaucratic collectivist system of communism, which employs the idea of socialism as an ideology—i.e., as a rationale for the rule of a bureaucratic class—first developed on the capitalist margin, in Russia, where the bourgeoisie was unable to carry out the bourgeois revolution.* The Party took the place of the entrepreneurs and corporations and pumped a surplus out of the direct producers by totalitarian force rather than by "freedom" of contract, as in the West.

The Russian experience took place in a relatively backward but still economically developed power. The trend toward collectivism in the Third World emerges out of much more desperate poverty and is visible in nations officially committed to capitalism, like Brazil and Taiwan or even the Ivory Coast, and in non-Communist socialist countries, like Egypt or the Sudan, as well as in Communist powers. The trend toward collectivism in the advanced countries of the West grows out of the inability of the capitalist institutional structure to cope, in a traditional (or classically capitalist) way, with the social, economic,

---

*The bourgeoisie did not actually make the bourgeois revolution in most capitalist countries—landed aristocrats carried it out in England, feudal plantation owners were its agents in Germany, a state bureaucracy played an important role in France, and so on—but even if it did not create the revolution, the bourgeoisie was strong enough to become the social base of the new order.

and political interdependencies of advanced capitalist production. Collectivization is significantly different within a framework of political democracy than under communism. There is, however, an underlying tendency at work in different ways in all of these societies: The increasingly social character of economic production requires conscious governmental intervention.

So markets give way to political decisions. In saying this, I assume the obvious: that completely free markets never existed and that impure markets are now becoming even more politicized. At the same time, bureaucrats, both private and public, become much more important than entrepreneurs or stockholders. The outcome of these changes is far from certain. In some respects, it conforms to Marx's powerful analysis of capitalist development and self-contradiction in the "Historic Tendency of Capitalist Accumulation" in *Capital*: The prediction that the private socialization of production would eventually pit the social means of production against the private mode of controlling them.

On the very first page of *The Communist Manifesto*, Marx and Engels indicated that they understood that these trends could lead to a tragic conclusion. Class struggles, they commented, always ended *either* with a revolution *or* with "the common ruin of the contending classes." If Marx recognized the second possibility in the abstract, he was clearly convinced throughout his life that socialism would triumph. However, by 1939 the other outcome was being viewed by serious Marxists as a very real, though intolerable, possibility. Even as he denied that the Soviet Union was a new form of class society, Leon Trotsky wrote, "Marxists have formulated an incalculable number of times the alternative: either socialism or a return to barbarism .... The real passage to socialism cannot fail to appear incomparably more complicated, more heterogeneous, more contradictory than was foreseen in the general historical scheme."[1]

But what Marx foresaw as an abstract possibility and Trotsky reluctantly recognized while denying its reality is now very clearly one of the two major options confronting humanity. Collectivism will indeed triumph, but it could take the form of two polar alternatives with a wide range of possibilities in between. On the one extreme, there could be an authoritarian, or totalitarian, collectivism run by a bureaucratic class; on the other, there could be a democratic communitarianism with considerable decentralization and self-management. The latter is what I mean by socialism.

The American economy is moving toward that fork in the road, but in a paradoxical way. On the one hand, the politicalization of economics proceeds apace, and both public and private bureaucrats play a more visible role in the formulation of policy. On the other hand, the system continues to operate primarily for the benefit of the possessors of wealth, even if the rich often leave the management of their corportions to hired hands. Daniel Bell is quite correct to write that "new men"—"the scientists, the mathematicians, the economists and the engineers of the new intellectual technology"—make many of the critical decisions. But he is wrong to say that those new men have a free hand, independent of the interests of the corporate rich.

In America, then, postbourgeoïs tendencies shore up bourgeois society. If left unchallenged, this trend would lead to the emergence of some kind of a bureaucratic collectivism, perhaps with a democratic facade. The new class would thereby triumph not in the name of socialism but from the workings of corporate collectivism, which is now the major movement in this society. The country would back into the future thoughtlessly, in precisely the manner that would maximize the possibilities of an elite system. Thus *late capitalism*, not socialism, is the precursor of an authoritarian society under the rule of the new class. Socialism, properly understood, is the *alternative* to such a development rather than the agency of it.

Because the collectivization trend is so large and so historically varied, it has given rise to positive and negative assessments from the Left, the Right, and the Center. Many of the definitions of a new class are impressionistic, transient, and incapable of sustaining the analytic weight imposed upon them. But, as George Lichtheim wrote,

> a new class, like a new culture, does not sprout overnight. There is clearly something in the notion that the functional separation of physical from mental labor may contain the germ of a new division along class lines. If this process should turn out to be irreversible, it would be necessary to conclude that the goal of a classless society is utopian, insofar as it assumes that the division of labor can be overcome. But whether or not this is actually the case remains to be seen. In any event it has no bearing on the exercise of power. Class analysis deals with long run processes, not with transitory political and ideological phenomenon.[2]

But even though we are dealing with an ongoing development within the framework of a concept, social class, which is as slippery as it is useful, the notion of a new class can make a modest contribution to our understanding of contemporary society. First, however, that notion must be unraveled. The following chart, which is far from complete, indicates just a bit of the complexity.

It is obvious that the issue is not quite as confused as this chart might at first seem to suggest. There are not thirty different definitions of the new class, since some of these analysts can be grouped together. There are the hopeful technocrats (Saint-Simon, Veblen, the Galbraith of the *New Industrial State*). Then there are various socialists and radicals who expected new strata to aid their cause. For example, during his debate with Eduard Bernstein in 1895, Karl

Attitudes Toward The New Class(es)

LEFT		RIGHT	
Good	*Bad*	*Good*	*Bad*
Saint-Simon	Bakunin	Pareto	Schumpeter
Karl Kautsky	Waclaw Machajski	D.P. Moynihan	Lewis Feuer
Louis Boudin	Lucien Laurat	Daniel Bell	James Burnham
Thorstein Veblen	Max Shachtman		D.P. Moynihan
David Bazelon	Milovan Djilas		Daniel Bell
J.K. Galbraith	Frankfurt School		Irving Kristol
C. Wright Mills	Andre Gorz		
Czech Academy of	Barbara & John		
Science	Ehrenreich		
Andre Touraine			
Andre Gorz			
Serge Mallet			
Roger Garraudy			
Santiago Carrillo			

Kautsky wrote that the intelligentsia within an emergent new middle class "one day would discover its proletarian heart" (although he felt that the state functionaries and the professionals within that class would adopt a bourgeois point of view). The American Marxist Louis Boudin falls into this category, as do C. Wright Mills and myself.[3]

Then there are European Left socialists and Eurocommunists, all of whom looked toward the new strata—sometimes called a new working class—to make common cause with the traditional proletariat. In this category I would include the Czechoslovakian Academy of Science in the period before the Prague Spring, the French leftist thinkers Alain Touraine, Andre Gorz, Serge Mallet, and Roger Garraudy, and the Spanish Communist leader Santiago Carrillo.[4] At least one member of this group, Andre Gorz, is also included among the Left critics of the new class, since he argued that this stratum could move either left or right.

On the Left, those hostile to the new class include the anarchists, like Bakunin and Machajski; those who saw the Communist bureaucracies as examples of new-class power (Laurat, Shachtman, Djilas); thinkers fearful of a bureaucratization of all modern systems (Adorno and Horkheimer from the Frankfurt School[5]); and New Leftists of the late 1960s and 1970s (especially the Ehrenreichs) who were critical of the class origins and tendencies within their own movement.

On the Right, those sympathetic to the new class include the Italian economist Vilfredo Pareto, who forecast the rise of a new elite from out of the working class. Then there is D.P. Moynihan, the neo-conservative, whose "The Professionalization of Reform" might be called a manifesto *for* the new class, but who also wrote a number of denunciations of the same class. Daniel Bell might also be counted in both the pro and con columns. Lewis Feuer, who makes the most far-ranging use of the concept of the new class, sees it as the key to most of social history. "Throughout human history," Feuer writes, "whenever people of a society have been overwhelmingly illiterate and voiceless, the intellectual elite has been the sole rival for political power with the military elite." And more traditional conservatives, like Irving Kristol, tend to equate the new class with liberal egalitarianism.[6]

These different perspectives also yield different definitions. Some see the new class as composed of engineers and "hard" scientists (Bell, Veblen); others as the educated class in general (Schumpeter, Bazelon, Harrington); others as the managerial class (Burnham, Galbraith, the Ehrenreichs); others as a new working class (Gorz, Mallet); others as a new bureaucratic class (the anarchists and the analysts of Stalinism). If space permitted, more complications could easily be added and many more thinkers could be introduced into this confused picture.

But does all this confusion mean that the concept of the new class is so imprecise as to be useless? No, particularly if one carefully specifies its members and adopts the modest attitude suggested at the beginning of this section. For the purposes of this essay, there is no great difference between designating a group as a new class or as a new stratum of a new middle class that began to appear around the turn of the century. So without making any claim to a rigorous and finished analysis, I will argue that there is an identifiable population, new to the social structure and with common views, that has already made a quantum leap in its impact on our political life in recent years and will continue to have an impact in the future.

One of the key indices to the existence of this class (but not its definition) is found in the statistics on education in America. In 1950, 1.2 million students graduated high school; in 1975, the figure had doubled to 3.1 million. In the late 1950s, 51.3 percent of the high-school graduates entered postsecondary education, and 25.8 percent received a bachelor's degree. In the mid-1970s, 57.4 percent of the vastly expanded pool continued their education beyond high school. In 1975, the last year for which figures on graduation are available, 31 percent of those who graduated high school four years earlier went on to earn a college degree. As a result of all this, the percentage of Americans between 25 and 29 years of age with a college degree nearly tripled between 1950 and 1970 (from 7.7 percent to 20.7 percent).[7] Even though this trend slowed in the 1970s, it defined a basic experience during more than two decades of American life.

Two initial thoughts suggest themselves. First, the spread of higher education has enormous social consequences; second, in and of itself, it does not prove the existence of a new class (or stratum). Is there any evidence that this group of college graduates then went on to adult careers sharing a common consciousness? I would say yes. In the years between 1940 and 1970, the number of "information workers" in the American economy sharply increased. That category, it should be stressed, is extremely broad: It includes electronic-machine operators as well as systems analysts; according to one estimate, it accounts for 46 percent of GNP.[8] Still, even though the "information workers" include many who are not conceivably part of the new class, this sector grew much faster than the total labor force between 1940 and 1970, and is moving ahead slightly faster in this decade.

A computation by B. Bruce-Briggs underlines this point. Between 1950 and 1970, the more elite occupations in the U.S. Census Bureau's "Professional, Technical, and Kindred Workers" classification grew from 6.9 percent of the labor force to 12.1 percent. If the more privileged and powerful individuals in management, sales, and farming are added, this population grows to almost 25 percent of the labor force. (The Ehrenreichs make a similar estimate of the size of the "professional-managerial class," but their analytic techniques are not as carefully worked out as those of Bruce-Briggs.[9])

It seems fair to assume that a significant portion of this vastly increased college graduate pool went into the new, nonmanual, *relatively* elite occupations in the burgeoning information sector. Others went into traditional middle- and upper-middle-class positions. Others simply used their credentials to get work that had previously been the province of the high-school graduate. But even with these and other complications, I think there is a new stratum/class in the American social structure; its members are characterized by college or graduate or professional education and *relatively* well-paid occupations, often in a new technological sector, with *some* opportunity for nonroutine work.

It is immediately obvious that this stratum is *not* a ruling class. In the Census year 1970, which Bruce-Briggs uses for his most recent computation of the "elite" professionals, managers, and others, the top income quintile in the United States began at $15,531 annually; the top 5 percent at $24,250.[10] Most of the people we have been describing are not even in the top 5 percent. That is why I stress that they have *relatively* elite occupations. Clearly, they are not involved in making the basic choices of the society. It is not so obvious, but just as true, that even those in the very top of this group—the highest level of salaried professionals and administrators—do not constitute a ruling class.

Let me simply summarize the argument I made in *The Twilight of Capitalism*. It is certainly true that nonowning managers and technicians play a much more significant role in late capitalism than they did in the earlier stages of this society. Yet the outcomes of the society continue to benefit primarily the possessors of great wealth; the talented and educated are tolerated in the "technostructure," or as "new men," only so long as they act to maximize the priorities of those who own. It is true that owners do not necessarily rule, in the sense of personally exercising political power; it is just as true that whoever rules, as long as the investment process is dominated by private owners, decisions will ordinarily promote their interests.

So a stratum of people in the American social structure has incomes, educational levels, and occupations that distinguish them from the working class and the poor; they are not, however, part of the corporate rich whose interests shape the basic priorities of the society. But isn't this stratum merely the same "new middle class" that was identified at least three quarters of a century ago? And if it is, why all the talk of a new class?

First, as David Bazelon pointed out some time ago, this stratum is engaged in planning, whether in the public or private sector. It is not the product of the emergent monopoly capitalism that created, at the turn of the century, a class of salaried managers within the corporate structure. It arises out of a much more developed phase of capitalism; it uses the "intellectual technology" of the times; it takes the cooperation of government and the corporations for granted. The New Deal, as Samuel Lubell understood, is part of its liberal heritage—whereas the original new middle class was Republican.[11]

Moreover, the social weight of this stratum has increased enormously. In Bruce-Briggs' computation, the elite section of the professional and technical category more than doubled between 1950 and 1970. This elite made the most striking gains within that 25 percent of the population defined earlier (which means that the "managers and administrators" stayed at roughly the same level during that two-decade period).

But my conclusions about the new class do not come merely from the study of statistical trends. As a participant in the civil-rights, antiwar, environmental, and feminist movements of the 1960s and 1970s, I observed the new-class composition of those very significant developments. One special circumstance—that these various protests coincided with the tremendous growth in the number of college students—might lead one to overgeneralize. Could not one account for that burst of social energy simply by attributing it to the presence of a large concentration of leisured, privileged students? The New Left would then be to the 1960s what swallowing goldfish was to the 1930s: a campus diversion. There would be no need to resort to elaborate theories about changes in social structure.

I obviously do not accept this interpretation, even though it contains a grain of truth (the concentration of students did tend to magnify and overdramatize the appearance of the new class). Contrary to widespread impressions, the activists of the 1960s did not disappear when SDS self-destructed, or even after McGovern's defeat in 1972. Many of the veterans of protest movements went into the Democratic Party structure, where they elected roughly a third of the delegates to the 1974 special Democratic convention and provided the basis for a number of Presidential primary campaigns in 1976, most notably the Udall effort. They are also to be found in a host of community organizing projects throughout the nation and have created a national network of state and local officials who are "graduates" of the 1960s.

These examples are out of my own experience. But there are also some hard data to back them up. *The Changing American Voter* by Norman H. Nie, Sidney Verba, and John R. Petrocik is a carefully documented study of changes in political attitudes and organization from the 1950s to the 1970s. The authors use the classic book, *The American Voter*, which appeared in 1960 and presented data from the 1950s, as a baseline to measure the changes that have taken place since then. Their conclusion is that significant, even dramatic, changes took place during those years.[12] Some of them are relevant to an analysis of the new class.

Between the 1950s and the 1960s, according to *The Changing American Voter*, voters became much less Republican, somewhat less Democratic, and much more independent. They also demonstrated much greater issue consistency (i.e., they had liberal or conservative attitudes on *both* domestic and foreign policy), and much more of a tendency to evaluate parties and politicians by ideological standards. The activists in the Democratic party became more youthful, and as a result the party's left wing went from 15 percent in 1956 to 26 percent in 1972, and the "moderate left" from 13 percent to 22 percent. In the 1960s, in every sectional and ethnic grouping except Jews and blacks, the young were more liberal than their elders, and in one case—upper-status Northern white Protestants—the older generation was conservative and the younger generation liberal.

These data should not be burdened with conclusions they do not support. So let me specify my argument carefully. The tendencies toward issue voting, consistency, etc., occurred at every age and educational level; not all these changes can be explained by the new class. Moreover, the most marked tendency was not toward realignment, as I had hoped in *Toward a Democratic Left*, but toward a decline in party loyalty and identification, with no clear replacement for them. Still, it is fair to see part of the changes documented in *The Changing American Voter* as providing a firm statistical basis for impressionistic personal judgments.

There is evidence that mass higher education and changes in the occupational structure have brought forth a new class/stratum with distinctive values and attitudes. This is not to suggest that a community of idealistic angels, devoid of any self-interest, is now abroad in American society. Such a notion is silly. Nor is this group a new "proletariat," in the sense that the young Marx used that term: a homogeneous, disciplined, and self-conscious class. It is, like every other class, internally ambiguous and even contradictory, and only a minority of its members are politically active. Moreover—unlike, say, the unions or the corporate rich—it is not united around clear economic realities that give rise to ongoing organizations.

Yet, with all of these qualifications, there are significant indices of the existence of this class. It has already played an important political role in this country. Does its growth mark the appearance of an antisocialist—or antiliberal—elite that uses socialist or liberal rhetoric for selfish purposes? Or is it a potential constituency for a genuine Left?

The notion that antisocialists can use socialist rhetoric is more than a hundred years old. In 1848, Mark and Engels devoted an entire section of *The Communist Manifesto* to just such an idea. They described a whole host of "socialisms"—bourgeois, petty bourgeois, feudal, reactionary—which they took to be frauds. In the years that followed, they extended this insight, analyzing the imperial "socialism" of Napoleon III and, most important, the "Bismarckian socialism" of their own homeland. And in 1893, Engels wrote to Adolph Sorge that the Fabians were "a group of strivers who are smart enough to recognize that the social revolution is unavoidable but who cannot trust this work to the raw proletariat and therefore are accustomed to place themselves in the lead." [13]

The irrepressible George Bernard Shaw echoed Engels, but with a completely different attitude, in his description of his fellow Fabian socialists. "There were practically no wage workers," Shaw wrote:

> the committee was composed of state officials of the higher division and journalists of the special critical class which produces signed feuilleton, they were exceptionally clever . . . . They paraded their cleverness . . . and openly spoke of ordinary Socialism as a sort of detention fever which a man had to pass through before he was intellectually mature enough to become a Fabian. Though at this time the idolatry of Marx by the Socialists was a hundred times worse than the idolatry of Gladstone by the Liberals, the Fabians in restating the economic basis of Socialism, brought it up to date by completely ignoring Marx. [14]

In a completely different development, an entire school of analysis viewed the Soviet Union as a society utilizing communist phrases to rationalize totalitarian exploitation of the workers. And more recently, there are Third World Marxists, like Issa Shivji, who regard the governments of the newly independent countries in a similar light. [15] The Russians have such a theory about the Chinese—and *vice versa*.

It is often argued that Bakunin was the originator of the theory that a new class used socialism for its own purposes. Paul Avrich points out that long before Machajski or Djilas or James Burnham, Bakunin had warned that "a new class, a new hierarchy of genuine or sham scientists" would establish despotic rule over the masses.[16] But when one looks at Bakunin's actual text, it turns out that he was criticizing representative democracy in general. The new class he conjured up would be elected, which means that his description hardly anticipates Communist totalitarianism.

Marx answered Bakunin briefly, and one point of his response is of more than passing interest. Bakunin had charged that the Marxists favored an "educated" or "scientific" socialism; since the masses were not scientists, that inevitably meant the rule of intellectual aristocracy. He had never spoken of "educated" socialism, Marx commented, and had used the term "scientific socialism" only in opposition to the utopians precisely because they had fantasies about the people rather than knowledge of social movements.[17] The exchange has contemporary relevance because Marx and Bakunin in effect *agree* that scientific expertise could become the rationalization of class privilege. That certainly happened with Stalinism—and it might even apply to liberal democratic theories about the "professionalization of reform."

A Polish revolutionary, Waclaw Machajski, has received a certain amount of attention as a prophet who saw a labor aristocracy riding socialism to class power. His writings were called to the attention of the English-speaking public by Max Nomad; the young Trotsky, in exile, encountered Machajski's views and later discussed them with Lenin when they first met in London in 1902.[18] And between the two wars, anarchists and left-wing Communists kept up a steady attack on the privileged life of the Soviet bureaucracy. In short, a socialist (or a democratic Marxist) has no problem recognizing the new class of the 1970s as pseudo-Leftist. But is that an accurate description?

First, consider an analysis from the Left: Barbara and John Ehrenreich's article on the professional-managerial class and the New Left.[19] I have serious methodological differences with the Ehrenreichs—above all their tendency to reify or anthropomorphize entire social classes and to make conscious class interests decisive in history (this is the "Beardian" reading of Marx that is quite popular in the United States). And yet I think there is a substantial point to their critique.

According to the Ehrenreichs, the professional-managerial class—or PMC, as they refer to it—emerged between 1890 and 1920. It was critical of the capitalists, who lacked science and culture, but also antagonistic to the workers, since the PMC reproduced the cultural and class relations of the society. This class was therefore Veblenesque and Galbraithian, and advocated reform from the top down. According to the Ehrenreichs, this perspective inspired the New Left of the 1960s. The Port Huron Statement of 1962, which effectively founded Students for a Democratic Society, called for "a left with real intellectual skills, committed to deliberativeness, honesty, and reflection as working tools. The university permits the political life to be an adjunct to the academic one, and action to be informed by reason."

So the Ehrenreichs' analysis describes a stratum with contradictory tendencies. As employees and subordinates, its members are hostile to corporate power and hierarchy. As relatively privileged professionals, they have a social stake in maintaining the relative position of the workers. To cite an example from my own experience: In Sweden, resistance to a socialist policy of "solidarity" with the poor, which consciously sought to transfer income to the bottom of the society, was more marked among professionals than among the blue-collar workers. And yet this same stratum, as the Ehrenreichs rightly argue, has been a major source of radicalism in the United States.

Many of these complex trends are at work in the American environmental movement. On the one hand, the environmentalists are sometimes totally unconcerned about the social consequences of some of their proposals—i.e., they effectively impose the cost of protecting the environment on the workers who will lose their jobs when a polluting industry is shut down. On the other hand, when groups like Environmentalists for Full Employment raise that issue within the movement, they get a sympathetic hearing. The new class, I am suggesting, is not inevitably and inherently on the Left or the Right. It has tendencies toward *both* liberal elitism *and* a democratic politics of alliance with working people and the poor. Which of these tendencies will prevail is not a question that can be settled theoretically. It will be decided politically.

The neo-conservative attacks on the new class miss these ambiguities. Moreover, they often contradict one another. Irving Kristol's influential *Commentary* article, "About Equality," stated a major theme of the intellectual faction grouped around that publication: that the new class objectively urges egalitarian policies even though what subjectively motivates it is a contempt for the absence of noble purpose in a business society. The college-educated new-class members "who though lacking intellectual distinction (and frequently lacking even intellectual competence) believe themselves to be intellectuals" are "most eloquent in their denunciations of inequality." Indeed, they are "engaged in a class struggle with the business community for status and power." In making this argument, Kristol makes two assertions that are both factually wrong: that "inequality of status and opportunity have visibly declined since World War II" and that income in America "and all modern societies" tends to be distributed along a bell-shaped, or "normal," curve. Yet, as I demonstrated in *The Twilight of Capitalism* (or as Paul Samuelson argues about the bell-shaped curve in his elementary textbook), the data do not support either claim.

Kristol's new class is ambiguously egalitarian. It uses egalitarian rhetoric and pushes egalitarian ideas, but for the dual purpose of countering the spiritual emptiness it feels in society and promoting its own elite power against businessmen. D.P. Moynihan makes the new class somewhat more mean-spirited. It resisted Nixon's (and Moynihan's) Family Assistance Plan because the proposal threatened its own class position. Those pseudoidealists were "*man-*

ipulating the symbols of egalitarianism for essentially middle- and upper-class purposes [emphasis added]." [20]

From the same general political perspective as Moynihan and Kristol, Penn Kemble and Josh Muravchik attacked this stratum for being uninterested in bread-and-butter questions altogether: The "affluent, educated constituency" of the "New Politics" is oriented toward an idealism unconcerned with New Deal issues.[21] That is a far cry from Kristol's charge of excessive, if ambiguous, egalitarianism, or Moynihan's description of the self-interested beneficiaries of the service strategy in the welfare state. And yet the very same tone prevails in all these contradictory analyses. Kristol is probusiness, Moynihan was identified with Nixonian reformism, Kemble and Moravchik are partisans of the Meany wing of the AFL-CIO—and all are united in their hostility to this emerging group, all deal with it in terms of a conspiracy thesis. The Ehrenreichs, even with their tendency toward simplistic categories and monolithic, conscious classes, are much more complex. They are also nearer the truth.

Finally, there is another aspect of the politics of the new class that practically everyone, including me, failed to understand in the late 1960s and early 1970s: its relationship to—the limitations imposed upon it by—the structural deficiencies of capitalist society.

All of the new-class theories, whether hostile or sympathetic, were developed during a period of affluence, or of the illusion of affluence. They therefore tacitly assumed that the society could continue providing relatively good jobs for all those college graduates forever. For example, Kemble and Muravchik argued that it would be possible for the "New Politics" to ignore economics altogether. But as the 1970s were to demonstrate rather rudely, this stratum has economic needs of its own. It is not simply ideologically or occupationally disposed toward planning for others: It requires planning for itself. And, for two reasons, this objective interest links it more with the great mass of the people than with the corporate rich.

First, Western capitalism is now facing problems of stagflation, which no government has solved. At the same time, there is evidence of a marked slowdown in the growth of the "information economy" that had absorbed so many of the graduates,[22] and there is even serious talk of a long-term downturn.

Even if the demographic *deus* does arrive *ex machina* in the 1980s—when the labor shortage created by a much smaller generation leads to full employment—it is likely that the graduates of the 1960s and 1970s will find their college degrees devalued in a limping economy.

These possibilities have already stimulated some critical revisions of "human capital" theory. In the 1960s, it was argued that more higher education would add to GNP and increase the incomes of individuals at the same time. The nation could thereby accomplish a social revolution without the inconvenience of changing basic structures. But then marginal analysis pointed up some sobering qualifications to those optimistic assumptions. In an economy based upon unskilled and semiskilled labor, an increase in high-school diplomas and college degrees would indeed raise productivity and incomes. But there is a declining yield to this process, and the result of increasing the graduates from 20 percent of the generation to 21 percent is quite different from raising their number from 5 percent to 6 percent. In brute economic terms, which do not dictate policy conclusions but are helpful in making them, it could cost society more to turn out those graduates than it receives from their enhanced productivity.

These developments, then, could turn the new class from planning for others (which is its elitist tendency) to planning for themselves and others, for the common victims of flawed social structures (a shift that would provide a basis for a social and democratic tendency). The "oversupply" of educated labor is an artifact of an American society that will only use it when it yields a proper return to corporate capital. New definitions—in reality—of "private" and "public" can change that.

And a second, related factor could reinforce the happier (from a Left point of view) of the alternative new-class tendencies toward planning: not the late capitalist economic limits to growth but the social limits to growth. In his stimulating book on that subject, the late Fred Hirsch argued that an egalitarian rat race is impossible. The first automobile is an aristocratic privilege; the ten-millionth automobile creates a traffic jam that totally undercuts any aristocracy whatsoever. Once the physical necessities are satisfied with manufactured goods that can be reproduced *ad infinitum*, the status necessities take over. One person stands on tiptoe to get a better view of the parade—a better position—and then everybody eventually stands on tiptoe, and no one has a better view, although everyone has expended more energy. But what if college degrees are our version of standing on tiptoe?[23]

I have merely summarized a few of Hirsch's major themes, but their relevance to my analysis should already be obvious. There are social limits to the individualism of the new class. That class—like every other class in America, including the workers and the poor—is normally thoroughly imbued with bourgeois values, even if it often has a reformist version of them. But what if bourgeois society becomes an impediment to the achievement of bourgeois values? That social order had always proclaimed that it could universalize its privileges. Alfred Marshall even said that everyone should be able to be a gentleman. But if there are no subordinates and no servants, no one can live as a gentleman should. And so the attempt to take capitalist illusions at face value can lead to anticapitalist conclusions.

I do not want to burden Hirsch with all of the value judgments of the preceeding paragraph. Let him speak in his own words. He raises the possibility that "privately directed behavior may lose its inherent advantage over collectively-oriented behavior *even as a means of satisfying individual preferences themselves*, however self-interested. It follows that the best result may be attained by steering or guiding certain motives of individual behavior into social rather than individual orientation, though still on the basis of privately directed preference."[24]

So there are current trends that could accentuate the "good" tendency of the new class toward planning—i.e., the democratic and social tendency. But the issue is far from settled, and it must be frankly said that the new class could be one agency in a worldwide movement toward collectivization that might well be elitist and authoritarian. In the not-too-distant past there were Fabians, like Shaw and the Webbs, who were taken in by Stalin—and even, in the case of Shaw, by fascism.[25] Such errors could certainly happen again.

Could the new class be a part of a Left coalition? That, too, is a possibility. But what are the alternatives to it? The critics of the new class in America tend to come from the neo-conservative Right. They reject bureaucratic collectivism *and* they are against the new class. The more classically conservative among them—say, Irving Kristol, who is not a "neo"-conservative at all—favor a free market and business society. But those, I would argue, are utopian illusions. For all of the conservatives' professions of faith in free enterprise, corporations are more and more intertwined with the government, as participants in planning from the top down rather than as servants of the market. Those who cling to the capitalist illusions will thus unwittingly rationalize an unconscious transition to the worst of the postcapitalist possibilities.

The "neo"-conservatives—i.e., those who came to their position from a liberal or socialist background, after being disillusioned of their Great Society dreams—often speak in the name of working people against intellectual elitists. D.P. Moynihan's model, for instance, is of a restored New Deal coalition. But that is to ignore the difference between the 1930s and the 1970s and 1980s. The college-educated stratum is larger; it has gone through political experiences; and it has a much greater social weight than ever before. In his primary race for the United States Senate, Moynihan just barely defeated a candidate who had mobilized those new-class forces.

I am not, then, simply saying that the new class *could* be a participant in a genuinely democratic Left. I am arguing that it *must* be if there is any hope that such a Left will provide nonauthoritarian responses to the inevitable collectivism of the late twentieth and twenty-first centuries.

NOTES

1. Leon Trotsky, *In Defense of Marxism* (New York, 1942), p. 31.

2. George Lichtheim, *Short History of Socialism* (New York, 1970), p. 310.

3. Karl Kautsky, *Bernstein und das socialdemokratische Programm* (Stuttgart, 1899), pp. 127ff.; Michael Harrington, *Toward a Democratic Left* (New York, 1968).

4. Radovan Richta, (ed.), *Civilization at the Crossroads*, trans. Slingova (White Plains, N.Y., 1969); Alain Touraine, *Le Mouvement de Mai ou Le Communisme Utopique* (Paris, 1968); Andre Gorz, *Reforme et Revolution* (Paris, 1969); Serge Mallet, *La Nouvelle Classe Ouvriere*, 4th ed. (Paris, 1969); Roger Garraudy, *Pour un Modele Francais du Socialisme* (Paris, 1969); Santiago Carrillo, *Eurocommunism and the State*, trans. Green and Elliott (Westport, Conn., 1978).

5. Most notably in *Dialektik der Aufklarung* (Amsterdam, 1947).

6. D.P. Moynihan, "The Professionalization of Reform," *The Public Interest* (Fall 1965), and *The Politics of a Guaranteed Annual Income* (New York, 1973); Lewis Feuer, *The Conflict of Generations* (New York, 1969); Irving Kristol, "About Equality," *Commentary* (November 1972).

7. U.S. Census Bureau, *Statistical Abstract of the United States: 1977*, pp. 136, 153.

8. U.S. Congress, Joint Economic Committee Staff Study, *U.S. Long Term Growth Prospects* (January 1978), pp. 3, 17-18.

9. Barbara and John Ehrenreich, "The Professional-Managerial Class," *Radical America* (March-April, 1977); B. Bruce-Briggs, "Enumerating the New Class," Appendix Table A-3.

10. U.S. Census Bureau, *Social Indicators 1976*, table 9/7.

11. David T. Bazelon, *Power in America: The Politics of the New Class* (New York, 1967), pp. 309, 331; Samuel Lubell, *The Future of American Politics* (New York, 1965), p. 71.

12. Norman H. Nie et al., *The Changing American Voter* (Cambridge, Mass., 1976); Angus Campbell et al., *The American Voter* (New York, 1960).

13. *Marx Engels Werke* (Berlin, 1968), XXXIX, p. 8.

14. Quoted in Yvonne Karp, *Eleanor Marx* (New York, 1976), II, p. 36.

15. Issa Shirji, *The Class Struggles in Tanzania* (Dar es Salaan, 1973).

16. In Sam Dolgoff (ed.), *Bakunin on Anarchy* (New York, 1972), p. xxii.

17. *Marx Engels Werke*, XVIII, pp. 635-36.

18. Max Nomad, *Aspects of Revolt* (New York, 1961); Leon Trotsky, *My Life* (New York, 1931), p. 129, and *Lenin*, (New York, 1959), p. 11.

19. Barbara and John Ehrenreich, "The New Left: A Case Study in Professional-Managerial Class Radicalism," *Radical America* (May-June 1977).

20. Moynihan, *op. cit.*, p. 357.

21. Penn Kemble and Josh Muravchik, "The New Politics and the Democrats," *Commentary* (December 1972).

22. *U.S. Long Term Growth Prospects*, p. 19.

23. Fred Hirsch, *Social Limits to Growth* (Cambridge, Mass., 1976).

24. See the articles by Hal Draper, James Fenwick, and Irving Howe on "The Neo-Stalinist Type," *The New International* (January 1948).

10

POLITICAL RESPONSES TO THE NEW CLASS

Kevin P. Phillips

The public reaction to the numerous socioeconomic dislocations surrounding the rise of the New Class (even without a precise definition of that term) has contributed greatly to recent American politics. And the decisive reaction may be yet to come.

All of the following trends have been linked, fairly or not, to the New Class (or to the larger phenomenon of post-industrialism—the increasing change in the U.S. economy to the production, consumption, and dissemination of knowledge):

1. rising taxes and expansion of the public sector of the economy;
2. inflation (stagflation);
3. no-growth/slow-growth cultural economics (antimaterialism, environmental extremism);
4. expansion of government bureaucracy and official regulation;

5. the knowledge revolution and its ramifications (the upsurge of planners, experts, and, in George Wallace's words, "pointy heads");
6. the communications explosion and its ramifications (societal destablization, media violence, commercial sex and pornography, media "negativism," and elite media bias);
7. societal permissivism and the revolution in behavior and values (sex, abortion, drugs, etc.);
8. racial and social engineering (busing, suburban racial balance, quotas, and the like);
9. defeatist foreign policy and deemphasis of national defense, national security, and military spending.

The connections between some of these phenomena and the rise of the New Class may be tenuous or exaggerated. Yet just as the post-industrial revolution and the New Class are creatures of the years since 1960, so are the political movements reacting to them.

The sequence of political reactions is itself revealing and suggestive of the escalating frustration of traditional American politics. Governor George Wallace was probably the first politician in the United States to respond directly to the impact of the New Class (without so labeling it), and he found a receptive national audience. Some analysts argue that Wallace's politics appealed purely to regional and racial interests. But that interpretation cannot explain the stunning vote Wallace received in the 1964 Democratic primaries in Maryland, Indiana, and Wisconsin. And it cannot explain the surprising extent of his third-party support (10-20 percent of the total vote) in 1968 in many of the Rocky Mountain strongholds of populism in the 1890s and 1900s—areas (like Idaho) that have since remained mostly on the Right. The day of the expert and the planner was dawning, and the appeal of Wallaceite rhetoric against bureaucrats, guidelines, planners, elites, and "pointy heads" struck a basic populist chord. In some ways, Barry Goldwater's rhetoric in 1964 about setting the Eastern seaboard adrift tapped similar sentiments. Antielite and elite voting patterns began a fundamental reversal that year.

A second, more moderate and broader-based reaction to the New Class was found in the politics and constituency of Richard Nixon and Spiro Agnew between 1968 and 1972. Wallace's complaint in 1970 that he should have been paid royalties for Agnew's speeches was well-founded. The Nixon Administration enforced and advanced desegregation, but other facets of its policy and rhetoric tapped what can be described, retrospectively, as anti-New Class themes and resentments. Agnew was often in the vanguard, but he had Nixon's support in opposing elitists, planners, the Eastern Media Establishment, Harvard and the Ivy League, nonprofit foundations like Brookings and Ford, campus activism, the drug culture, pornography, and the like. These targets read like a laundry list of middle-class resentment in the 1960s. National defense and patriotic *rhetoric* (if not always *substance*) bolstered the substantial anti-New Class image of the Nixon-Agnew Administration. GOP theorists, myself among them, saw in the votes for Nixon and Wallace (57 percent of the total) a "New Majority."

The opportunity for such a majority, pivoting on public reaction to New Class-related issues, came when the Democrats nominated George McGovern in 1972. Some 40 percent of the McGovern delegates to the 1972 Democratic convention had master's degrees or better, and much of McGovern's doctrine was quintessential New Class ideology. Samplings of faculty and student opinion in Ivy League universities showed substantial pro-McGovern majorities. Meanwhile, places like the Mississippi pineywoods, the Colorado Plains, and the Idaho mining country, locales that previously had always supported antielite politics, *supported* the Nixon-Agnew ticket by a four-to-one majority. Some 80 percent of those who voted for Wallace in 1968 backed Nixon in 1972. Cultural polarization over the New Class was by no means complete in 1972, but it had reached substantial proportions.*

Prominent among the groups disenchanted with McGovern and joining with the GOP in talk of a new political alignment was the "neo-conservative" school of former liberal Democrats centered around magazines like *Commentary* and *The Public Interest*, organizations like the Coalition for a Democratic Majority and the Social Democrats, U.S.A., and the presidential candidacy of Senator Henry Jackson. In a more subdued and/or academic vein, neo-conservatives voiced many of the same criticisms made by conservative Republicans, although their tone was different and the overlap was perhaps only 50-60 percent. In 1972, a few prominent neo-conservatives like Irving Kristol saw the Democratic party on its way to becoming an American equivalent, dominated by the New Class, of the leftist Social Democratic parties of Europe, with the GOP having the opportunity to gather opponents of the New Politics under a broad new tent. Watergate destroyed that opportunity, but as scandal undercut the GOP, the (almost entirely Democratic) neo-conservative movement surged to the fore of anti-New Class criticism. Since about 1973, neo-conservatives have provided the great majority of the intellectual critiques and analyses of the New Class, its themes, and its failures. However, the 1976 presidential candidacy of Senator Jackson, the neo-conservative standardbearer in the Demo-

---

*Contrary statistics can be offered: The conservative Catholic mill towns of New England generally supported George McGovern, and Seymour Martin Lipset and Everett Carll Ladd have shown that over 40 percent of the American professoriat, unhappy with what McGovern represented, backed Nixon. But on the whole, the 1972 election represents the sharpest polarization over the New Class to date. Most of the core New Class was on one side, and ten million or so conservative and conservative-populist Democrats crossed over to the GOP for reasons that were implicitly and explicitly hostile to the New Class or attitudes linked to the New Class.

cratic party, got no further than his effort in 1972. Neo-conservatism is predominately an intellectual movement with little record of success in Democratic presidential politics.*

In contrast, the "New Right," another political group that has emerged since Watergate, represents a very different and much less fashionable set of forces. While neo-conservatives harass the New Class in magazine articles and intellectual discourse, but lack a mass constituency and make little effort to defeat New Class politicians and programs, the New Right is essentially nonintellectual and deals in populist mobilization of grassroots lower-middle and middle-class constituencies on issues like abortion, busing, education, textbooks, school prayer, the Panama Canal, and property taxes. In lieu of "New Class" terminology, the New Right talks about "producers" and "nonproducers" (essentially the New Class) and couches its political appeals in rhetoric that mixes patriotic and traditional conservative slogans with populist opposition to elites and "big" this or that—Big Business, Big Labor, Big Government. The New Right is partly a continuation of the GOP "New Majority" syndrome, partly a continuation of the Wallace movement. But as of mid-1978, its impact on issues from situs picketing and gay rights to the Panama Canal has been enough to prompt a frightened countermobilization by New Class liberals. A 1978 Americans for Democratic Action pamphlet predicts that "the coming war against America's New Right will make the McCarthy struggle look like a street fight."

Watergate was a crushing victory for the New Class. The upheavals of 1973-74 destroyed the Republican "New Majority" that might have encompassed or contained *both* neo-conservative intellectuals and New Right populists in a larger coalition able to respond to New Class excesses in a moderate yet effective manner. So *both* neo-conservatism and the New Right seem to be political movements or schools of opinion without a party; both are loathe to identify actively with the GOP. The post-Watergate Republican party, with a shrunken base of the commerical elite (Old Class) and regarded by many as an endangered species, no longer appeals to the populist-conservative "New Majority" of the Nixon-Agnew days or has much of the chance, so richly available in 1972, to put together a national majority coalition of moderate conservatives able to articulate and implement anti-New Class perceptions. The prospects seem dim for re-creating that majority coalition, although there is always the chance that the GOP could elect a president in 1980 (just as Jimmy Carter's collapse in October 1976 almost made Gerald Ford the winner).

However, despite this lack of an obvious institutional vehicle, political reaction still abounds against ideas directly and indirectly linked to the New

---

*While only a minority of Democrats are of the New Class, its influence within the party is pervasive, even in the administration of a somewhat conservative Southerner like Jimmy Carter.

Class—in many cases, even a majority opposition. Most opinion polls emphasize the popularity of political positions *opposed* to the New Class trends listed at the beginning of this article. Bureaucracy, social engineering, taxes, and extreme government regulation (from OSHA to protection for snail darters) have probably never been more unpopular than now. It seems unlikely, however, that such anti-New Class attitudes can find effective expression in the future through a single broad-based party, as they might have in 1972. True, there is always the possibility that the post-Watergate GOP, under sufficiently pressing national circumstances, might surmount its cultural narrowness, grassroots atrophy, and Old Class nonarticulateness, but I think it unlikely.

A larger possibility, at least through the early 1980s, would be a disintegrating party system, in which reactions against policies linked to the New Class play a powerful role without reconstituting or realigning the two-party system. Poll data from late 1977 and 1978 suggest an ongoing, perhaps even intensifying, public disillusionment with government, politicians, and political institutions.

Harris Polls -
"People running the country don't really care what happens to you."

Percentage of Respondents	1966	1968	1971	1972	1973	1974	1976	1977
Agreeing	26%	36%	41%	50%	55%	48%	59%	60%

Although this point has been made by Louis Harris from what might be called a New Class perspective, it has also been made by a leading GOP pollster, Robert Teeter. In a talk to the Republican State Chairmen's Association in April 1978, he indicated that the cynicism of the Vietnam and Watergate eras lives on.

Perhaps more important still, in 1978 the American electorate seems to be caught up in a new form of "disestablishmentarian" politics. Tired of seeing their opinions ignored, issue after issue, by the established political powers, voters are embracing populist political mechanisms. They are trying to force their views upon policy makers by such devices as initiatives, referenda, and demands (by state legislatures) for a federal constitutional convention, and they are trying to control the tenure of presently serving executives and legislators, through recall movements, two-term limitations, and the like. The victory in June 1978 of Proposition 13 in California, which lowered the state property tax, was a significant populist victory. In state after state, commentators have begun to note a populist upsurge. Most important, the issues involved typically bespeak populist-conservative complaints against New Class-related policies: limiting taxes, blocking busing, restricting abortions, requiring a balanced budget, repealing gay-rights ordinances, and so forth. The columnist David

Broder has gone so far as to say that initiatives and referenda have become ''the playthings of the New Right.''

Further evidence can be found in public-opinion surveys. Gallup recently reported a solid popular majority (a 57-to-39-percent majority) for a constitutional amendment to establish a national referendum device. (Three-to-one majorities already exist for anti-busing and balanced-budget amendments.) And polls by Louis Harris in mid-1978 suggest that Americans, who in recent years have been strongly negative about the institution of Congress while still approving of their individual representatives, now—for the first time—give even the *individuals* a negative rating (by a 43-to-39-percent majority). It is too early to be sure, but these may be the first signs of a fundamental public disillusionment with politicians, parties, and institutions that no longer seem to work. The malaise of the 1960s and of the Watergate era, were transitory; this discontent may be much deeper.

Any such upheaval is likely to oppose the New Class rather than submit to its leadership, given the extent to which New Class beliefs conflict with popular/ populist opinion. However, if one speaks more broadly of a post-industrial adversary culture, one can argue that elements of the New Right leadership are also an adversary culture, with respect to the prevailing national political and cultural elites. One prominent New Right tactician, Paul Weyrich (of the Committee for the Survival of a Free Congress), has bluntly stated that the New Right are not old-type conservatives but radicals out to displace the existing power structure.

The New Right is sometimes described as ultraconservative, but that is a great oversimplification. Most of the New Right organization leaders have at one time or another criticized big business, especially multinational corporations. Several leaders of the old-line American Conservative Union have criticized the willingness of the New Right to abandon conservative economic doctrine and to support middle-class welfarism. Overall, it seems fair to say that the New Right is a vehicle less of conservative ideology than of neopopulist social insurgency. Donald Warren, a sociologist at the University of Michigan, has used the term ''Middle American Radical'' to describe the 25-30 percent of the U.S. electorate that (like the New Right) is politically, culturally, and socially alienated—but from a *traditional* perspective. And Dale Vree, at the Hoover Institution, has suggested that while antiestablishment insurgency is called ''right-wing'' in the context of U.S. politics, it would be called ''left-wing'' in the Third World.

The current party structure or leadership of the ''New Right'' may ultimately be unimportant; both may have little to do with the final expression of ''Middle American Radicalism'' or populist-conservativism. The larger, perhaps even pivotal, question is whether the general wave of populist and conservative alienation, building since the late 1960s and 1970s, will ebb, persist, or grow.

Advocates of the two-party system hope that it will pass, and that postindustrial dissidents can be lured back into a party system resting on *industrial-era* economic classes and cleavages. But if the malaise of the 1960s and 1970s continues to intensify, the ultimate popular reaction to the New Class, the post-industrial revolution, America's socio-moral upheaval, or whatever one wants to call it, may very well become an increasingly volatile force outside traditional party or institutional channels (especially since the great chance for party reform or realignment was lost in 1972).

If the attitudes and politics of the New Class are leading us to such an extra-institutional crossroads, then labels of conservative or liberal, left and right may be irrelevant and even confusing. Some years back, Seymour Martin Lipset described the politics of middle-class frustration—whether in Germany, Italy, Pierre Poujade's France, or Joseph McCarthy's America—as "Center Extremism." Fascism itself was essentially a middle-class phenomenon, its origins blurred by left and right labels. And anti-New Class politics in the United States could be similar—nationalistic, majoritarian, work- and productivity-minded, inclined to a strongman, and disposed to bypass institutions in which the public had lost faith.

History suggests that nations do not easily absorb upheavals like post-industrialism or the emergence of the New Class. Free institutions in Britain did survive the chaos of the Industrial Revolution. But it does not seem idle to speculate that a more worrisome situation may be shaping up in post-industrial America.

11

USING PUBLIC FUNDS TO SERVE PRIVATE INTERESTS:
The Politics of the New Class

Aaron Wildavsky

An old joke tells of a physicist and an economist marooned on a desert island with an ample supply of cans but without a can opener. The physicist thinks of heating the cans and calculating their trajectory as they burst. The economist, in the manner of his trade, says simply, ''Assume a can opener.'' What follows is entirely in the latter tradition, for I do not intend to ask whether there is a new class, but to assume there might be.

If there were a new class, what would it be up to?

In a word, this new class seeks what every other class does—namely, privilege. What, then, distinguishes this new privileged class from the old? In a word, asymmetry. Previously, whether wealth brought status or status wealth, they came together and both brought political power. Being on top meant exactly that: not only having more money but enjoying higher status and greater political power than most other people.

So let us assume that America's new class has money (though not the most money) but not corresponding status or power. Its defining existential condition is that high income and professional standing alone do not enable its members to maintain the status and privilege to which they aspire. Their money cannot buy them what they want; so their task, as they define it, is to convince others to pay collectively for what they cannot obtain individually. Thus government lies at the center of their aspirations and operations.

Fortunately, it is not necessary to advance a new theory to explain and predict new-class public policy, because the rudiments already exist in Fred Hirsch's *Social Limits to Growth* (Cambridge, Mass., 1976). The basic difference between Hirsch and me is that he thinks collective choice is the way for everyone to discipline his desires, whereas I think collective choice is a way of getting everyone else to subsidize the new class. But his underlying mechanism is the same as mine, and he was first.

According to Hirsch, consumption has social limits because the quality of certain goods deteriorates with use or, more accurately, with users. The more people who enjoy them, the less enjoyable they become. Everyone is aware that the more the people who acquire higher education, the less a degree is worth, and the more expensive it becomes. When every plumber's son can buy a boat, to use an example from my own observation, and the Sacramento channel gets clogged up, of what use are richer peoples' boats?

This "break between individual and social opportunities" occurs because of "competition by people for place, rather than competition for performance." If people compete to improve performance, all may do better, but if they compete for position, only one can come out on top. Absolute accomplishment can be increased for all, but higher relative shares are available only for a few. In such situations, Hirsch says, "Getting what one wants is increasingly divorced from doing as one likes."

The distinguishing characteristic of what Hirsch calls positional goods is "that satisfaction is derived from scarcity itself." When everyone learns about that wonderful little restaurant with the superb service, its value declines. As Hirsch says,

> what the wealthy have today can no longer be delivered to the rest of us tomorrow; yet as we individually grow richer, that is what we expect. The dynamic interaction between material and positional sectors becomes malign. Instead of alleviating the unmet demands on the economic system, material growth at this point exacerbates them. The locus of instability is the divergence between what is possible for the individual and what is possible for all individuals. Increased material resources enlarge the demand for positional goods, a demand that can be satisfied for some only by frustrating demand by others. The intensified positional competition involves an increase in needs for the individual, in the sense

that additional resources are required to achieve a given level of welfare. In the positional sector, individuals chase each others' tails. The race gets longer for the same prize.

All this is plausible, possibly correct. Hirsch and I part company over his claim that the prevalence of positional issues makes markets inferior to government for increasing social satisfaction. For the new class, whose money cannot buy position, I would agree, but for the society that subsidizes these amenities, I would not.

Let us suppose that there are people ordinarily called the relatively rich but whom I will now call the positional poor. They make between, say, $30,000 and $100,000 annually but find they cannot attain a level of amenity corresponding to their economic income. They lack distance from lower-class competitors and lack the social position that they think they should occupy but that Hirsch's theory tells us they can no longer attain on their own. Since my subject is class privilege, how might the new class convert the resources it does have (a modest affluence, a high-status occupation) into what it lacks (distance and position)?

It is all too true that the intertwined advantages of geographic distance and social position can no longer be obtained by a modest affluence. Clean air, safe streets, virgin wilderness, household help, political power, social deference— all these and more, which were once the private property of the upper-middle-class professional (it came with status, so to speak), are out of the reach of individual effort. These amenities, these ancient accoutrements of position, require huge resources and coercive authority that can conceivably come collectively through government but never privately through personal perserverance.

What Hirsch did not see was class privilege. For the very reason he gave, valuable amenities could never be available for all. But Hirsch did not know how right he was; only collective action could restore the distance and position the new class was in danger of losing to the rising middle-masses. Whereas in the past upper-middle-class professionals kept their distance and maintained their position by individual initiative, now they do so by collective action. What has changed is not class interest, but class strategies: Collective decisions are now made to serve personal purposes.

I bring up this inconvenient extension of Hirsch's theory, not to belittle an original mind, whose contribution enables all who come after to move ahead,* but rather to purge it of its one imperfection: the notion that personal

---

*Hirsch employs the analogy of people in a crowd who stand on tiptoe, so that in the end no one can see better. Personally, I would rather take the more elevated line, attributed to Sir Isaac Newton, that he was able to see so far because he stood on the shoulders of giants. (Robert K. Merton's seminal *Standing on the Shoulders of Giants* [New York, 1965] is devoted to the origins of this aphorism.)

motives—distance and position—would not continue to operate in public as well as in private decision making. My task is to inhale the pure Hirsch, as it were, and exhale the consequences for public policy of a new class whose task it is to preserve old individual amenitiès by pouring them into collective bottles.

First the easy examples: the physical environment, transportation, and industrial safety. Unless a person can afford to live in exceedingly remote areas, he cannot control environmental values—the purity of air, water, and wilderness. Nor, in the midst of campers and dune buggies, can he limit access to the wilds. But the government can and does. Vast areas can be closed off to further settlement. Industry can be forced to clean up or compelled to leave. Who, today, can afford to maintain white-water canoeing, or make utilities burn expensive low-sulphur oil, or install more expensive scrubbers to clean the smoke? Only government.

Now everyone benefits by purifying the environment, but the costs are paid more by the old masses than the new classes. Since most of the people make most of the money, they pay most of the taxes and an ever larger share of the price increases, as costs of compliance are passed on to the consumers. And the jobs lost by slowing down economic growth are labor intensive (lumberjacks, machine operators) whereas the jobs gained are managerial and professional (devising regulations, monitoring compliance).

The trade-offs in terms of jobs also help explain the interest of the new class in industrial safety. By diverting funds from production to safety and from individual to collective responsibility, the national product declines, thus slowing up the mass entry into the middle class that creates competition for position. The new jobs that are created, moreover, call for regulation and inspection, just the kind to be filled by the professional new class. Job substitution means less competition. Besides, as production falls, new-class employment rises.

Transportation policy is tricky. Members of the new class are interested in making it easier for themselves to go to work and harder for others to drive on vacation. Subsidizing mass public transportation has twin virtues: others pay to get the new class to work on commuter railroads but find it more difficult (more expensive and less comfortable because big cars are too costly) to drive to the wilderness—where, in any event, access is limited to those who have time to walk or money to fly into the remote interior. (Here, as elsewhere, I have benefited from conversations with B. Bruce-Briggs.) Since the new class can afford the fancy equipment, it uses less crowded roads and parks at public expense. A nice deal, if you can get it.

Even nicer, because so wonderfully indirect, are the mechanisms for increasing political power and household help. At first blush, it appears strange for a monied class to limit the size of campaign contributions or replace private contributions entirely with public subsidy. But once one understands that the new class is well off but not wealthy, and numerous but not enormous, it figures. Limitations on campaign contributions reduce the political power of the opponents of the new class—the real rich, the corporations, and the trade unions. By weakening intermediary organizations that might mediate between the citizen and the state, like political parties and labor unions, individual political entrepreneurs from the new class, with professional skills in communication and plenty of free time, have a much better chance to run and to win. And should they be short of cash, public financing, paid for by millions of others who do not necessarily share their views, is available to keep them running.

But have they really managed to hang on to household help? Of course: After all, the alternative was worse—conflict between the sexes. In the good old days, this conflict was muted either because women expected to clean house, or because help was cheap. The loss of help to the rise of affluence may have precipitated the change in household expectations. In any event, both husband and wife were upper-middle-class, verbally well-armed, and tactically well-matched. So they divorced or they divided the housework. But why fight when others can be made to do the work or pay the cost?

My experience is that almost all upper-middle-class people have at least part-time household help, and many have more than they admit. How do they make appear what according to folklore has disappeared? By taking their opportunities where they find them. The supply of household help increases by a hidden mass immigration from poor countries attracted by jobs left vacant as the working class moved into the middle class, thereby threatening the position of the new class. These immigrants from Central and South America or the Pacific—the poorer South invading the richer North, to use the vocabulary of North-South differences—are not only relatively cheap to employ but rather dependent as well. They are illegal, therefore they want no official notice, therefore they pay no taxes, hence they cost less. That is why their existence is deplored, but nothing is done about them.

The additional cost of hiring them is made up by the entry of new-class women into the job market. To some extent, which may be considerable, these capable women replace or displace less capable men, which may account for the extraordinary persistence of high unemployment, especially among minority men, in the face of a substantial growth in total employment. No doubt this displacement has the double effect of swelling the welfare rolls, thereby also increasing the supply of unofficial household help. Now we see them, now we don't; now we know why this help does not appear in official statistics, and remains unacknowledged to interviewers, but nonetheless appears when we make unexpected daytime visits to our (what shall we call them?) class-mates.

If this new class, like other classes, pursues its own self-interest, however, how can we account for its overt espousal of minority interests, such as establishing quotas at the Democratic National Convention? A closer inspection of the category called "minority" will explain why. For one thing, these quotas include biographical groups, like women and youth, who, having pushed themselves forward, are bound to come disproportionately from new-class families. For another, the "representatives" of ethnic minorities are bound to be more highly educated, more professional, and more like the new class in attitude than are other delegates. Affirmative-action programs, for some strange reason, have largely been successful in finding high professional positions for middle-class but not working-class minorities. And a third reason—the discovery of deprived minorities—is of most interest.

In earlier decades, deprived masses were in oversupply, and aspiring elites were in shorter supply: They were few in number and they faced considerable risk. By the 1960s, however, because of relative prosperity and the growth of social-welfare programs, deprived masses had dwindled, but elites had multiplied. The theory of the oppression gap, as I once called it, predicted that as the political price of elites dropped, efforts would be made to drive it up again, by a version of Say's Law—supply creates its own demand. The supply of oppressed minorities was increased, in fact, by relaxing the definition of boundaries (women, over half the population and with most of the money, were counted as a minority), by making stages of life (youth, old age) into sources of exploitation, and by other devices too numerous to mention.[1]

All of this account, it must be admitted, is too pat. Interests are rarely calculated correctly, at least not the first few times. Unanticipated consequences are the rule, not the exception, of social action. In sum, interests are not usually pursued so blatantly or as successfully as has been suggested here.

The blatancy factor depends on the ability to disguise and diffuse the actual costs of new-class politics. If the thesis advanced here is correct, for example, I would predict that these costs would not appear as items in the federal budget but would be paid indirectly by tens of millions of taxpayers and consumers. This is the path taken by regulations adding costs to cars, houses, and business—costs paid for in part by taxes, but mostly by higher prices.

It is hard to believe that the new class always gets its way or is never surprised or always consciously calculates its interests. Common consciousness comes from common position, not from acting in concert. It is not conspiracy but common interests that create common policies. As for correctly anticipating consequences, that is doubtful. The stupidity theory is generally more accurate than the conspiracy theory. It may be, for instance, that lower economic growth will adversely affect not only the absolute but the relative amounts of new-class income. If the question is raised, as Lenin put it, of who will do what to whom, the new class may find itself lacking in the required forceful qualities. But class delusion is an old story.

These speculations assume the politics of the new class is similar to the

Marxist interpretation of the politics of the old classes; getting others to pay for your privileges. Sometimes this interest masquerades as environmentalism, sometimes as safety, other times as equality, but it always ends up creating greater distance between class and mass.

NOTE

1. For an elaboration see Aaron Wildavsky, ''The Search for the Oppressed,'' *Freedom At Issue* (November-December 1972).

12

TWO "NEW CLASSES" OR NONE?

Andrew Hacker

Each age has its own conceits. Today's tend toward the sociological. We see society as surpassingly complex: even the most minimal comprehension requires sophisticated methods of analysis and measurement. Income, education, and employment are correlated with age, ethnicity, and sex to yield unending columns of statistics. Entire careers have been built by permuting categories or by labeling boxes and arrows and calling the collage a "theory." In an era so impressed with analysis, the idea that we now have a "new class" in our midst should not be surprising. As it happens, there are two contenders for the title (interestingly, with almost no overlap in membership). The claims of both will be examined in the light of two overarching questions. First, is either in fact a "class" in any meaningful sense? And second, if new social conditions are actually emerging, are they best explained in class terms? The intellectual inspiration for this examination derives in large measure from the writings of Karl Marx. However, the epigraphs come from Edmund Burke. These two writers had an enduring understanding of class. We underestimate them at our peril.

A "NEW CLASS"?—I. "NEW POWER IN NEW PERSONS"

The rise of the manager has been heralded for close to half a century. In *The Modern Corporation and Private Property* (1932), Adolf A. Berle and Gardiner C. Means showed how the growing dispersion of stock ownership gave increasing autonomy to corporate administrators. Since the authors' concern was mainly with the legal and economic implications of these developments, little attention was devoted to the individuals holding executive positions. At no time were these men referred to as a class; indeed, they were hardly mentioned at all.

The class designation came nine years later, when James Burnham coined the phrase now linked with his name. *The Managerial Revolution* was a revision of Marxian analysis. Burnham agreed with Berle and Means that ownership no longer coincided with control. But since he remained commited to the idea of class rule, he had to find a group to replace the proprietors. The proletariat was not ready for that role; indeed, it might never be. So Burnham made the managers his "new ruling class," dialectical successors to the bourgeoisie. They form a coherent group that, "as against the rest of society, has a greater measure of control of the access to the instruments of production and a preferential treatment in the distribution of the products of those instruments." In other words, the managers not only run the economy, they also insure themselves a comfortable life.

While Burnham's theory had Marxian origins, it was echoed elsewhere. One year earlier, *Fortune* published an article, "30,000 Managers," which contained the following passage:

> No one can say for certain how many of them there are, but 30,000 more or less is a fair enough estimate. They are the men who guide the business activity of the U.S. The decisions they transmit give jobs to the millions; and take jobs away. When they pass the word, smoke comes from the tall chimneys, lathe chucks purr in streaming oil; mill workers blaze through the night shift; and in the yard the switchers chuff, the boxcars clank together. When their judgment becomes clouded old governments fall; when their judgment clears, new governments respond to their influence.[1]

The last sentence is particularly intriguing. Governments respond, rise, and fall, depending on the decisions of these managers. This notion meshes well with Burnham's view. He argued that in all advanced economies, business would nominally come under public ownership; his "new ruling class" of managers would in fact be government officials. However, in a corporate state where politics no longer had hegemony, they would be the real rulers, not subservient to political officeholders. As Burnham put it, "all major parts of the economy will be planned and controlled by the single integrated set of institutions." As a vision, it has much in common with Engels' description of the postrevolutionary dictatorship: "The government of persons is replaced by the administration of things and the direction of the process of production."[2]

According to Marx and Engels, the entire proletariat was to seize the state apparatus and expropriate private property; the bourgeoisie would then automatically disappear, leaving society with only a single class, which would govern according to Engels' formulation. In time, the state would "wither away," as would the last class of human history. At no time did Marx or Engels say that a particular group would hold administrative positions or direct the productive process.

Milovan Djilas was a man in power during the aftermath of an actual revolution. According to his book, *The New Class*, however, it is not the proletariat as a whole but rather a class of officials who rule in socialist states. "Government of persons" continues, says Djilas, with "special privileges and economic preference" for a "special stratum" of administrators. Djilas is prepared to call them a class because they have "control of the national income and national goods." In this he echoes Burnham's revision of Marx: a ruling class need not consist of owners; having control is sufficient in contemporary circumstances.

Yet Djilas parts company with both Marx and Burnham in one important respect. The real "new class"—the one that counts—consists not of industrial managers or even economic planners but of the "party or political bureaucracy." So it is not control over the modes of production that creates the new ruling class, but staffing the political apparatus. For Djilas, politics is not superstructure but rather the source of power and class rule.

Even if his analysis is correct for Communist regimes, Djilas' conception of a "new class" seems only marginally applicable to the American experience. While government engages in many activities and consumes much of the nation's income, our "political bureaucracy" is not really a ruling class. Cabinet officials and higher civil servants, for example, do not cohere as a single stratum. However, elements from among them can be seen as participants in a wider ruling system.

This was the view of C. Wright Mills in *The Power Elite*. Writing at the same time as Djilas, Mills coined the phrase to describe the leading personnel of America's major institutions. In the United States, production, distribution, and exchange are still conducted as private enterprises. At the same time, other organizations that are not businesses have substantial social influence. So the "power elite" has several coordinate branches besides corporation executives—for example, top military managers. Generals and admirals are, of course, employees of the government. Yet Mills felt that their positions have become so institutionalized that they are insulated from outside interference; overall, the military is essentially an independent corporation. The same is true of many civilian agencies administered by career officials.

All these managers, said Mills, can be seen as a single elite. Even so, he took care not to call them a class. On one occasion, he described them as "men of the higher circles;" on another, as "commanders of power." He also specified that certain officeholders did *not* belong to the elite: among them, trade union leaders and members of legislative bodies. The structures in which such individuals operate necessarily makes them responsive to popular constituencies; as elected officials, they can be voted out of office by rank-and-file citizens. Their bases are thus too democratic for the insulated exercise of power, a requisite of elite rule.

Mills did not mention other elite centers of control, largely because they were just beginning to flower during the period he was writing. I have in mind various private institutions that remain relatively autonomous even though much of their funding comes from public sources: universities and foundations, medical centers and research institutes, and a long list of quasipublic authorities. Eli Ginzberg once called these nonbusiness, nongovernment institutions America's "third economy."[3] They have budgets well into the billions of dollars and provide employment for millions of workers. Insofar as they participate in decisions that help give shape to society, executives of these institutions appear entitled to membership in Mills' power elite.

However, most writers concerned with class rule or elite power find the largest share of mastery resting in the nation's corporation boardrooms, partly because of the conviction that the United States is still essentially capitalistic, with the decisions of the business community determining in large part the direction of the nation. Other institutions are seen as ancillaries supporting business operations or assuming tasks business finds unprofitable.

But do the men at those mahogany tables constitute a class? They do according to writers like G. William Domhoff, whose first book, *Who Rules America?*, published in 1967, gave an answer to the question posed by its title: "There is a ruling social class in the United States . . . . This class is made up of the owners and managers of large corporations." In a subsequent study, *The Bohemian Grove*, he listed about 2,000 such individuals.

What is interesting about Domhoff's description is that he sees an older, propertied class continuing in power, even in an age of corporate capitalism. His "ruling class" contains not only managers but also owners. Unlike Berle and Means, or Burnham, or Mills, Domhoff postulates that America still has a bourgeoisie: a class with sufficient personal holdings to control major business enterprises. If asked, Domhoff would say that classical capitalists still own and run America.

At this point ideology comingles with analysis. If the vitality of Marxian theory is to be affirmed, capitalism today must be portrayed as having a ruling class whose power flows from the actual ownership of the means of production. Hence the search for contemporary counterparts of Rockefeller, Carnegie, and Harriman: scholars like Philip Burch, Maurice Zeitlin, and Robert Fitch and Mary Oppenheimer have scoured corporate records in the effort to identify individuals or families or estates with enough stock holdings to control the largest corporations in the country.[4] They usually find what they are seeking, and can thus conclude that any "new class" of managers must answer to the actual owners of capital.

My own investigations have persuaded me that these holdings are largely illusory. For example, the 8 May 1978 *Fortune* analyzed the 5,995 directors of the 500 industrial companies in its 1977 listing. Fewer than 100 of them were major stockholders. There are, of course, the Fords and Graces and Du Ponts, or the Mellons, with their shares of Gulf and First Boston and Alcoa. Yet the Mellons and Du Ponts are now nieces and nephews and grandchildren of the original capitalists; many of their holdings are locked up in trusts. In fact, this generation exercises far less control than the banks and insurance companies and investment houses on which corporations depend for financing. Indeed, directors representing such institutions ousted Robert Sarnoff as chairman of RCA, despite his status as successor to the company's founding father.

Our largest business organizations operate within the matrix of corporate capitalism: an institutional system of power. What, then, of the human participants? Should we call them a class? Quite obviously, a class must consist of people: corporeal and sentient beings, with names and addresses and telephone numbers. To what extent should we interest ourselves in individuals holding high corporate positions? In previous eras, family holdings, inherited ownership, and personal property were the rule; it thus made sense to study the people at the top. Power reflected personality, biography was an important adjunct to history, and the imprint of a dominant class turned on the character and quality of its members. But in an age of corporate property, individuals are much less important.

I would propose that we regard corporation managers as well-paid employees, the counterpart in the private economy of our higher civil servants. The great majority come from unprepossessing backgrounds. Only a few attended exclusive prep schools or Ivy League colleges. More likely, they majored in engineering or accounting at a local state university and then went straight to work—without gaining whatever benefits follow from graduate study in business administration. While few are of proletarian origin, they are hardly products of privilege.

Most advance at a moderate pace and sometimes switch companies or serve an occasional stint of outside service. They tend to become chairmen or presidents at about the age of fifty-eight, and serve a seven-year term until retirement. Those who reach top positions do receive impressive annual salaries. Still, it should be stressed that corporation careers provide relatively few opportunities for amassing personal wealth. Generally speaking, an executive can begin to build an estate only after reaching the summit. Only then will he have enough after-tax cash to exercise the stock options offered him. For example, Clifton Garvin had only $380,000 in stock when he became president of Exxon after twenty-eight years of service. Thomas Murphy owned less than $300,000 in General Motors shares when he became its chairman, and it had taken him thirty-seven years to fill that portfolio. These are really quite modest holdings, less than those of many physicians and lawyers. Moreover, the vast majority of executives finish well below Garvin and Murphy, perhaps with a comfortable pension but nothing substantial in equity.

I record all this simply to indicate that fortunes are not made in corporation careers. The exceptions are executives who begin with firms that then enter an era of expansion. People who signed on early at IBM, Xerox, and Polaroid, and bought stock at ground-floor prices, found themselves millionaires. But they are not typical, nor are those adventurous spirits who see where the action is moving and quit to set up companies of their own.

Are they not men of power, if not wealth? My own assessment is that rulership resides in the structure. Institutions hire an assortment of individuals to perform functions requiring a human touch—men and women who sit in assigned chairs and make decisions for the organizations that employ them. Thomas Murphy, by himself, has no personal power worth mentioning. The institution for which he works is certainly a center of power, and the office in which he sits has controls that its occupant operates. But any one of several dozen people could sit at that very same desk, and the outcome would be approximately the same. In short, the office has a degree of leeway in deciding where the organization will move, and a human being occupies that office. But to understand the power of General Motors, we should not even ask for the name of its chairman. All corporations have people, much like Murphy, who are a necessary factor in the productive process.

Nothing about these employees warrants collecting them in a class. Even though they meet and greet one another in clubs or committees or boardrooms, they do so not as individuals but as representatives of the institutions that employ them. For this reason, C. Wright Mills chose to call them an "elite." The people he wrote about exercise significant power. But, Mills went on, they would not

> were it not for their positions in the great institutions. For such institutions are the necessary bases of power . . . . No one, accordingly, can be truly powerful unless he has access to the command of major institutions, for it is over these institutional means of power that the truly powerful are, in the first instance, powerful.[5]

Mills' term, "elite," is clearly preferable to "class," since it refers to individuals only for as long as they remain the occupants of particular institutional positions. It has been part of the ideology of our time to stress the importance of individuals, just when we should be learning to examine institutions. The very conception of a "ruling class" militates against understanding capitalism today.

As it happens, Marx himself knew better. Not only did he and Engels see corporate capitalism emerging, they understood its implications for their theory. The future, Marx wrote in Volume III of *Capital*, would bring "an enormous expansion of the scale of production and enterprises, which were impossible for individual capitals." From this would result "the highest development of capitalist production . . . as the common property of associates"—in short, the huge corporation as we have come to know it.[6] (All that needs to be added is that the dominant "associates" are now parallel institutions: banks, investment firms, insurance companies, pension funds, and so forth.)

But what happens to class rule? Engels took up this topic in the *Anti-Duhring*. With "the conversion of great organizations for production," he said, "the bourgeoisie can be dispensed with." As holders of corporation shares, rich people will revert to being "mere owners." Their chief activities will be "the pocketing of revenues, the clipping of coupons, and gambling on the stock exchange." The institutions of corporate capitalism will be managed, said Engels, by "salaried employees"—or, as Marx described them, "administrators of other people's capital." At the same time, Marx and Engels declined to call these administrators a class. Marx spoke of them as "mere managers"; because they have "no title whatever to the capital," there is a "separation of the wages of management from the profits of the enterprise."[7] Even with occasional bonuses and options, their basic remuneration is salary. This is hardly the way Marx would choose to describe history's next class of rulers.

So Marx and Engels seem to be suggesting that with the coming of corporate capitalism, class rule will reach its end. But what of their overall theory of history? "The history of all hitherto existing societies is the history of class struggles." So went the opening words of their *Communist Manifesto*. What form is this struggle to take in an era of impersonal institutions? The proletariat will remain, to be oppressed, debased, exploited. Yet it will suffer not at the hands of a ruling class, but from the power of corporate organizations. Struggle may continue, but not in its classical form. The new combat will pit human beings against institutional structures. Needless to say, Marx must have realized how much harder it would be to rouse a revolutionary consciousness against such an inanimate enemy. Earlier proletariats were exhorted to expropriate the expropriators. But now it is hard to know what to hate. Where does one mount a barricade against Tenneco and Textron and Teledyne?

Like Marx, I am unprepared to regard the salaried managers of our time as a "new class" of rulers. They are simply highly placed employees, and there are hardly enough of them to make a class. I prefer a simpler phrase of Edmund Burke's: We are dealing with "new power in new persons." But let us remember that the power is corporate rather than corporeal. No one realizes this better than the men we have been examining. They know they are creatures of constraints, modern analogues of Prometheus—restrained by senior vice-presidents and cordoned by chains of committees.

A "NEW CLASS"—II. "THE WHOLE CLAN OF THE ENLIGHTENED AMONG US"

Even if we reject the notion that the United States has a "new class" of rulers at the top, it is still possible to discover changed configurations lower down. Hence the attention accorded a rather different "new class" of Americans: persons who are not in ruling positions but have increasing influence on society at more intermediate levels. Commentaries on this "new class" tend to agree on its members' economic status (comfortable), level of schooling (college or above), occupations (more or less professional), and ideology (more or less liberal). Moreover, they take no small pride in being open-minded and up-to-date. In short, this "new class" represents the most recent metamorphosis of the country's upper-middle class.*

Government statistics, opinion surveys, and occasionally election returns can be used to show that this "new class" encompasses an increasing segment of the population. Moreover, its influence has been imprinted on areas of policy and conduct once left to other authorities. For instance, the spheres of "education" and "welfare" have become essentially "new class" preserves. No one will dispute that recent decades have seen the emergence of new forms of employment. Indeed, we are often told how many current occupations did not exist a generation ago. More than any other single factor, these new occupations have been the force shaping contemporary attitudes and behavior. Here again I will take my text from the writings of Marx—this time a passage from *The German Ideology*:

> As individuals express their life, so they are. What they are, therefore, coincides with their production, both with what they produce and with how they produce.

---

*In earlier generations, the phrase "upper-middle class" brought to mind proprietors of medium-sized businesses, or local lawyers or physicians. They were the people Charles Beard had in mind when he called the United States a "business civilization;" a class of burghers who expressed themselves by building their own enterprises. To be sure, this group is still very much with us, especially at our economic frontiers. Even so, an entrepreneur is not usually whom we have in mind today when we speak of the upper-middle class.

The outlooks of individuals derive chiefly from the production in which they engage. In previous periods of history, work took place mainly at farms and factories. For most people, production consisted of raising crops or turning materials into finished articles. The advance of technology has made many of these occupations obsolescent. Between 1945 and 1975, the number of man-hours required to produce 100 bushels of corn fell from fifty-three to six. Human input per bale of cotton went from 146 hours to twenty-three. Even chickens did their part: their "rate of lay" rose from 161 to 228 eggs per bird.[8] In industry, there were similar changes. Between 1954 and 1977, the work forces of three major petroleum companies—Exxon, Shell, and Standard Oil of Indiana—actually declined, during a period when both oil production and overall employment rose markedly. Because of technological innovations, all those derricks, tankers, and refineries needed fewer human attendants.

Service industries have followed suit, from the first grocery with a shopping cart to the latest fast-food franchise. With electronic switching, the telephone industry needs fewer operators. With computerized billing and reservations systems, rising demands for various services can be met with the same number of employees.

What does an economy do as it achieves efficiency in production? By and large, the process takes place gradually; there are few sudden or large-scale firings. Attrition does much of the job: as people leave, no one is hired in their place. (At the same time, it is not uncommon for a firm to close an older factory and open elsewhere a new one requiring considerably fewer workers.) But for the economy as a whole, reductions in the blue-collar force have been balanced by creating new white-collar positions.

The creation of these new occupations has been justified on a number of grounds. It has been argued that more sophisticated technologies require more personnel at higher organizational levels—for instance, additional workers to plan and program and coordinate the operations of modern industry. We are also told that the growing complexity of knowledge calls for intricate layers of specialists. In short, it is contended that these new occupations are necessary. The people who fill them are said to be producers, albeit of a new and different sort. What they do is essential for overall output. Or so the argument goes.

Other new occupations are justified by claiming that they enhance the quality of our lives. More services are available, ranging from psychiatry and ski instruction to sex therapy and higher education. Restauranteurs and news-casters and travel agents provide a more varied and adventuresome existence. These people do not make anything, but bring about experiences for others. Professors, especially those in the liberal arts, certainly belong in this category. So do accountants and attorneys, whose activities it is said, increase the sum of orderliness and justice in society. We are better, broader people because of the availability of all these services.

What we are, Marx said, coincides with our production, with what and how we produce. So what is the "production" of these new occupations? They are said to provide services, often of professional quality. They generate information and explanations. But they are chiefly engaged in the creation of symbols: words, numbers, and other modes of notation. The medium can be talk (vibrations in air), writing (ink or graphite on paper), or electronic impulses (on plastic tape, cathode screens, integrated circuits). These services require a combination of technical and social facility, the ability to explain ideas and interpretations to others. The committee, the conference, and the seminar are modern equivalents of the marketplace.

As we express our lives, so we are. When we are removed from settings where goods are produced, the intervening distance increases the possibilities for distortion. An oil company executive once told me he had been with his industry for thirty years and had never seen the stuff. He was paid to produce talk about oil. But with 1,500 miles between himself and the nearest wellhead, he can no longer be sure that the symbols he creates describe the product they refer to. Theories, concepts, and symbols have become entities with logics of their own. Conversations deal less with reality and more with conceptions ("poverty," for example, or "crime," or "national security") claiming to characterize it, ("Vietnam" was one case; the "population explosion" will be another).*

The production of symbols originally arose as an adjunct to technology. Words and numbers helped improve machinery; symbols thus mirror the rationale of engineering, following rules of computation, efficiency, consistency. (What we call the social sciences reflect these industrial origins.) Most new occupations conceive their purpose as decreasing disorder, illogic, and in some cases injustice. Their common ideological underpinning, insofar as they have one, could be characterized as the "rationalist attitude" (to borrow a phrase from Joseph Schumpeter): the use of symbols—verbal, mathematical, etc.—to create and then impose an order that is beyond the capacity of reality to absorb. Overweening efforts of this kind are by no means unique to our time. Intermittently throughout history, people have come to believe they have discovered new powers of rationality. It is a short step from such a belief to the presumption that social improvement can come from these reasonings. Who could deny that we desire rational solutions to social problems? No one argues for unreason, so that is not the issue. Certainly all of us seek policies that will bring the results we want. But even at our best, we understand much less about

---

*The scholarly word for all this is "reification," long a staple term in academe, where scholars are supposed to guard against taking their symbolic creations too seriously. However, we now face situations where what once were "real world" policies and decisions are being made on the basis of reified conceptions. In short, the problem is no longer academic.

the world than our conceptions suggest that we do. The same is true of our ability to alter our world to our liking.

This kind of rationalist attitude flourished in France during the period we call the Enlightenment and in its aftermath, the French Revolution. Edmund Burke referred to "the whole clan of the enlightened among us," who are so impressed with their intellectual prowess that

> they are in no sort of fear with regard to the duration of a building run up in haste; because duration is no object to those who think little or nothing has been done before their time, and who place all their hopes in discovery.

As a consequence, Burke wrote, "very plausible schemes, with very pleasing commencements, have often shameful and lamentable conclusions."[9]

The rationalist attitude of Burke's time had imposing political aims: liberty, equality, and popular sovereignty—all to be achieved with eye-dazzling immediacy. Our period has been less grandiose in its goals. Even so, they have an impressive ring: "War on poverty," for example, or "community control," or "new math," in tandem with "teaching machines," or "winning hearts and minds" as a military strategy, or "synergy" for corporate conglomerates.

These examples should indicate that, in our age at least, the rationalist attitude cuts across conventional lines. It would be a mistake to confine our comments to the left side of the political spectrum. Most indictments of the so-called "new class" center on the excessive rationality of the liberal camp. Witness D.P. Moynihan on academic solicitude for juvenile delinquents, or B. Bruce-Briggs on banishing the automobile in favor of mass transit, or Nathan Glazer on achieving racial justice via arithmetic formulas.[10]

Reviewing much of this literature, one would conclude that the "new class" consists almost entirely of comfortably situated citizens who work out personal feelings of guilt by claiming compassion for the oppressed. Entire professions have indeed emerged with the purpose of making human relationships more rational, so urgings of conscience coincide with opportunities for building careers. In this regard, the "new class" is seen as largely liberal or radical in persuasion. In particular, its members strike an antibusiness posture and are highly critical of capitalism, both in philosophy and performance. So it is not surprising that critics of this "new class" are chiefly conservatives, or "neoconservative" alumni of an earlier, more limited liberalism.

The success of capitalism certainly engenders an anticapitalist mentality. Joseph Schumpeter showed how this economic system, itself born of revolution, cannot help creating first what he calls "a critical frame of mind," and then "the rationalist attitude":

> Capitalism creates a critical frame of mind which, after having destroyed the moral authority of so many other institutions, in the end turns against

its own . . . . The rationalist attitude does not stop at the credentials of kings and popes, but goes on to attack private property and the whole scheme of bourgeois values.[11]

Yet Schumpeter, though a conservative, was also a good Marxist. He thus could not attribute the rise of the rationalist attitude solely to capitalism as a system of private ownership; technology played at least a coequal role. "The development of modern industry," wrote Marx and Engels, "cuts from under its feet the foundation on which the bourgeoisie produces and appropriates." And "modern industry" means new machines, new chemistry, and new modes of computation, creating attitudes that eventually undermine the edifice that brought them into being. For this reason, I must disagree with those who see a "new class" as composed mainly of verbally versatile people with a penchant for social planning. The tendencies I have been describing infuse an array of modern occupations. If there is a "new class," it also includes much of our current military establishment and significant segments of corporate industry.

We currently pride ourselves on having a "professional" military, which means that officers possess new and sophisticated skills. In order to obtain promotion to lieutenant colonel, for example, an officer should have earned a graduate degree, complete with a footnoted thesis. So the higher reaches of our armed services are becoming populated with officers presumably adept in the art of symbols. But this means we have appreciably fewer leaders of the older, more roughly hewn school.

Back in the early 1960s, I came to know an army major who had been sent as a master's degree candidate to my university. He soon found that he was simply unable to come to grips with the materials assigned in his seminars, and he could no more write an academic thesis than learn to be a ballet dancer. So, at the end of the year, he told me that he would probably be passed over and retired at the rank of major. Yet he had been a gallant and effective officer in Korea, inspiring his men to feats they had never believed possible. His parting words to me were these: if we ever again found ourselves in Asia, the outcome would not be to our liking.

By linking military promotion to graduate-level proficiency, we run the risk of excluding less literate men who are nevertheless natural leaders. In Saigon, we had people who could program computers with aplomb. At the same time, however, our infantry could not match the enemy's maneuvers in the field. This situation largely resulted from the frequent rotation of personnel as an aid to officers' careers. Great emphasis was also placed on an officer's ability to conduct briefings, again demanding fluency in symbols. But our opponents outfought us where it counted, even though their officers had never seen a footnote.

We now have a military overqualified for the kind of combat still encountered in many parts of the globe. In the meantime, the production of symbols has become as common in councils of war as at social-welfare seminars. We would do well to wonder whether our failure in Southeast Asia had any causes in common with our experience with the war on poverty at home.

Business is another setting for the rationalist attitude. Many of our major business schools now make calculus a requirement for admission, thus excluding from their channel of mobility countless students who have real entrepreneurial talents but cannot master mathematical models. To be sure, in many if not most cases the emphasis on mathematics is simply a cover for making decisions through intuition. Citing sets of equations is easier than defending a personal judgment. Even so, we must wonder whether the emphasis on symbols may not turn out to be a source of weakness in an increasingly competitive world. The issue is not being for or against research or data or analysis as an accompaniment of business decisions. The question rather involves the overall attitude of those who staff American industry. The peril is one of remoteness: It is hard to visualize a party of American salesmen snaking a rented launch up the Zambezi River to promote their product in Mongu and Senanga—especially if the alternative is conducting systems analysis at air-conditioned headquarters stateside.

But do people afflicted with the rationalist attitude constitute a "new class"? Again, the participants themselves are unimportant; what counts is the structure in which they are situated. The individuals in new occupations entered them because the openings were there. They produce words and numbers and notations because that output is expected of them. If anything, they belong to a very old class: they work for their living, just as most people always have. The color of their collars may have changed. They have larger vocabularies and greater verbal facility. They receive comparatively generous salaries; many live varied and interesting lives. Yet when all is said and done, they remain workers beholden to the organizations employing them. Many may be upper-level employees. But they are still at the upper level of our proletariat, and do not constitute a special class by themselves.

What is new, therefore, is not a class of people but the occupations they currently fill, which are symptomatic of an important event of our epoch: the turning back of technology on itself. It is one thing to produce symbols, which in itself cannot do too much harm. It is another to persuade yourself that your output is essential or important. In that case, the damage is mainly to yourself. But it is quite another thing to act as if reality can adapt itself to your constructs. This last presumption is laden with mortal danger.

In *The Social Contract*, Jean-Jacques Rousseau wrote of "nations which make themselves illustrious and wretched with so much art and mystery." We have plainly arrived at that point. Whether we ever had a choice in the matter will remain a matter for argument. But to indict a "new class" as the culprit is an act of self-deception. Its members are bit players who do not even choose their own lines.

NOTES

1. *Fortune* (February 1940), p. 58. (The article is unsigned.)

2. Friedrich Engels, *Anti-Duhring* (Moscow, 1954), pp. 388-89.

3. Eli Ginzberg, *The Pluralistic Economy* (New York, 1965).

4. Philip Burch, *The Managerial Revolution Reconsidered* (Lexington, Mass., 1972); Maurice Zeitlin, "Corporate Ownership and Control: The Large Corporation and the Capitalist Class," *American Journal of Sociology* (March 1974); Robert Fitch and Mary Oppenheimer, "Who Rules the Corporations?" *Socialist Revolution* (October 1970 and January 1971).

5. C. Wright Mills, *The Power Elite* (New York, 1956), p. 9.

6. Karl Marx, *Capital*, ed. Engels (Moscow, 1959), III, 436-37.

7. Engels, pp. 385-86; Marx, pp. 387-88.

8. U.S. Census Bureau, *Statistical Abstract of the United States: 1977*, p. 695.

9. Edmund Burke, *Reflections on the Revolution in France* (London, 1910). pp. 58, 84.

10. Daniel Patrick Moynihan, *Maximum Feasible Misunderstanding* (New York, 1969); B. Bruce-Briggs, *The War Against the Automobile* (New York, 1977); Nathan Glazer, *Affirmative Discrimination* (New York, 1975).

11. Joseph Schumpeter, *Capitalism, Socialism, and Democracy* (New York, 1942), p. 143.

13

THE NEW CLASS:
A Muddled Concept

Daniel Bell

The term—the idea—"the new class" is a linguistic and sociological muddle. It mixes together two concepts: the emergence of a new social *stratum* and the stridency of a cultural *attitude*. It is true that, within an emerging post-industrial framework, a new professional and technical stratum has expanded in recent decades, largely in the knowledge field (education, health, research, engineering, and administration), and that the greatest growth in employment has been in the public sector. It is also true, though more ambiguously so, that cultural and political attitudes highly critical of traditional capitalism (though more reform-minded than revolutionary) have spread among the educated classes and now seem to dominate the cultural periodicals. But the relation between these two developments is less clear. The proponents of the idea of a new class, principally David T. Bazelon (who has concentrated on the social stratum) and Irving Kristol (who has concentrated on the political and cultural attitudes), believe that the two trends are integrally related. I do not agree, and in this essay I intend to trace these two developments and see how they relate to each other.

The idea of "the new class" is actually an extension of Joseph Schumpeter's and F.A. Hayek's discussions of the intellectuals. In his *Capitalism, Socialism and Democracy*, Schumpeter argued that capitalism undermines itself by its "rational and unheroic" mode of life. Since "the stock exchange is a poor substitute for the Holy Grail," the intellectuals take the lead in attacking the system. Who are the intellectuals? The Duke of Wellington's dismissive remark, "the scribbling set," is too narrow, yet it provides a starting point for Schumpeter:

> Intellectuals are in fact people who wield the power of the spoken and written word, and one of the touches that distinguishes them from other people who do the same is the absence of direct responsibility for practical affairs. This touch in general accounts for another—the absence of that first-hand knowledge of them which only actual experience can give. The critical attitude [arises] no less from the intellectual's situation as an onlooker—in most cases also as an outsider . . . .

> The intellectual group cannot help nibbling, because it lives on criticism and its whole position depends on criticism that stings; and criticism of persons and of current events will, in a situation in which nothing is sacrosanct, fatally issue in criticism of classes and institutions . . . .

But why worry about these intellectuals? Because, says Schumpeter, "the mass of people never develops definite opinions on its own initiative. Still less is it able to articulate them and to turn them into consistent attitudes and actions. All it can do is to follow or refuse to follow such group leadership as may offer itself."

Public policy, because of the social atmosphere, becomes more and more hostile to capitalist interests and "a serious impediment to its functioning." And, at this point, the role of the intellectual becomes more important:

> The intellectual group's activities have however a relation to anti-capitalist policies that is more direct than what is implied in their share in verbalizing them. Intellectuals rarely enter professional politics and still more rarely conquer responsible office. But they staff political bureaus, write party pamphlets and speeches, act as secretaries and advisers, make the individual politican's newspaper reputation which, though it is not everything, few men can afford to neglect. In doing these things they to

some extent impress their mentality on almost everything that is being done.[1]*

The argument is made even more strongly by F.A. Hayek. In his essay, "The Intellectuals and Socialism," Hayek writes:

> In every country that has moved toward socialism the phase of the development in which socialism becomes a determining influence on politics has been preceded for many years by a period during which socialist ideals governed the thinking of the more active intellectuals. In Germany this stage had been reached toward the end of the last century; in England and France, about the time of the First World War. To the casual observer it would seem as if the United States had reached this phase after World War II and that the attraction of a planned and directed economic system is now as strong among the American intellectuals as it ever was among their German or English fellows. Experience suggests that once this phase has been reached it is merely a question of time until the views now held by the intellectuals become the governing force of politics.

Why is this so? Because the intellectual is the broker of ideas and makes the market for ideas. As Hayek puts it,

> There is little that the ordinary man of today learns about events or ideas except through the medium of this class; and outside our special fields of work we are in this respect almost all ordinary men, dependent for our information and instruction on those who make it their job to keep abreast of opinion. It is the intellectuals in this sense who decide what views and opinions are to reach us, which facts are important enough to be told to us and in what form and from what angle they are to be presented. Whether we shall ever learn of the results of the work of the expert and the original thinker depends mainly on their decision.

> The layman, perhaps, is not fully aware to what extent even the popular reputations of scientists and scholars are made by that class and are inevitably affected by its views on subjects which have little to do with the merits of the real achievements . . . . This creation of reputations by the intellectuals is particularly important in the fields where the results of expert studies are not used by other specialists but dependent on the political decision of the public at large. There is indeed scarcely a better

---

*This contradicts Schumpeter's other remark that intellectuals lack a first-hand acquaintance with political affairs. Actually, these are two different kinds of intellectuals—let us say Noam Chomsky and Ralph Nader—but what unites them is a highly moralistic attitude to politics.

illustration of this than the attitude which professional economists have taken to the growth of such doctrines as socialism or protectionism. There was probably at no time a majority of economists who were recognized as such by their peers, favorable to socialism (or, for that matter, to protection) . . . . Yet it is not the predominant views of the experts but the views of a minority, mostly of rather doubtful standing in their profession, which are taken up and spread by the intellectuals.[2]

What is striking about these formulations of the central role of the intellectuals is how much they mirror the Marxist conception. In his *Poverty of Philosophy*, Marx wrote: "Just as the *economists* are the scientific representatives of the bourgeois class, so the *Socialists* and the *Communists* are the theoreticians of the proletarian class."[3] And in his canonical work, *What Is To Be Done?*, which lays out the argument for the vanguard role of the Party in tutoring the masses, Lenin invokes the authority of Karl Kautsky, the literary executor of Marx, regarding the role of the intellectuals and socialist consciousness in combating a trade-union ideology that "means the ideological enslavement of the workers by the bourgeoisie." Lenin quotes Kautsky, as follows:

> Socialist consciousness is represented as a necessary and direct result of the proletarian class struggle. But this is absolutely untrue . . . . Socialism and the class struggle arise side by side and not out of the other; each arises under different conditions. Modern Socialist consciousness can arise only on the basis of profound scientific knowledge. Indeed, modern economic science is as much a condition for Socialist production as, say, modern technology, and the proletariat can create neither the one nor the other, no matter how much it may desire to do so; both arise out of the modern social process. The vehicle of science is not the proletariat, but the *bourgeois intelligentsia*.[4]*

And yet it is also true that in many countries intellectuals were a force for social stability, most notably in Victorian England. In the latter half of the nineteenth century, the English intellectual class functioned exactly like the "clerisy" that Coleridge envisaged: it furnished the educated leadership in both

---

*The distinction between the *intelligentsia* and *intellectuals* has confused so much of the discussions, since many writers, including Schumpeter and Hayek, use them interchangeably. Let us say that "intellectual" refers to a kind of *activity*, while the "intelligentsia"—in the older, Russian, use of the term—are a social group whose members detached themselves from their class and were critical of society. I shall use "intellectual" to mean those engaged in knowledge and scholarly activities, and "intelligentsia" to mean an ideologically-minded group.

Church and State that would tame the fanaticism inherent in human nature and the extremes of economic group interest.

The distinctive feature of this new intellectual aristocracy—the Trevelyans, Macaulays, Huxleys, Arnolds, Darwins—was the high moral purpose, deriving from Evangelical religion, that animated them. And, as a class, they diffused through the leading administrative, educational, and intellectual institutions to form an Establishment that "gentled" the harsh features of English life.[5]

Even the image of the Russian intelligentsia as either revolutionary, nihilistic, or dilettantish neglects the fact that other "intelligentry," drawn from the children of the gentry, often vehemently opposed Westernization on Slavophile or religious grounds. In the 1860s and 1870s, a Russian conservative movement, detesting abstractions, attracted important writers like Danielevski, Katkov, Leonte'ev, and Pobedonostev, as well as Dostoevsky. And in the early twentieth century, one of the most notable declarations in Russian intellectual life was *Vekhi* (Landmarks), a collection of essays—by, among others, the religious philosophers Berdayev and Bulgakov and the eminent liberal thinkers Peter Struve and M. Gershenzon—that called for the regeneration of intellectual life through the primacy of moral and religious principles.[6]*

In the first four decades of the twentieth century, intellectual life in most European countries was usually dominated not by the Left but by the Right, as an aggressive political force, or—less stridently, but more importantly—by humanistically inclined or religious intellectuals. In the Anglo-American world there were Ezra Pound, T.S. Eliot, Wyndham Lewis, D.H. Lawrence, W.B. Yeats, Irving Babbitt, Paul Elmer More, and the notable school of "Southern Agrarians" and "Fugitives." In France there was the *Action Francaise* of Charles Maurras and Leon Daudet; the aggressive fascists like Drieu la Rochelle, Bardèche, and Brasillach; the bitter, soured writer Louis-Ferdinand Céline; aristocratic conservatives like Henry de Montherlant; and fervent Catholics like Paul Claudel and George Bernanos, influenced initially by Charles Peguy, who came to his moral purity through the rejection of socialism. In Germany there were irrationalists like Julius Langbein and Moeller van den Bruck, romantics like Ernest and Friedrich Junger, the aesthetic circle of Stefan George, and the disillusioned doctor-poet Gottfried Benn. In Italy there were the strident voices of Marinetti and the Futurists, the romantic nationalism of

---

*The extraordinary collection of essays *From Under the Rubble*, edited by Alexander Solzhenitsyn, is directly modeled on *Vekhi*. As Max Hayward remarks,

> by modelling their collection of essays on *Landmarks*, Solzhenitsyn and his associates demonstrate their conviction that in order to talk meaningfully about present-day Russia it is essential to cross back over the intellectual void of the last sixty years and resume a tradition in Russian thought which is antithetical to the predominant one of the old revolutionary intelligentsia, particularly as it developed in the second half of the nineteenth century.[7]

D'Annunzio, and the complex skepticism of Pirandello. Major intellectual figures such as Croce, Bergson, Unamuno, Ortega y Gasset, Thomas Mann, and Jacques Maritain disdained what Julien Benda called, in a famous essay, *La Trahison des Clercs*—the intense politicization of intellectual life.

While many of these individuals and movements were strongly anti-Left or even reactionary as well as humanistic, almost all the leading intellectual figures in the twentieth century despised bourgeois life. The English intellectual aristocracy had "tamed" the bourgeois spirit by emphasizing the role of the gentlemen or by insisting that artistic pursuits were more important than money. The Italian humanists lived in what Croce called the tiny but aristocratic *respublica literaria*. Yeats rejected Marxism and materialism—both Russian communism *and* English life—in favor of authoritarian rule, supported by religion, to cleanse society of the anarchy of values produced by democracy. Romantic or traditionalist, Enlightenment or irrationalist, vitalist or naturalist, humanist or racialist, religious or atheist—in this entire range of passions and beliefs, scarcely one respectable intellectual figure defended the sober, unheroic, prudential, let alone acquisitive, entreprenurial, or money-making pursuits of the bourgeois world. This is the major cultural fact in the history of the last seventy-five years.[8]

Historians rarely like or acknowledge the idea of a *caesura*, a "turning point" in history. Logically almost no event emerges like a *deus ex machina*, and any set of changes, no matter how sudden or even unexpected (like the Russian Revolution in October 1917), has obvious sources—once the historian, by hindsight, knows where to look. Yet one might say that 1945 signified the opening of a new axial period in Western history. As far as the idea of a "new class" and its putative character are concerned, there have been four significant historical changes:

1. The first is the collapse of any major right-wing, reactionary, or protofascist influence in the intellectual community. Since World War II had the character of a "just war" against fascism, right-wing ideologies, and the intellectual and cultural figures associated with those causes, were inevitably discredited. After the *preponderant* reactionary influence in prewar European culture, no single right-wing figure retained any political creditability or influence. Yeats was appreciated as a poet but no one discussed his politics; his great poem, "The Second Coming," which had been written against Christian values and democracy, was now read as a prophetic announcement about the decline of the West. Pound retreated into silence. The older European voices of humanism and aesthetic retreat were stilled.

The major cultural figure after World War II was Jean-Paul Sartre, with his doctrine of political engagement and hatred of the bourgeoisie. In the early 1950s, his wartime collaborator Albert Camus broke with Sartre because he would not condemn the Soviet concentration camps, since he did not want to seem to endorse the United States against the Soviet Union. Even though disillusionment with communism was widespread among members of the old left intelligentsia, such as Ignazio Silone, Arthur Koestler, and Manès Sperber, few of them moved "right." In the early 1950s, Silone said that the major ideological conflict would be between the communists and the ex-communists. In a significant sense this was true of the decade between 1955 and 1965, the period of the cold war. But after 1965 the rise of the Third World ideology proved to be the stronger magnet,[9] playing on liberal guilt about racism and imperialism and the moral claims for redressing poverty and exploitation— even though, as in so many instances, the new revolutionary elites ruling in the name of the people in Algeria or Libya or Cuba were themselves a "new class."

If the Soviet Union and Marxism had been the avatar of young Western intellectuals before World War II, the mesmerizing influence of "national liberation" and "antiimperialism" and the still hypnotic idea of "revolution" attracted young intellectuals to support Castro, Ché Guevera, Ho Chi Minh, and Mao Tse-Tung. It was no longer the "orthodox" appeals of Marxism that attracted the new young intelligentsia, but rather the lumpenproletariat appeals of Frantz Fanon, the insurrectionary romanticism of Ché, the elitist Marxism of Georg Lukács, the sardonic tone of Bertolt Brecht, and the heady ideas of cultural transformation in the "new man" promised by Mao.

In the 1970s for some of the intellectuals—as with the "new philosophers" in France—there began a new cycle of disillusionment. And, in the United States a so-called neo-conservative movement began to emerge among the intelligentsia. Yet the fact remained that the dominant tone in the intellectual community was a liberalism in which issues such as equality, racism, imperialism, and the like took precedence over other values like liberty and free enterprise.

2. The years after 1945 saw the emergence in the Western countries of what I have called post-industrial features in the techno-economic order. In one respect, post-industrial values reflected a growing dislike of materialism and an emphasis on the quality of life—e.g., a concern with the environment, pollution, and the like. Such values reinforced the basic liberalism that has dominated the Western polity for the past half-century. But the *structural* aspects of post-industrialism—and the transformation of the occupational structure of the society—derive from techno-scientific changes in the organization of the economy: the strategic centrality of information and knowledge, the new innovative role of *theoretical* knowledge for research and development as well as policy, the growing importance of the science-based industries in last half of the twentieth century (e.g., electronics, computers, optics, polymers), and the rise of "intellectual technology" as the main feature of these developments, as machine technology was to industrial society in the past.[10]

The socioeconomic changes can be illuminated by a few brief indicators:

a. *A shift from a goods-producing to a service economy in the distribution of employment*. By 1970, more than 65 percent of the labor force was in services, about 30 percent in manufacturing, and under 5 percent in agriculture. "Services" is a large, even residual category; it masks a wide variety of employments, from domestic service to research and science. However, the main feature of the change was the expansion in human and professional services, rather than those that are auxiliary to industry, such as transportation, utilities, finance, and so on.

b. *A white-collar and professional-technical occupational force*. Contrary to Marx's belief in the expansion of an industrial proletariat, the major feature of the last decades has been the centrality of a white-collar labor force and, within it, the greater expansion of the professional, technical, and managerial classes. The expansion came in two stages. In 1900, farm workers made up the largest segment (37.5 percent) of the labor force, while manual workers (excluding services) made up 35.8 percent, and white-collar workers 17.6 percent. By 1940, farm workers had declined to 17.4 percent; manual workers predominated, with almost 40 percent of the labor force. Since 1950, however, the proportion of the blue-collar force has declined, while that of the white-collar workers has been rising.

Table 13-1
Employment by Major Occupational Groups, 1940-85
(in thousands)

	1940	%	1974	%	1985 (projected)	%
White collar workers	15,500	(31.0)	41,700	(48.6)	52,200	(51.5)
Professional & technical	3,750	(7.5)	12,300	(14.4)	16,000	(15.5)
Managers & administrators	3,650	(7.3)	8,900	(10.4)	10,900	(10.5)
Sales	4,800	(7.6)	5,400	(6.3)	6,300	(6.1)
Clerical	3,350	(6.7)	15,000	(17.5)	20,100	(19.5)
Blue collar workers	19,900	(39.8)	29,700	(34.6)	33,700	(32.6)
Craftsmen	6,000	(12.0)	11,400	(13.4)	13,800	(13.3)
Operatives	9,200	(18.4)	13,900	(16.2)	15,200	(14.7)
Laborers	4,700	(9.4)	4,300	(5.1)	4,800	(4.6)
Service workers	5,900	(11.7)	11,300	(13.2)	14,600	(14.1)
Private household	2,350	(4.7)	1,200	(1.4)	900	(.9)
Other service	3,550	(7.1)	10,145	(11.8)	13,700	(13.2)
Farmers	8,700	(17.4)	3,000	(3.5)	1,900	(1.8)
TOTAL	50,000	(100)	85,900	(100)	103,000	(100)

The actual *numbers* employed in each category are equally interesting, and often neglected. In 1940, there was a total of 50 million workers in the labor force; in 1974 the figure had risen to more than 85 million; by 1985 it should reach more than 103 million. Table 13-1 provides the salient comparisons for occupational shifts, in percentage and absolute terms.

A number of crucial changes should be noted:

—In 1940, about 25 percent of the male labor force were self-employed as farmers, artisans, or small-business proprietors. By 1975, more than 90 percent of the labor force were salaried and working in organizations.

—In 1940, the industrial labor force made up almost 40 percent of the working population, a total of 20 million workers. While the absolute number had increased to almost 30 million persons in 1974 and will still rise to 33.7 million in 1985, the industrial share of the labor force will decrease to about 32 percent in 1985.

—Professional and technical workers, and managers and administrators, comprised 7.4 million persons in 1940 (14.8 percent of the labor force). By 1974, they were 21 million workers, or one-fourth of the labor force. And in 1985 they will amount to almost 27 million.

c. *The rise of an "information economy."* The categories of agriculture, manufacturing, and services grew out of older social-accounting systems. They do not, however, allow one to see the rise of significant new sectors, particularly the rising knowledge and information sectors. Although these categories are broad and are now being refined, they include the large spectrum of activities ranging from data processing to creating new knowledge in the society. In 1962, Fritz Machlup estimated that about 29 percent of GNP was accounted for by the "knowledge industries." Studies by Marc Porat, issued by the Department of Commerce in 1977, indicated that more than 55 percent of the GNP and of the labor force was within the "information economy."

Since these categories lack statistical validation, and there are few reconstructed time-series for making historical comparisons, one can only note what one intuitively discerns—that the U.S. economy today primarily turns on the processing of information and knowledge, even within the traditional sectors.

d. *The expansion of the nonprofit sector.* Most of this expansion in professional and technical employment is due to the expansion of government services, particularly in the areas of education, health, and welfare. But much of the growth of research and development, even when conducted by private firms, is underwritten by the government. It has been estimated that seven out of ten *net* new jobs in the 1960s were created in the nonprofit sector, and that almost two-thirds of all scientists and engineers working on research and development projects were funded by the federal government. In 1965, Eli Ginzberg and his associates estimated that 35 to 40 percent of all employment is within the nonprofit sector—including, of course, government, hospitals, universities, social services, and research organizations.

3. The "revolution" in education. In the last forty years, the United States has gone from an elite- to a class- to a mass-system of higher education. Whatever one thinks of the quality of the education of the population, education has significantly become one of the largest *industries* in the United States, more than half the youth population does some college work, and a large number of persons are engaged in teaching (about 3.2 million), almost 600,000 of them teaching in institutions of "higher learning."

In 1940, about 30 million persons were in school, but less than 1.5 million of them were enrolled in higher education. By 1975, about 60 million persons were in school, 8.5 million of them in higher education. In 1940, less than 15 percent of the group eighteen to twenty-one years of age entered college; by 1975, the figure was almost 50 percent. In 1940, only 4.6 percent of the populace twenty-five years of age and over had completed college; by 1975, almost 14 percent of those over age twenty-five had completed college. Of the group twenty-five to twenty-nine years of age, almost 22 percent had completed college by 1975.

This is not the place to discuss the reputed impact of college education. But sociologists have consistently noted that those with higher education tend to be more "liberal" on noneconomic issues and more independent in voting. Equally important, the expansion of education also creates a "scale" effect that allows more militant minorities to organize more effectively. S.M. Lipset has argued that the number of active student radicals, both in the 1930s and the 1960s, usually came to no more than 5 percent of the student population; but 5 percent of a student body of 1,000 is a tiny knot of only fifty persons, while 5 percent of 10,000 is 500, a number that can become effectively organized within a larger, diffuse, and unorganized body.

In the late 1960s, there was an eruption of student unrest that has clearly had an imprinting effect on those who lived through those turbulent years. As a number of observers have pointed out, in the 1960s the size of the youth cohort had jumped more than 50 percent by the mid-decade, creating an extraordinary "generational" self-consciousness that combined with the new militancy of the blacks and the antiwar agitation (stimulated greatly by the threat of conscription hanging over the heads of all young men) leading to a series of chain reactions on hundreds of campuses. For the student activists—who numbered in the hundreds of thousands—this era will be the decisive experience of their lives, like the Depression and the war for previous generations. But this student activism, coming after previous waves of radicalism and liberalism on the campuses, was also a form of "vocational training"—in organization, mobilization, speaking, lobbying, and the like—that will stand them in good stead in future years. It is likely, and is already apparent, that some of the extreme militancy has faded, and their political views have become less militant and extreme. Yet each new student generation begins several paces, so to speak, to the left of the previous ones, and even though each generation may experience a softening of mood or a conservatism of spirit, the entire "slope," or the axis of political attitudes, moves further to the left on a historical scale.[11]

4. The adversary culture. The phrase, the thought, is that of Lionel Trilling. In the preface to *Beyond Culture* (1965), Trilling remarks that "any historian of the literature of the modern age will take virtually for granted the adversary intention, the actually subversive intention, that characterizes modern writing." Trilling, it should be noted, was not polemicizing against this intention. As an early proponent of modernism, he had appreciated its liberating force. But over the years he had begun to question some of its effects. When Herbert Marcuse argued in *An Essay on Liberation* that art communicates an objective truth that is not accessible to ordinary experience, Trilling asked (in a way that even "rather surprised" himself): What if "art does not always tell the truth or the best kind of truth and does not always point out the right way?" What if art "can even generate falsehood and habituate us to it . . .?"

The adversary intention, in the past, was restricted to a small group of persons and works. The situation today, as Trilling pointed out, has changed. Thirty years ago, the university figured as a citadel of conservatism. Few would make that claim today. A quantitative difference has emerged in the relation of the adversary culture to the society:

> The difference can be expressed quite simply in numerical terms—there are a great many more people who adopt the adversary program than there formerly were. Between the end of the first quarter of this century and the present time there has grown up a populous group whose members take for granted the idea of the adversary culture. This group is to be described not only by its increasing size but by its increasing coherence. It is possible to think of it as a class. As such, it of course has its internal conflicts and contradictions, but also its common interests and presuppositions and a considerable efficiency of organization, even of an institutional kind.

For Trilling, the growth of an adversary culture, its adherents now sufficiently large to be a class, posed two problems. One was the relation of the adversary culture to the middle class. As Trilling noted, the "legend of the free creative spirit at war with the bourgeoisie" must now be regarded ironically. Even more, if the adversary culture "has not dominated the whole of its old antagonist, the middle class . . . it has detached a considerable force from the main body of the enemy and has captivated its allegiance."

The second problem—and perhaps the most important one for Trilling, a believer in the humanities and literature as a major mode of intellectual life—was the relation of the adversary culture to its own members and ideals, particularly its power to create a new conformity. As Trilling wrote about this largely neglected theme,

> If I am right in identifying [the adversary culture as a class] then we can say of it, as we say of any other class, that it has developed characteristic habitual responses to the stimuli of its environment. It is not without power, and we can say of it, as we can say of any other class with a degree of power, that it seeks to aggrandize and perpetuate itself. And, as with any other class, the relation it has to the autonomy of its members makes a relevant question, and the more, of course, by reason of the part that is played in the history of the ideology by the ideal of autonomy. There is reason to believe that the relation is ambiguous.[12]

These four changes in the culture and the social structure frame the question of the character of the "new class," to which I now turn. What does one mean by a "class?" That is the bedeviling question. When Noel Annan speaks of the intellectual aristocracy in England as a class, he has in mind a distinct notion of behavior and social status. He writes:

> Class on the impersonal level is the key to conduct because it defines the way in which a man is treated by his fellow-men and how reciprocally he treats them. It is justifiable to stress its importance because in England especially, a man's social status has always been a touchstone to his standard of values.[13]

This usage is akin to the idea of a "social class" and is coeval with Max Weber's idea of a "status group." But it does not tell us the basis of class, though it does emphasize the mechanism of continuity, which is the family. Trilling is looser in his formulation of class, though he points to such elements as size, coherence, power, and the effort to perpetuate itself. Yet in this instance, too, there is little sense of the basis of class, other than education and, presumably, position in the intellectual community.

Marxist definitions, since they emphasize location in the structure of production, do point to an objective foundation, but they lack any sense of the mechanisms of consciousness (other than the "external" factors of crisis and conflict that presumably generate solidarity). Aside from his empirical descriptions of social groups in *The Eighteenth Brumaire*, most of Marx's definitions (and there are several) are too formal.

To be useful for the modern world, a definition of class has to be found in the *social structure* in some institutional arrangement providing the basis for differential position and power/authority/influence and reward. And it must comprise, as well, a *cultural* outlook providing a coherent view, a common consciousness, and, implicitly, some legitimation for the class itself. In brief, a "class" exists when there is a community and continuity of institutional interest and an ideology that provides symbols of recognition (or codes of behavior) for its members.

If one looks at capitalist society in these terms, the bourgeoisie formed a class because of its community of interest in the system of private property, the continuity of the system through the family, and the justification of private property through the doctrine of natural rights (or, in Locke's terms, through the fact that man has endowed nature with his labor and is entitled to the fruits of his labor and the right to pass those fruits along to his heirs).

The major difficulty with contemporary capitalism arises, first, from the breakup of "family capitalism." The firms created by the original capitalists or entrepreneurs bore the family names, such as Swift, Grace, or Ford, and were continued through the ownership of private property. The managerial revolution sundered ownership from management. Ownership is a right, but management is a function. Yet management has increasingly become more and more powerful in the corporation. The second major difficulty with the character of capitalism is that ownership is increasingly vested less and less in family groups, even those divorced from management, and more in mutual funds, pension funds, trust funds, and the like. These are "owners" in the legal sense of being stockholders, yet they are not owners in the sense of having any psychological identification with the firm. They are principally investors seeking a return, who can and will "walk away" from the firm if it is not providing the return that is sought.

In this respect, there is a breakup of the class system of capitalism. There is an upper class of wealth, but a managerial class of function; while the upper class can pass on its wealth (subject to the tax laws) to its children, the managers cannot pass on their positions (though they may provide cultural advantages) to their children. The result is that the *continuity* of the system is in the enterprise itself, not in the families whose intermarriages and interconnections had provided a social cement and continuity to the system.[14] At the same time, the justification of the system, to the extent that it rests on the idea of private property and ownership, is called into question. The issue necessarily arises: What is the Corporation? Those who have spent their lives within it, whose social life and status are tied up in the corporate life? Or those who are technically the "owners," but who can, and do, walk away from the enterprise?

All of these analytical problems arise in trying to define the emerging class system. If property and inheritance form the basis and mode of access in the capitalist system, then technical skill and education are the base and mode of access to position and power/authority/influence and reward in a post-industrial system.* Yet do those whose positions rest on skill and education have enough common interests to form a "class?" And what would be its ideology?

The ideology is the easiest to identify—it is the idea of the career open to talent, the idea of a meritocracy. Its justifications are in the democratic ideal and in the idea of equality of opportunity that have underlain Western society in the past hundred years. Yet curiously, at the moment when the economic and educational systems have become more open because of the need for professional skills and the breakdown of family and social-class barriers, the idea of a meritocracy has come under attack on the very ground that it would create a new privileged class system and thus exclude those who are unable to meet the educational or skill requirements. A meritocracy emphasizes individualism, competitiveness, and ability. Yet the argument against it, as John Rawls has put it in his *Theory of Justice*, is that ability is inherited, like tallness, and ability in itself, like tallness, should not command a differential reward, but should be placed at the disposal of the community as a whole. And those who have found themselves disadvantaged in the educational competitions are now demanding "equality of outcomes" and places allocated on the basis of group attributes. Although those who would benefit are largely the minority groups, the "theoreticians" of the new equality are largely intellectuals from the meritocratic class. In this, one sees again the repetition of history: a section of the emerging new class detaches itself and provides the ideological leaders for a disadvantaged group.

But history does not repeat itself so simply. Not only does the political system decisively introduce complicating variables (the conflict *between* nations, particularly between north and south, forces different organizational forms on the national societies), but it is questionable whether the amorphous bloc designated as the "knowledge stratum" has sufficient *community* of interest to form a class, in the sense understood for the past 150 years. If one starts from the "social structure" and seeks to identify the information and knowledge sector, there are four broad strata:

1. The information processors and the technical and professional workers. These can be regarded as *occupations*. These are individuals, with some higher education, who handle tasks that require some certified competence.
2. The intellectuals and knowledge workers. These are individuals concerned with the creation, evaluation, and, at the research level, transmission and application of knowledge. These are the scientists and scholars, mathematicians and economists, research physicians, and law teachers who decide

---

*I do not assume that this exhausts the question of a modern class system. The most important variable—the role of politics, and the control that derives from the political system—is left out of this analysis. I have tried to deal with some of those questions in *The Coming of Post-Industrial Society*, Chapter 6, especially pp. 358-66.

through peer review who is qualified for recognition in the intellectual community, and whose consensus determines which paradigms of knowledge or theories carry greatest weight.

3. The creators and critics of culture: novelists, painters, musicians, and critics who form the peer-review system in the arts.
4. The transmitters of culture and knowledge: cultural and intellectual periodicals, museums, publishing houses, libraries, etc.
5. The appliers and transmitters of knowledge: engineers, physicians, lawyers, teachers, and social-service workers, who are often organized as professions or guilds and have certification requirements for entry into each field.
6. Managers and administrators in economic enterprise, public bureaucracies, and nonprofit institutions (e.g., hospitals, schools, universities).
7. News and entertainment workers: reporters, journalists, and broadcasters in the print and electronic media; the movie makers, show-business people, and the like.

The preceding is a functional classification, even though there are inevitable overlaps, and all the other categories are included in the first, overall category. One can also establish a set of cultural-political categories:

1. The clerisy. The guardians of orthodoxy in the society, religious or scholarly. In the older sense of the term, the Establishment.
2. The policy intellectuals. Specialists and advisors, attached to elites or government, utilizing their knowledge for purposes of policy and action.
3. Ths ideological intellectuals. Those who seek to mobilize ideas and values, to attack or defend existing institutions, who are *engaged* in the combat of ideas.

The intention of these distinctions is not to establish a set of formal categories. One can do so, and classify activities as *instrumental, creative and evaluative, normative and critical*, or by some different set of criteria.* One could then chart the modes of recruitment, the patterns of advancement and recognition, the role of the major professional and intellectual institutions and academics in defining modes of conduct, and the like. It is my intention to show that, in these diverse activities, there are few institutional arrangements that bring these groups together, in structural terms, as a coherent class. If the question of *interests* is decisive, for example, then there are two kinds of

---

*S.M. Lipset and I have done so in some working papers for an ongoing comparative study of intellectuals in four countries. The classifications I have used are for illustrative purposes. They are not the ones used in our working papers, which are much more elaborate; we have made an effort to fit them, more formally, into sociological theory. Yet they encompass the kinds of groups enumerated here.

attachments. The first is what could be called professional *estates*, or statuses. Within the knowledge stratum, there are four functional estates:

1. Scientific and scholarly
2. Technological (applied skills)
3. Administrative
4. Cultural (artistic and religious)

The crucial institutional locations, however, are what I have called *situses*, or vertically organized locations of *interest-bound* activities:

1. Economic enterprises and business firms
2. Government (bureaucratic-administrative; judicial)
3. Universities and research organizations
4. Social complexes (hospitals, social service, community organizations)
5. The military

The point is that the professional groups, the estates, although loosely organized in "corporate form," are *distributed* among the different situses. Thus some scientists work for the military, others for business, others are in the universities and research organizations. Similarly, the technological professions are distributed among the situses. The controlling argument is this: When the state becomes the decisive arena for the allocation of resources and for the decisions that provide differential power to different activities, the *situses* are the major factors within that arena, because they are the claimants and the constituencies in that game.*[15]

If *interests* provide one criterion for the conditions of class, it is not clear what the common interest of the diverse "information and knowledge" occupations would be.† The same problem bedeviled James Burnham when he was grappling with the problem of identifying the "managers" as the new class that would succeed the capitalists in the great historical organizational change. The

---

*While the bureaucracy and the intelligentsia do form a "new class" in the Communist countries, most sociological and political analysis is largely in terms of these *situs* groups: the Party, the government bureaucracy, the central planners, the factory managers, the cultural institutions, the heads of collective farms, etc. In this respect, my depiction of the stratification system of "model" post-industrial strata, as well as the analysis of Communist, and even all state-directed systems, derives more from "elite" than "class" theory.

†B. Bruce-Briggs has argued that while the technologists and administrators might be attached primarily to their *institutional* locations, the scientists and cultural persons would be more likely to identify with their "estate" or professional group. As a psychological fact, I think this may probably be true, but when interests are at stake, because the financing of these activities derives largely from the state, the major claimants become the more powerful institutional situses.

term "managers" proved quite elusive; Burnham said he meant the "production managers," "administrative engineers," "supervisory technicians,"* but not the finance executives, following Veblen's *Theory of the Business Enterprise*, which distinguished between industry and finance. In the overall context, the economic administrators, not the political bureaucrats, would run the society; but then, Burnham concludes: "To say the ruling class is the managers is almost the same thing as to say that it is the state bureaucracy." This is because the managers "will exercise their control over the instruments of production . . . through their control of the state which in turn will own and control the instruments of production."[16] No wonder Gerth and Mills called Burnham "a Marx for the Managers"—and he was no more right than Marx was.

Moreover, economic (or occupational, or structural) interests are not necessarily the decisive determinant of political, and certainly not of cultural, attitudes, which are more diverse and varied than the specific interests identified with an economic position. Political and cultural attitudes often derive from traditional family attachments, religious or ethnic identification—or the reactions against them, as individuals cut loose from their early moorings and define themselves on the basis of new cultural imagos (e.g., "liberation") and new cultural styles. As I have argued in *The Cultural Contradictions of Capitalism*, the standard demographic variables that sociologists have used for social-class identification in order to predict voting behavior, child-raising patterns, buying habits, and the like are less reliable as the culture increasingly fosters "discretionary social behavior," and individuals choose to "make themselves" on the basis of varied imagos drawn from the mass media.

Looking at the divisions in American politics, one can make a division, as Richard Hofstadter first did, between economic-interest (or "class") politics and sociocultural (or "status group") politics. Along the axis of economic issues, one can make a left-right distinction, and, along the axis of cultural issues, a liberal-conservative distinction. The first axis divides those who want state intervention and planning and the curbing of business power from those who defend laissez-faire and free enterprise. The other axis divides those who cling to traditionalist, usually Protestant, small-town values from those whose values are urban and more cosmopolitan and espouse relaxed restrictions on morals and cultural styles, the hallmarks of "modernity." Yet there is often little congruence between the two axes. The American working class might be "left" on economic issues, yet conservative on cultural issues. The managerial groups in the society might be "right" on economic issues, yet "liberal" on cultural issues. The important question, at any time, would be which issues were salient and why.[17]

---

*This definition reappears as the "technostructure" in John Kenneth Galbraith's *The New Industrial State*, one of his contributions to the theory of a "new class."

	Left	*Right*	
Liberal	Urban intellectuals	Managers	Cultural
			Issues
Conservative	working class	Old Capitalists	

Economic
Issues

If one considers the present-day issues that mix economic and cultural questions—such as ecology (the trade unions and blacks are largely indifferent, but the middle-class professional is not), affirmative action (the unions and liberal Jewish community and the blacks are on opposing sides), community control of schools, busing, decentralization of political power, planning, and the like—any effort to correlate social status or economic interests with positions on cultural questions is bound to be tangled.

In short, if there is any meaning to the idea of a "new class," as posed by Bazelon, Kristol, et al., it cannot be located in social-structural terms; it must be found in cultural attitudes. It is a mentality, not a class.

The dominant cultural mentality in the Western world—I refer largely to the intellectual milieu of the leading periodicals and the moral temper expressed in the arts—is the idea of the antinomian self: the individual, not an institution, is the source of moral judgment; experience, not tradition, is the source of understanding. The idea of an "authentic identity" is the norm that individuals should follow; institutional and organizational life, which bends a person into "roles," is inherently depersonalizing and destructive of the "whole man." While the nineteenth-century ideal emphasized "liberty," the idea of being free of ascriptive ties, the twentieth-century ideal emphasizes "liberation," the freedom from all institutional restraints.

Yet both ideas have deep roots in the strongest traditions of Western thought. Antinomianism has roots in Christian thought and received reinforcement during the Reformation in the Protestant insistence that individual conscience, not the institutional authority of the church, be the basis of faith. And the idea of the "self" derives from the liberalism of Kant, with his insistence that the moral foundation of behavior is autonomy, or the idea that an individual being is "self-determining," not "other-determined."

What is distinctive about the modern temper is the way in which these ideas have been carried to extremes. To begin with, both attitudes, albeit anti-institutional, were *within the framework of religion*. The antinomianism of Luther was a spiritual antinomianism in which the individual was made responsible for the "decision" to come to Christ. And the autonomy of Kant derived from the idea of a "rational religion" in which Reason was the ground of a moral imperative. And it is in the very nature of religion to impose a set of limits on the way in which an idea can be expressed in practice.

Yet a double process of detachment was at work in the nineteenth and early twentieth centuries. For the advanced social groups—the artists and the educated social classes—the legitimation of social behavior passed from religion to the expressive culture. Nothing was sacred, and the exploration of all impulses became an aesthetic norm. Thus "the culture" was freed from the domination of religion and from traditional moral norms.

In the economy, the "rugged individualism" of the first entreprenurial classes was held in check by some of the religious norms that formed the Protestant ethic. Yet as the Protestant ethic itself began to give way, the sense of acquisitiveness, the other root of capitalism, could be held in check only by the countervailing efforts of trade unions, who resisted the unilateral power of the capitalists to determine the rules of work and reward, the efforts of small business to hold out against the trusts, and the efforts of an educated middle class to resist the spoilation of the environment (an issue that goes back to the conservationist movement of the Progressive era).

In the last fifty years, cultural styles have taken the initiative in promoting social and economic change—at first in the "high culture," as the experimentalism of the modernist movement provided an extraordinary surge of creativity, and then for the middle classes, in new "lifestyles" and other appurtenances of the consumer society. In all this, the legitimations of orthodoxy, traditionalism, and bourgeois life have gone by the board. Capitalism, as its most trenchant defenders from Schumpeter to Kristol have noted, lacks any "transcendental justifications," since it is simply instrumental and rational, and creates no values of its own. The idea of liberty, which would guard against the centralization of power and bespeak a pluralist society, has given way in the culture to the idea of "liberation," which often paradoxically gives way to submission—because the individual who seeks to "escape" himself can often do so most readily by submerging his anxious self into "community" and some "whole way of life" that radical movements seem to promise.

The "new class" consists of individuals who have carried the logic of modern culture to its end. Serious and committed, as many are, or trendy and chic, as others may be, they make up a cultural phenomenon that mirrors the breakdown of traditional values in Western society. It is not a "new class" in any social-structural sense. It is the endpoint of a culture in disarray.

Chanticleer thought his crowing had caused the sun to rise. The "new class" has a somewhat similar relation to the structural transformation of capitalism. It is surprising that the critics of the "new class" attribute such powers to it.

Modern capitalism has been transformed in two ways. One is the growth of state power and the increasingly decisive role of the state in managing, if not directing, the economy. Inevitably, such an extension of state power limits the role of the corporation class and, given the increased bureaucratization, even inhibits capital formation and, through the extension of cumbersome regulation, limits the flexibility of economic enterprises to adapt to market conditions. (However, not all enterprises are eager to accept market freedom when the time comes—witness the unwillingness of many airlines to accept deregulation of routes and fares.) But the growth of state power and the centrality of the political system in managing the society do not arise from any ideological pressures. They are responses to the "systemic" impact of the structural changes in capitalist society. The last seventy-five years have seen four major changes extending state power.

The first has been the requirements of defense. Gearing a society to war requires a degree of control over resources, from stockpiling to allocation, and the subordination of major economic activities to national needs. By its very nature, defense matériel is a "public good" that can be ordered and used only by the state. Since 1940, the bedrock of American capitalism has been a permanent defense economy.

The second change has been the rise of social services and large state expenditures for welfare, medical care, support for education, and the like. The acceptance of the principle of welfare (though not necessarily the extent of the expenditures) arises from the necessity of *inclusion* of disadvantaged groups into citizenship in the society. From Bismarck and Disraeli through Franklin D. Roosevelt and Dwight D. Eisenhower, the very idea of "one nation" rather than "two" has dictated the acceptance of the idea of a welfare state, and with it the principle of entitlement.

The third factor, arising from the technological revolutions in transportation and communication, is the increasing degree of interdependence in the society, so that spillover effects are no longer local but national. Problems of economic dislocations and adjustments to change and industry-wide or national rules to deal with pollution and environmental issues necessarily involve federal authority. It may well be that the actual operational measures could, in a more innovative way, be left to market mechanisms, rather than to cumbersome bureaucratic regulations. But federal authority is initially necessary for the establishment of policy.

And finally, in the growing interdependence of a world economy, basic economic issues—such as the relative value of money, the price of commodities, the changes in the international division of labor—can only be negotiated among nation-states, and national economic policy becomes a cardinal consideration for the political order.

Along with these structural changes, modern capitalism has been transformed by a widespread hedonism that has made mundane concerns, rather than transcendental ties, the center of people's lives. Although the new legitimations derive from what had once been an adversary culture, the engine of modern capitalism has taken over these cultural styles and translated them into marketable commodities. Without the hedonism stimulated by mass consumption, the very structure of the business enterprises would collapse. In the end, this is the cultural contradiction of capitalism: Having lost its original justifications, capitalism has taken over the legitimations of an antibourgeois culture to maintain the continuity of its own economic institutions. Capitalism is a very different social system now than it was one or two hundred years ago.

The ties of character structure, social system, and culture, which had given capitalism coherence in its bourgeois phase, have unraveled. A very different social form—in the sociological structure, the legal character of the corporation, the growth of state power as an independent force, and the hedonism of the culture—is still to be named. It is not the product of "the new class." Nor will the "new class" be its master. In seeking to map the course of social change, one should not mistake the froth for the deeper currents that carry it along.

NOTES

1. Joseph Schumpeter, *Capitalism, Socialism and Democracy* (New York, 1942), chapters 12 and 13. Quotations have been transposed to compress and strengthen Schumpeter's description. The actual sequence of quotations is: pp. 137, 147, 151, 147, 145, 154.

2. F.A. Hayek, "The Intellectuals and Socialism," *University of Chicago Law Review* (Spring 1949), reprinted in George B. de Huszar, ed., *The Intellectuals* (Glencoe, Ill., 1960), pp. 371-73.

3. Karl Marx, *The Poverty of Philosophy* (New York, 1963), p. 125.

4. Quoted in V.I. Lenin, *What Is To Be Done?* (1902; Moscow, 1947), p. 52. Kautsky's essay appeared in *Neue Zeit*, 1901-02, XX, I, No. 3 (the official theoretical organ of the German Social Democratic Party). The italics in the quote are in the original and are so noted by Lenin.

5. See *The Collected Works of S.T. Coleridge, Lectures 1795 on Politics and Religion*, ed. L. Patton and P. Mann (Princeton, 1971), pp. xvi, 137. Also S.T. Coleridge, *Biographi Literaria* (New York, 1939), pp. 101-02; Noel Annan, *Leslie Stephen* (Cambridge, Mass., 1952), p. 1. Also, Noel Annan, "The Intellectual Aristocracy," in *Studies in Social History*, ed. J.H. Plumb (New York, 1955), p. 244.

6. See Richard Pipes, "Russian Conservatism in the Second Half of the Nineteenth Century," (XIII International Congress of Historical Science, Moscow, August 1970); Leonard Schapiro, "The Pre-Revolutionary Intelligentsia and the Legal Order," in *The Russian Intelligentsia*, ed. Richard Pipes (New York, 1962), pp. 29-30; Leonard Schapiro, "The Vekhi Group and the Mystique of Revolution," *Slavonic and East European Review* (December 1955).

7. Alexander Solzhenitsyn et al., *From Under the Rubble* (Boston, 1974). Introduction by Max Hayward, pp. v-viii.

8. On this subject there is a huge literature. For useful reference: John R. Harrison, *The Reactionaries: A Study of the Anti-Democratic Intelligentsia* (New York, 1967); George L. Mosse, *The Culture of Western Europe: The Nineteenth and Twentieth Centuries* (London, 1963); Fritz Stern, *The Politics of Cultural Despair* (Berkeley, 1961); Joshua C. Taylor, *Futurism* (New York, 1961); H. Stuart Hughes, *The Obstructed Path: French Social Thought Between the Wars* (New York, 1968); John L. Stewart, *The Burden of Time: The Fugitives and Agrarians* (Princeton, 1965).

9. For a prediction of the powerful new role of the Third World ideologies, see my book, *The End of Ideology* (Glencoe, Ill., 1960), pp. 373-74.

10. These features are discussed at length in my book, *The Coming of Post-Industrial Society* (New York, 1973; paperback edition, with added Foreword, 1976).

11. The statistical material in this section is taken from standard sources, principally *Historical Statistics of the United States*, and the *Statistical Abstract, 1976*. The projections of the occupational labor force to 1985 are from the *Monthly Labor Review* (November 1976). On the nonprofit sector, see Eli Ginzberg et al., *The Pluralistic Economy* (New York, 1965).

12. Lionel Trilling, *Beyond Culture* (New York, 1965), pp. xii, xiii, xv, xvi.

13. Annan, *Leslie Stephen*, p. 2.

14. For a more detailed analysis of this phenomenon, see my essay, "The Break-up of Family Capitalism," in *The End of Ideology*.

15. I have conjoined here arguments that are divided between my two recent books. An elaboration of the idea of *situses* can be found in *The Coming of Post-Industrial Society*, pp. 374-78. On the role of the State, see the section on "The Public Household," in *The Cultural Contradictions of Capitalism* (New York, 1975).

16. James Burnham, *The Managerial Revolution* (New York, 1941).

17. Daniel Bell (ed.), *The New American Right* (New York, 1955).

14

CONCLUSION:
Notes Toward a Delineation
of the New Class

B. Bruce-Briggs

Can this diffuse material be integrated? Despite many difficult problems, I think it can. But to view the figure of the New Class, a good deal of underbrush must be cleared away first.

A major obstacle to vision is that noxious French weed transplanted to American soil by William James—the term "intellectual." To most Americans, the notion that intellect or intelligence is the special preserve of any particular group is pretentious, even hilarious; but a tiny band wears the label proudly—a few thousand people at most—including a core of a few hundred, most of whom live or did live in New York City, and write for a handful of arcane, low-circulation journals. They like to think of themselves as "passionate" about ideas—as one of them, Richard Hofstadter, wrote, "dedicated to the life of the mind"—or as "creators of culture," in Lipset's oft-cited definition.[1] Well, is not the song writer a "creator of culture"? Is not the fundamentalist preacher or the Talmudic scholar living "the life of the mind"? Is not the redneck "passionate" about the idea of race? The very annoyance of broad elements of society at what intellectuals say is evidence of a widespread concern for ideas, or at least words.

In fact, the intellectuals only count among their number people who are concerned in certain ways about certain kinds of ideas. Just as doctors are not those who treat the sick (we all do that) but those who are accepted as doctors by other doctors, intellectuals are those who are recognized as such by other intellectuals (the certification of doctors is, of course, protected by government, which is not the case for intellectuals, except in the "centrally planned economies.")

No one seems to disagree that most intellectuals have a highly critical attitude toward society. But disaffected people are found among all elements. The alienation of a few thousand, drawn from a universe of millions of educated persons, seems attributable to individual personality, personal or family history, or perhaps the ordinary variability of humanity, and does not require any grand macrosociological theory. Of course intellectuals are disaffected; they only admit to their ranks the disaffected (who, once admitted, may become less so as they mature).

Today, most of the disaffected are on the Left. But as several contributors to this volume have pointed out, intellectuals used to be critical from the Right. There is a very simple and plausible economic explanation for this shift. Intellectuals are highbrow journalists who write for an audience with a high level of literary education. In former times, they were almost exclusively recruited from the privileged classes, not only "intelligentry" (the delightful neologism Bell has coined for this volume) but bourgeois rentiers as well. Until about the First World War, almost all intellectuals (and almost certainly their audience) had independent sources of income. They were part of a leisure class living on capital—i.e., they were members of families or classes that were on the way down, and their hostility to their society can be most easily explained as the understandable revulsion of the declining toward the *parvenu*.

Today, one still cannot make a living as an intellectual; their magazines are almost all run at a loss and pay trivial or no fees to contributors. But almost all members of the New York intellectual community now have faculty appointments, and it is generally believed that a substantial portion of their readership is university professors, and almost all of it is university graduates. Judging from circulation figures, the market is at most a few hundred thousand, and a good number of these readers presumably consider themselves intellectuals as well. Many other things have happened in the intellectual milieu during the last sixty years, but let me suggest that the switch from Right to Left may be a function of a change in the market.[2]

Next in the intellectual pecking order are what Lipset calls the "distributors of culture"—employees and subcontractors of more broadly-based upper-middlebrow periodicals and book publishing firms catering to an educated but less demanding market, which is large enough to support a few thousand salaried journalists and editors and a few hundred freelance writers, all of whom operate in a tough, competitive business. Formal feedback mechanisms in this market are very primitive. There is no easy way to determine what the consumers will buy. Success or failure depends on inspired entrepreneurship; the fortunes of the enterprises ride on the judgment of a handful of editors. How do they gauge the market? They know one another and talk with friends, again mostly living in or near New York City, who are mostly of similar social background, education, and values. Among their friends are the intellectual community described earlier.

At least in New York and Los Angeles, these culture distributors are part of a larger society, a sort of "high bohemia," which takes pride in its wit, taste, freedom from traditional restraints, and adherence to the latest fashions in clothing, entertainment, and ideas. Most of the money in this milieu seems to come from selling luxury goods and services to the prosperous—including books, periodicals, films, plays, and art. These luxury vendors resemble nothing so much as the hangers-on of a Renaissance court—but the prince is dead. Within this circle appeared what its chronicler Tom Wolfe called "radical chic." My observation suggests that few of these people believe in anything except power, celebrity, and the pleasures of the flesh. Should "Nazi chic" appear, jeweled swastikas would be hot items in the boutiques of Madison Avenue and Sunset Boulevard.

I suggest that the market for these culture distributors is formally educated people—professors, schoolteachers, other professionals, staff people of various sorts, *and their wives*. In other words, those who have been labeled the New Class. The changing values/ideology of the media might be explained in market terms. The interplay of producers and consumers is incredibly complex and indeterminable, but those who bristle at Galbraith's thesis that General Motors controls the market for automobiles should not blandly believe that Galbraith controls the market for economic theory.[3]

A step farther down are another group not considered intellectuals—mass media journalists also working in a highly competitive business, as close to an ideal free market as exists in American today, a market in which nobody has to buy (in fact, less than half of the population buys any journalism at all). Their market, one may assume, is white-collar workers. These journalists are, on the whole, rather stupid fellows, but that is not especially relevant or important. Their job is to produce assemblages of words and pictures that people will buy. Again, it does not seem particularly useful to attack them for believing that the ideas *they* consume might be adapted for mass consumption.

Let us take the market analogy one step further: Like any businessman, a word-producer must differentiate his product from his competitors, but a product that is too deviant cannot sell, except perhaps to a very narrow, specialized audience—such as, say, the readership of the intellectual magazines. A new product must deviate only carefully from the norm, and only the most perceptive or fortunate entrepreneur/editor can successfully introduce a radically new line.[4]

The post-World War II period saw many successful idea promotions: "McCarthyism," "the Radical Right," "nation building," "the illegal-and-immoral-war-in . . . ." Harrington had a winner with "poverty" (which displaced Galbraith's "affluent society"). As Bartley points out, Ralph Nader has found a huge market for "consumerism." All these can be said to have been promoted by intellectuals. But not all recently successful ideas were intellectual promotions—the case of the "counterculture" is perhaps arguable, but how about "the Communist conspiracy" or "law-and-order"? And we forget the intellectual product failures. Whatever happened to "white ethnics" and its follow-up, "blue-collar blues"? But the Edsel of the recent idea market was "equality of results." Lord knows this was pushed heavily; but despite reams of learned research and impassioned articles, it went nowhere. (At a conference in Massachusetts in the early 1970s I heard the editor of the Boston *Globe* claim that income distribution would be *the* issue of the 1970s. Too much of his market research was done in Cambridge and too little in Brookline and South Boston.)

I have taken a stubborn line merely to make a straightforward point. To those who claim the world is ruled by ideas (and therefore by the idea producers and distributors), I ask: Why *those* ideas? Of all the ideas available, why are those particular ideas accepted, even believed? There are certainly many reasons, but one obvious one is that certain ideas are in the interest of certain groups, and that a major interest is economic interest. There is nothing sinister about this notion. Few people have the strength of character to be genuine cynics. Most honestly believe that what is good for them is good generally. Max Weber labeled this coincidence of idea and interest "elective affinities." Since it is widely accepted that it is no accident that independent businessmen believe in laissez-faire economics, and that working men are generally well-disposed toward theories of the beneficence of collective bargaining, it should not be difficult to accept the idea that other people in different economic situations should hold different economic views. Furthermore, those who accept the notion that certain cultural views are consistent with the situation of the bourgeois or the proletariat should entertain the possibility of a similar relationship to other economic groups.

Now, none of the ideas that many of the contributors find obnoxious is new, so let me suggest that their recent circulation is the result of changes in the market, which is now found among educated people who have been labeled the New Class.

I suggested above that the academy was a major market for the producers of words. The second major group identified as "intellectuals" is the university community. The incredible expansion of the faculty and the student body detailed by several of the contributors might in itself account for some of the striking changes in the market for words. But why should the university be so receptive to these ideas? One explanation that can be discarded is that the scientific method necessarily generates a critical turn of mind, which is then applied to society as a whole. Consider Lipset's data: it is not professors in the "hard" sciences, but those in the humanities and so-called "social sciences" who have dissident values. For example, a 1913 study found that physicists were far more likely to be deists than sociologists and psychologists.[5]

There is a simpler explanation for disaffection in the universities. While well rewarded (especially considering their hours*) relative to the public at large, most professors are ill-paid in comparison to other professionals—doctors, lawyers, architects, and especially corporate managers and even independent businessmen. While the professoriate has made a heroic adjustment to this condition by adopting a style of genteel poverty that rejects vulgar (and expensive) display, it rankles.† As Lipset has demonstrated, the applied disciplines are the least disaffected, and these have the most opportunities for business jobs or consultancies.

Now, I must expand on some of the contributors' evaluations of the social role of the universities. Certainly we need scholarship, research, and education. But most civilized societies support dedicated scholars who perform no immediate practical function; this handful can be maintained in many ways. We do need the knowledge that universities produce, but it can be generated in research organizations, without the distractions of students or of publish-or-perish. And within the universities, the most needed researchers are not the most disaffected. Look at the far right hand side of Lipset's table on p. 76. The enormous productivity of American agriculture results not from the sweat of labor, the ingenuity of entrepreneurs, the workings of the free market, or (not yet) the spin-offs of theoretical research, but from the painstaking empirical

---

*As any student can tell you, the professors do not seem to be around much; they are "working at home," doubtless because of the primitive working conditions they labor under. (Professors are well paid, but most lack the amenities and perquisites of business employees, and cannot believe the quality of secretarial and support services businessmen take for granted—another quite justified source of dissatisfaction.)

†And while the professoriate is highly regarded by the public-at-large, I suggest it is less so by these same doctors, lawyers, and businessmen—its reference group, its "classmates."

work of men who are, for the most part, blissfully innocent of the cultural attitudes discussed here. The same is true, but less so, in decreasing order, of engineers, medical teachers, and hard scientists. Academic dissidence is concentrated in the subjects that are least necessary to the workings of the industrial/capitalist system.

The claim that the universities produce trained manpower needed by the corporations must also be heavily qualified. Yes, they need managers, engineers, chemists, geologists, etc., and it is among these disciplines that the least alienation is found. Private business needs few sociologists, historians, and English majors, and it is among these disciplines that adversary attitudes are most likely to be found. Furthermore, since so many students are attracted to them—because they are usually easier and have more palatable content (what is more fascinating than the study of man and his art?)—these fields have a production of graduates far in excess of what the private sector can absorb, who must seek employment in the nonprofit sector, especially of course, education and government, and seem to have reasonable cause to be less enthusiastic about ''free enterprise'' and to complain of its distorted values.

Lipset's speculation that the concentration of intellectuals in universities might provoke difficulties for post-industrial society similar to those caused in industrial society by the concentration of proletarians in factories warrants closer examination. Not only is it unnecessary for the teaching and research functions to be combined in one place, it is difficult to see why any intellectual activity requires the concentration of workers that some industrial processes do. Economies or efficiencies of scale are few in intellectual work, which is accomplished by individuals and in small teams. There is surprisingly little interplay among academics at the same university, perhaps because of increasing specialization or the intense competitive nature of contemporary scholarship.*

While noticeable economies of scale are present in the library, laboratory equipment, and the computer center, technological advance portends to make the last of these obsolete and perhaps the first also. The advantage to students of a large university are those of a supermarket—they have wider choices, but little incentive or information with which to exercise those choices, so they mostly take what is offered. None of these reasons seems to account for the incredible size of many universities. The actual reasons were dystopian incrementalism (it was cheaper to add on to existing facilities than to build new

---

*This may explain the odd professorial view of competitive capitalism. Their assumption that business must be more of ''a rat race'' than academia is probably wrong. Unlike intellectual endeavor, most successful economic activity requires the coordination of the efforts of large numbers of people. The businessman competes at cooperation. The most obvious counter-example, however, is the media business; most films depict businessmen as if they were all Hollywood sharks.

ones) and politics (existing universities can lobby, nonexisting ones cannot). Still, these large centers of ''intellectuals'' do exist and are unlikely to go away.

Of course, the universities have many other vital social functions in addition to education and research. Most students are there because university attendance is expected of them or because they believe, with good reason, that they must obtain a diploma in order to gain entry to most jobs that offer the good things of life in contemporary America. In addition, universities continue to perform their traditional functions of transmitting the culture of the dominant classes, providing a playground and mating ground for their children, credentialing and ''socializing'' the recruits from the lower orders required by any healthy oligarchy, and supplying the sinecures for the less aggressive scions of the privileged classes that every society has. In this last function, however, the university is performing less well than in the past. It is internally much too competitive today, another reason for the malaise of the professoriate. (A fundamental problem of ''the meritocracy'' is that the sinecures are drying up. One cannot even count anymore on a soft and profitable life in a stock brokerage house or a Wall Street law firm.)

The students are as they have been for 800 years—a very few really concerned with learning, who will become the next generation of genuine scholars; a much larger group of serious careerists (many of whom in the 1960s considered academia the preferred career); a vast mass more interested in sex and artificial stimulants; and a substantial rowdy minority.

The university does perform two vital functions for business, or more precisely for the managers who run it. First, it simplifies personnel procedures. Like any bureaucracy a large corporation finds it too expensive to discriminate very carefully among individuals, so it needs simple screening devices, the more straightforward and measurable the better—for some jobs you require a high school diploma, for others a college degree, for others an MBA.

But growing in importance is the university's role in resolving what I believe to be a fundamental problem of a society based upon the principle of equality of opportunity—if you like, an internal contradiction of the meritocracy. Let us consider the social situation of an archetypal contemporary, well-off American, John Merit. He is not a great man, as he well knows, but in a rather tough, competitive struggle, he has achieved some degree of preeminence and the consequent privilege, income, and standard of living. While he may nominally be a member of some religious denomination (especially when his children were growing), he is basically a man without faith and has no hope for The World To Come. He can achieve immortality only through his children. But he has no productive property, and will almost certainly leave them none, because he must live the last decade of his life on his small capital and provide for another ten years of his widow's support. Furthermore, since he has won in a competitive struggle, he has some unusual abilities—he may be smarter, more productive, more personable, or more ruthless than his peers—that he cannot transmit to his children, who are probably less talented and will be less successful than their father (unless they should show some extraordinary ability in some other field), whether because they lack the same challenge or because they have moved closer to the genetic mean. So how can John Merit guarantee his beloved son a suitable place in this world? He can buy him education and can agitate for the wider society to pay for it—hence the upper-middle class obsession with "good schools."

John Junior's problem is even worse. Since it is highly unlikely that he will measure up to his father, he must settle for a sinecure, or perhaps reject the old man's values, turn his back on "the rat race," and drop out into a trade, a service business, or a proprietorship. It is wonderful how many former dropouts are trying to make a living as small businessmen. This is a great tragedy to most parents, but from a social point of view, it is an excellent development. In order to provide room at the top, a meritocracy needs suitable vehicles for downward mobility and its appropriate justifications.

In this regard, it is most unfair to blame the intellectuals for the counterculture, the New Left, and the campus disruptions of the 1960s. Most of the professoriate and the New York intellectuals, while constitutionally tolerant and occasionally wavering, were appalled or disgusted by the extreme manifestations of the decade, especially the drug-fornication-rock-oriental religion-unreason scene. But there was a link to student unrest. Students in the 1960s knew that they could earn tolerance for revolt if they used the correct *political* ideas/words. Ladd and Lipset found an enormous amount of sympathy for campus unrest among the professoriate, which certainly would not have been there had the students mouthed right-wing slogans.*

Bell is quite right to disavow a direct connection between the extreme movements of the last decade and his knowledge class/professional and technical intelligentsia/knowledge stratum. Of course the values useful ("func-

---

*One manifestation of the New Class that seems impossible to rationalize in economic terms is the moral outrage that appeared among adults during the 1960s. One cause of the Great Schism among the New York intellectuals was the Vietnam War—but not over whether the United States should support the South Vietnamese government, for almost all the intellectuals favored an American pullout. This will sound incredible to the general reader, but the intellectuals split into two warring camps over the *reason* for withdrawal: one group, who thought Vietnam the-wrong-war-in-the-wrong-place-at-the-wrong-time, were savaged as amoral by those who saw the war as a-horrendous-crime-against-humanity. Similarly, the controversy over decentralization in New York City, which appeared to the outsider to be a naked struggle between blacks and Jews for school jobs, was treated as the *Gotterdammerung* in the intellectual press.

But Jeane Kirkpatrick also correctly identifies the tendency toward political passion with the radical Right, few of whom are intellectuals in any occupational or educational sense. Berger's concept of a need for a substitute for religion may provide an explanation, at least for part of the population. Even in the Age of Faith, only a few sought the Holy Grail. Or perhaps some part of the population cannot handle the internal conflict between selfishness and high principle without a short circuit.[6] I don't know; the idea of the New Class need not explain *everything*.

tional") to it are reason, melioration, order, prudence, planning—in other words, Bell's own values. Yet, these are unsatisfying and unnatural, especially to the young. Primitive societies marry off the girls at puberty and let the young men brawl in bachelor houses. On the other hand, the needs of the meritocracy require that young people devote their most vigorous years to at least the pretense of scholarship, a function that is the province of greybeards in most societies.

Tolerance alone, however, cannot account for the campus radicalism of the 1960s. Equally unsatisfactory is the explanation that student activism increased because of the large absolute numbers of radicals, even though they represented a tiny and relatively fixed percentage of the campus population. This account has not stood the empirical test of the 1970s: There are as many students now, but where have the flower children gone? Perhaps it was the rate of change that was the determinant, but measuring that would require a social calculus that does not exist. Maybe the student revolution was a success—the draft is kaput; it would seem students study less than ever before; parietal rules have been abandoned; and "dropping out" has been accepted, like marijuana. This explanation is less satisfactory, but I think that revolt resulted less from the New Class than from a natural reaction to a life dominated by rational values.

Writers as diverse as Ludwig von Mises, Peter F. Drucker, and Christopher Lasch have commented on how unsatisfying bureaucratic life is; although most people most of the time will pay for security with liberty, some will rebel some of the time, and a few all of the time. Most of the veterans of the fight against dehumanizing bureaucracies are now well-ensconced in bureaucracies—and smoking a little pot, voting for the most "liberal" candidate they can find, and probably breeding the next generation of college radicals. The worst that can be said of the New Class is that it failed to come down hard on destructive campus rioting, but is it to be expected that a group will be punitive toward its own progeny? And in retrospect, the campus strategy of the meliorist meritocrats of the multiversity was correct—against the Left who saw the millenium and the Right who saw anarchy, they argued wait-it-out-and-it-will-blow-over, and it did. Certainly a movement that was blown away by cancellation of the draft and a single volley of musketry cannot be thought of as a threat to society or as hope for its secular redemption.

As I suggested, the New Class is characteristically identified with the bureaucracy. In the absence of a paper on the subject, let me assemble a few scraps of data that seem to fit the New Class hypothesis. There has obviously been a major expansion of the power of government since the early 1960s. Who has gained most from this is a partisan question, but an obvious beneficiary has been the high bureaucracy. Beginning with the Kennedy Administration their pay has been increased, "supergrades" have been created, staffs have proliferated in the executive and the legislative branches, and civil service entry has been modified to favor college graduates, so that the federal bureaucracy has moved from the old police-style everybody-starts-from-the-bottom to the military-style division between officers and the other ranks. Government employment is no longer the province of a few gentlemen of independent means in the diplomatic service and a majority of ill-paid and ill-regarded hacks; it is now a well-rewarded career offering interesting work, and power. Ambitious young lawyers will come to Washington for half the salary they could get in leading private firms.

To what degree a bureaucracy is an independent force is a fascinating, unanswerable question. Obviously, responsible bureaucrats have and should have considerable leeway to perform their functions; equally obviously, they do and should quake when called by the Congress or the White House, the presumed representatives of the people. For our purposes here, it suffices to note that bureaucrats are also voters, supporters of causes, extremely well-positioned lobbyists, and consumers—of goods and words. One must assume they are the major market for the *Washington Post*. One need not imply sinister intent to note that they benefit in power, prestige, income, and opportunities for promotion from expansion of government, and to assume that they are a market for ideas that justify the same. However, it would be a serious mistake to see them as a monolithic block.

The largest single bureaucracy remains the Department of Defense. I know there is widespread sentiment there against the "adversary culture" associated with the New Class. In regard to economic organization, bureaucrats in DoD are generally not strong partisans of either free enterprise or equalitarian socialism; as one would expect, they are strong statists, mostly taking for granted the huge, nominally private, managerially run, tightly government-regulated corporations that are their major contractors. These bureaucrats are very similar to military officers or corporate executives, highly but technically educated, and not usually from the best schools. If we measure the New Class by education, they are part of it, but by common worldview or political cohesion, they are not.*

The domestic/social-welfare/regulatory bureaucrats are a more mixed lot. Most are still time-serving hacks, but there are some of those people labeled the New Class, who will use government to remake the nation in their image. It is these people who best fit Lipset's description of those who look to the university as a reference group. Many of them are in the bureaucracy because they could

---

*A glaring weakness in trying to make an economic link to the appearance of New Class attitudes is the apparent conflict between neoisolationism and the wonderful opportunities offered by the foreign policy-intelligence-defense business. A partial explanation is that the bulk of those jobs were technical, and the "soft" disciplines were blind with envy; another was the political necessity of limiting the traditional liberty of the favored classes from conscription. But these explanations do not seem sufficient.

not get university jobs. I believe they use universities as contractors more than the national security apparatus does, but if Moynihan was correct in maintaining that they are promoting welfare, that seems inherently no more reprehensible than the Pentagon promoting defense, and liberal society can be throttled by the generation of dependency as well as by militarism.

It seems to me, however, that the ideal New Class organizational setting is not government, but the nonprofit private sector. Government is too answerable to outsiders. But in the foundation or the endowed research organization, as in the university, the employees are answerable only to themselves; the second best arrangement is contract research to social-welfare bureaucracies. The nonprofits, at least in the Northeast, are thick with the remnants of the intelligentry, persons of good family and modest trust funds—the audience of the *New Yorker*.

As for politicians, they are elected by constituencies; to the degree that a New Class is growing, politicians should respond to it in a democratic system. Scattered observation suggests that the congressional representatives of areas with concentrations of people in presumed New Class occupations—e.g., Manhattan, the Washington suburbs, and major university cities—are the most liberal, even left-wing. Some politicians represent the New Class and many are from the New Class. It is startling how many were once professors (but rarely the best scholars[7]). A university connection is very valuable to a politician, and a complete study of the university posts occupied by defeated or displaced politicians would be fascinating. I suspect it would show a disproportionate number of liberals/Democrats. But this is hardly sinister, because a disproportionate number of conservatives/Republicans will get business jobs. If these are accurate characterizations, however, there would be some substance to the idea that liberals are the political manifestation of the New Class, just as conservatives are of the business class.

Likewise, the unsuccessful journalists become journalism school teachers, or get foundation grants, or become government or corporate public-relations men. Successful journalists receive some university patronage in the form of visiting lectureships and fellowships, and scattered anecdotal data suggest that recipients are rarely right-wingers, again indicating some community of interest.*

It seems fair to regard lawyers rather like politicians. They both serve constituencies/clients. As pointed out by Glazer, the percentage of lawyers serving public or other nonprofit organizations is growing, which would seem

---

*On the whole, journalists are contemptuous of academics (universities supply few "stories," and scholarly standards are an affront to those of journalism) but journalists do directly endorse universities by presenting a professor's views as a disinterested source, very like the manner they treat a "public advocate."

to reflect a shift in the clientele. Moreover, like politicians, all lawyers, no matter whom they serve, benefit from the expansion of government.

Let me add to Glazer's analysis a broader reason for the recent shifts in judicial opinion: the federal judiciary is performing exactly the role intended by the Founding Fathers—to be the branch of government most independent of the populace, and therefore most reflective of upper-class opinion.[8] If it has become more "liberal" and more agreeable to government intervention in certain areas and to the removal of restraints in other areas, we may accept this as reflecting shifts in upper-class opinion—all the more so because on many issues the courts in the 1970s are tracking mildly in a conservative (or better said, neo-conservative) direction, again reflecting educated opinion. Furthermore, while the state courts are for the most part popularly elected, efforts are being made to modify the democratic processes—through subterfuges like "the sitting judge principle"—and there is intense agitation by lawyers, apparently supported by other educated people, to substitute some indirect means of selection by lawyers or "blue-ribbon" panels of "citizens."

Alone among the contributors, Bell would have us concentrate on the scientist, who is of particular interest because he is the only *new* occupational type discussed here. Every other type—the scholar, the alienated cleric, the establishment apologist,[9] the hippie, the rowdy student, the provider of entertainment services to the rich, the bureaucrat, and the manager—appears full blown at least as early as the High Middle Ages. To a considerable degree, the scientist has displaced the priest in popular regard because of his demonstrated capacity for magic and prophecy. But Bell is right in being skeptical of the scientist's abilty to transmit prestige into the sort of moral and political power the priest had. Most scientists are immersed in their own work and have wonderfully conventional personal lives and political attitudes. The few scientists who have ventured into wider public policy issues have all too frequently taken extreme and absurd positions and have been hampered by an insufferable intellectual arrogance. The scientific administrators are necessarily among the nation's shrewdest operators, because they must handle such touchy prima donnas, but few have achieved power or position outside "the scientific estate."

Just above I finally used a word that has been avoided—"liberal." Ladd's data have convinced me that it no longer means anything specific. "Liberalism" in the nineteenth century was a clearly defined body of thought, which remains fossilized in the tiny Liberal parties of continental Europe. In the Anglo-Saxon world however, it has come to be a label for policies and programs that are constantly in flux. In the lifetime of most readers, "liberal" has gone from meaning internationalism to neoisolationism, from reasoned anticommunism to unreasoned anti-anticommunism, from belief in the color-blind state to advocacy of racial quotas. Journalists could not understand how Senator Henry Jackson could be "liberal" on some issues and "conservative" on other issues, although his positions were a standard liberal syndrome as late as 1964. Today, we see liberalism making another shift, this time to the right. In his race for mayor of New York, Congressman Koch justified capital punishment as a liberal policy initiative, on the grounds that it showed "concern for people."

Let me suggest that what liberal now means is adherence to the conventional wisdom/attitudes/programs of the educated classes. To say that college professors are disproportionately liberal is very near to a tautology. I have become persuaded that Bazelon's notion—that, in a considerable sense, self-perception as "liberal" characterizes conscious membership in the New Class—is worth serious consideration. Conversely, as taken as given by Ladd, "conservative" means opposed to "liberal."

The Ladd data explain a phenomenon that has long bemused me: Why do individuals in "high bohemia," who cannot master a simple syllogism, assume that opposing views, however carefully argued, represent ignorance or low-class attitudes? "Liberalism" has become a form of snobbery. But why should a well-off "high bohemia" support radical ideas? Perhaps this could be one reason: Although Bell is correct in noting that cultural liberalism need not necessarily accompany leftism or economic liberalism (e.g., the classical social democratic proletariat), among the higher orders it usually has. Cultural and political radicalism have been joined among artists, writers, and other denizens of bohemia since the time of Byron; if such people do not, as I observe, possess any firm ideas on anything, anything could be sold them under the label "liberal," even revolutionary socialism.

If my suspicion is right and if Ladd is correct in defining contemporary liberalism in social terms, then the prevailing liberalism among the educated need not necessarily be a source of alarm to defenders of capitalism. But note that Ladd has been very careful to stick to the available data. Pollsters are also members of the New Class,* and presumably they ask the kind of questions that concern liberals, so practically no recent poll data are available on New Deal-type liberal issues.

The New Class need not favor government ownership—control is sufficient, even better because it entails less responsibility—but it need not even want this. Like all groups, it wants government to serve its interests. If, indeed, it lives from government or from supplying ideas to people who live from government then it should support increased government spending as Ladd suggests. But I

---

*In 1976, a leading pollster found that a major issue troubling the electorate was "morality in government," which he interpreted as Nixon-Watergate. When I suggested that it also might mean revulsion against perceived government indifference to pornography, abortion, and crime, he got the point immediately—but it would not have occurred to him independently.

would not be quite as strong as his interpretation of his data (pp. 109 and 110). Note that the distinction between education groups is not very large and that two of the domestic spending indicators are crime and drugs (also crime)— traditional areas of government responsibility, conservative issues, and areas in which the New Class collects little from government spending. An occupational or industrial breakdown might have discriminated better.

Ladd's principal argument that level of education is a better predictor of opinion than occupation or source of income is so persuasive that I must nibble at it a bit. First, occupation and education are much the same thing. Few people go to school to be enlightened, rather to be trained or to earn credentials. Second, the majority of all people with postgraduate education are in three occupations—medicine, law, and education, especially higher education. Similarly, the private/nonprofit distinction I suggested to him is inadequate, if only because nonprofit fails to take into account the defense workers and nonprofit sector entrepreneurs in other industries who live off government.*

And, as many readers have surely noticed, the correlation of higher education with certain attitudes can be interpreted without recourse to the idea of the New Class—

1. If you like those values, it is clear that education is doing exactly what it is supposed to do, making people more perceptive and more critical of archaic prejudices.

The critical approach is a powerful weapon, but like a howitzer, it can only demolish what it is aimed at. How can one improve on James Agee's, "How can anyone who has swallowed the doctrines relating to penis-envy, or the withering away of the State, strain at the doctrine of Transubstantiation?" (Of course, this applies also to counterbattery fire—journals adverse to the adversary culture edit out material which argues the other way, "to sharpen the argument.")

2. If you dislike the values, higher education is obviously indoctrination.

A minor contemporary mystery is what actually goes on in the classroom. Clearly, a substantial portion of the students are not listening at all, and most of the rest are concerned with obtaining the maximum grade with the minimum

---

*However, Ladd's analysis is supported by a remarkably similar data base. Toward the close of the study, David T. Bazelon graciously made available a copy of the thesis of his student James T. Barry,[10] who manipulated a NORC survey of college students of the class of 1961, 4,400 of whom were resurveyed in 1968. Barry attempted to test Bazelon's hypothesis that there is a New-Class-in-formation by comparing occupational groups classified roughly according to Bell's estates and situses. While Barry modified census occupational categories in a manner very similar to that which I suggested to Ladd, I find some other difficulties in his method and interpretation; nevertheless, that group of 28 year-olds with graduate degrees displayed little difference in opinion by occupation and industry, with one exception—as in Ladd's data, the academics were far more "liberal" than other groups.

investment of effort, which is to feed back to the professor what the student thinks he wants to hear. But what effect has the instruction on the students' perception of the world?

The socialization of the "better" students is also mysterious. Not that there is much overt discrimination against those who deviate from the professor's norm, although dissidents of the Left or Right complain that the hurdles are higher for them—but this may be sour grapes. I have seen the enforcement of conformity displayed nakedly in two disciplines—architecture and city planning—but to what degree it exists in others I must leave to other researchers. We know there is an input of professors who are likely to think of themselves as liberal and an output of graduates who become more likely to think of themselves as liberals, but the *process* is obscure.

Ladd has wrestled magnificently with the data available to him, but he agrees that we cannot hope for conclusive answers to these questions without a sample large enough to break down into statistically valid subpopulations by age, income, occupation, industry, education, and source of income. For example, Ladd looked at his data base to try to verify Glazer's speculation that lawyers were self-employed and conservative, but only thirty-eight lawyers were in the NORC sample of 9,100. A proper survey of a huge sample is required and its results, properly manipulated, could resolve many important questions of social science.*

Now let us turn to the relationship between these phenomena and capitalism. In my view, Schumpeter's influence on the understanding of this subject has been unfortunate. His specious mixed metaphor, "the stock exchange is a poor substitute for the Holy Grail" is better put, "The stock exchange is a poor substitute for a pirate raid, but a tenured professorship is a fine substitute for a canonry, and civil service is a vast improvement on being a toady to a titled gangster." The notion that capitalism is inherently rational, calculating, and unheroic is belied by business practice. Successful businessmen smile at the notions of rationality attributed to them by economists. The free-wheeling entrepreneur—Commodore Vanderbilt, Henry Ford, Howard Hughes, Aristotle Onassis—*is* heroic; the calculating nobleman was contemptible—Louis VII was a saint, but Louis XII was "the spider king." The heroic figures are those who overreach without stopping to count the cost. In all systems, the unheroic is the calculator, the bureaucrat, and the critic.

That capitalism undermines religion also will not bear scrutiny. While many of the early capitalists were at best deists, the golden age of capitalism was a period of religious expansion. The capitalists themselves promoted religion for

---

*Patrons of research, please note: I am prepared to attempt it, but it will be *very* expensive.

obvious reasons. In the last century, the Methodists, the Baptists, the Mormons, the Roman Catholics, and numerous other denominations and sects have proliferated. How much of this is real faith and how much is "religiosity," literally God only knows, but the same can be asked of the earlier "age of faith." There has been a rough correlation between involvement in the capitalist system and religious adherence. Yes, the professors and the intelligentry and *their* clergy drifted into avowed secularism. But what have they to do with capitalism? And even if capitalism did generate rationalism, lack of faith, and absence of heroism, it is not immediately obvious why these attitudes should appear most notably among "intellectuals," who *most* thoroughly despise not only heroism but the martial, family, and other "feudal" values and are the most strongly antireligious and anticapitalist. While capitalism does permit hostile intellectuals by providing the *necessary* conditions of affluence and liberty, that is not a *sufficient* explanation. The argument that these people dislike capitalism because it does not buy and sell enough of what they want to sell and buy strikes me as much more reasonable.

As for the assertion that late capitalism has generated hedonism, Max Weber said that it should be taught that greed preceeded capitalism; perhaps we need to add to the curriculum that the desire to consume and display, to get high and get laid existed before Madison Avenue. Those elements we associate with the New Class are set against the sorts of things that big business wants to sell. In addition to their affection for foreign goods, they make a point of what some perceptive person called "conspicuous inconspicuous consumption"—Volvos rather than Buicks, beads rather than flashy jewelry, peasant blouses instead of furs, custom-made, labor-intensive services instead of capital-intensive, mass-produced goods—while those people most tied into the contemporary industrial system are the most conventional in their consumption patterns. Consider the traditional, non-New Class "businessmen and officials" on p. 115—they are even squarer than the working people. Capitalism has an interest in consumption *and production*.

Yes, capitalism is merely instrumental, and so is cooking, but so what?

Hacker is the only writer to expand on the high-level business managers. I know many such men, and like generals and police chiefs whose superior abilities have taken them to the top, they delight in basking in one another's company as further demonstration of their membership in an "elite." Whether this commonality makes them a class is arguable, but they cannot be an unclass merely because they derive their power and income from occupying a position. A duke derived his power from his position as a land-owner and law-giver; a capitalist derived his power from his position as a factory-owner and order-giver. Managers are obviously powerful, but are less so now than when Berle and Burnham spotted them as the coming men. Their freedom of action has been limited by the trade unions, and increasingly in recent years by government, so much so that Murray L. Weidenbaum has written of a "second managerial revolution."

Lipset has speculated on their relationship to the universities. While Galbraith is correct in saying that they are not as annoyed by intellectualdom as are entrepreneurs,[11] more discrimination is needed. Within the corporations are the line managers who direct production and distribution, but also the growing staffs in public affairs, government relations, internal education, and long-range planning, and in trade associations or research organizations who deal in ideas/words. These staffs look to the university (and to the media) as a reference group. They are not (or not yet?) a dominant element in the corporation, but they are growing in numbers and perhaps in influence. My contacts with many of these men over the years has convinced me that, unless they are properly instructed ideological conservatives, Bartley is right to suggest that they are the Fifth Column of the New Class within the capitals of capitalism. Many of them were pushed aside from major career tracks and have reeducated themselves by imbibing deeply from the wells of contemporary conventional wisdom.[12] Since the technical departments have used chemists as experts in chemistry, the staff departments draw upon social scientists as experts on society.

Like their counterparts in the military and internal security agencies, the staff are what Bartley's friend R. Emmett Tyrrell calls "intellectualoids." This should not surprise us, because whether or not they should be counted in the New Class, they owe their existence to the New Class through a perverse dialectic: intellectual attacks on business require intellectual apologetics; an active bureaucracy requires aggressive lobbyists; as Glazer points out, government regulation generates legal defenses.

Not long ago I organized a series of education seminars for the high command of a major corporation (what a quintessential New Class activity!) and recruited a neo-conservative speaker who gave a thoughtful and persuasive account of the forces being mustered in Washington—economists, policy analysts, etc.—against the enemies of business, but, as one of the executives pointed out afterwards, "he sees politics as purely a struggle between intellectuals."

I have also frequently offered a pop version of the New Class idea to business audiences. Entrepreneurs love it (they understand economic motivations and class-consciousness), managers are nervous (they prefer conspiracy theories), and the staffs are infuriated. Since the staffs are responsible for recruiting these sessions, of course, I never get a follow-up invitation.

Now, to what degree can any of these disparate elements be considered "a class"—i.e., to what degree will they perceive a common economic interest and make common political cause? As usual, Bell has posed the right question in his matrix of "estate" versus "situs." Will these people adhere to their occupational peers or to their institutional peers? Clearly, it varies—managers, including political managers, are expected to put the organization first; lawyers, reflecting their medieval origins, are supposed to champion their clients, but only according to the rules of The Law (i.e., other lawyers). But in suggesting that intellectuals are not like lawyers, Glazer is expressing an ideal more than a reality. Scientists, other "experts," and publicists will now line up on all sides of all issues—most of them firmly believing they represent disinterested truth and high ethical values, though "institutional requirements" will often press them too hard. One solution is to tell the truth, but not the *whole* truth, yet the tensions are often severe. For example, I heard that the most troublesome element in a certain great corporation is not black militants on the assembly line, but the technical workers in the research labs. When I repeated this to an official at one of these labs, he replied that researchers were troublemakers because they reported their findings regardless of corporate policy— i.e., the standards of science ("estate") had a higher value than the requirements of the corporation ("situs"), but dysfunctional results are suppressed, and also leaked. We see this in journalism as well—producing for your peers is "professionalism" and or "sincerity," producing for your patron or market is "selling out."

Another way of regarding the same issue is as a widening circle of interest. Everyone is first of all loyal to his own interest (or that of his immediate family, which amounts to the same thing), then to his specific organization in competition with like organizations, and then to his industry vis à vis others. But he usually is also loyal to a tribal/religious group, and to a broader economic group, especially when it is challenged.

Perhaps this point can be made clear by resort to the analogy of the classical capitalist. The bourgeois compete among themselves, but the bourgeoisie stands together against the aristocracy or the proletariat; for short-term gain, some elements will make common cause with their enemies. Some French aristocrats saw their interest in going over to the Revolution; bourgeois officers commanded the Red Army. As this is written, one auto company is lobbying the hated auto safety agency to block a technological innovation that would give its competitors a short-term edge. I hate to add to the definitions of "class," but let me suggest that it is the residue of economic interest remaining when more direct interests are subtracted, and is only of concern when it operates on a broad scale.

Consider another "class" seen by Kristol to be in opposition to the New Class—"the business class." He does not have to define it, because we know what it is—small proprietors, middlemen, salesmen, big business, managers, active and passive rentiers, and financiers with disparate interests, who could be at one another's political throats, and usually were during the early Republic. Their alliance and cohesion was created by two perceived threats—the Southern slaveocracy, which the Republican Party was created in 1854 to thwart, and the appearance of an organized proletariat, which the Republican Party was reorganized *circa* 1896 to fight. Let me suggest that the New Class would gain unity only if challenged, and to be challenged it must be identified.

Now, although Bell accepts many of the concepts related to the idea of the New Class, and indeed is largely responsible for their circulation, he considers their juxtaposition a "muddled" idea. Certainly this would be so if anyone had identified the emerging technicians with anticapitalist cultural and political ideas. Fortunately, except for a single wee slip by Kristol in separating "scientists" from the qualifying "in the public sector" by a few sentences (see p. 89n.) no serious commentator has done so; discussion of the subject has concentrated on intellectuals or word producers (e.g., Podhoretz, Kirkpatrick, Kristol) or on the entire salariat or scholariat (e.g., Bazelon, Harrington, Ladd), but not on number workers. Bell may have even contributed slightly to the confusion in *pop* versions of the post-industrial society by seeming to identify the universities with "the scientific estate," when *real* scientists are a minority of professors, and professors are a minority of scientists, and by identifying "post-industrial values" with a separate "cultural estate" that does seem to be mostly academics. Writers who fall short of Bell's enormous secular learning may also be excused for labeling the "professional and technical stratum" as "an intelligentsia" or "a class," since he has repeatedly done so in earlier versions of the post-industrial society.

In order for the New Class to be a class-in-being, Bell suggests that an ideology is necessary, and correctly nominates "meritocracy." That idea might be extended further—define booklearning as "merit," school grades as "talent," formal education as "skills," words and numbers as "theoretical knowledge"; claim that "knowledge work" produces a large amount of GNP by including everything from the manufacture of telephone cable to the cleaning of day-care centers; include in the growing "knowledge class" everyone from go-go dancers to proprietors of Carvel stands; label professors' salaries as "human capital"; maintain the objective "necessity" of "planning" (planners); and pin the blame for certain apparent disharmonies in the system on capitalism and Christianity. But seriously, when an ideology is needed, one will surely appear—the market provides.

Bell has suggested that egalitarianism is inconsistent with the interest of the New Class—not necessarily so. In answer to my question regarding the level at which confiscatory taxation should begin, egalitarians have uniformly said about $50,000 (in 1978 dollars), which of course is the highest salary a knowledge worker can reasonably expect. Poor McGovern misinterpreted a program to pull down those above the New Class into a program to really help the lower classes, the cost of which would have fallen on the New Class, which accounts for his disappointing showing on campus. This is a reasonable explanation for the apparent anomaly mentioned by Harrington of American professionals supporting leveling and their Swedish equivalents opposing it. In Sweden, the New Class has already pulled down the entrepreneurs and managers, so much so that a chief of one of the Swedish zaibatsu advises me that he cannot obtain managers with money, but only with perquisites, power, and interesting work. Consider the emphasis of the American egalitarians on the distribution of money income; *other* income will presumably be distributed on the basis of one's contribution to the needs of society. And almost ignored in the struggle over equality was the attempt to eliminate racism by imposing "objective" criteria—diplomas and written tests. When black organizations began to demand proof that these were relevant to job performance, enthusiasm for affirmative action evaporated, rather as did that for civil rights when "black power" demanded the "commissions" in the war against poverty.

Hacker has suggested that the New Class is all of us. This might be answered by reference to the Marxist thought he cites—if capitalism permeates all elements of society and its culture, it is reasonable to project that "intellectualism" does also. Not long ago I fell in with a group of Pennsylvania school bus drivers on holiday and was horrified (but not surprised) to learn that to be licensed they had to undergo a formal course of education—not, of course, in driving a school bus, but in classroom work followed by a written examination.

To Wildavsky, the New Class is effectively all of favored America, regardless of its source of income or level of education. The significance of the social-limits-to-growth movement is a problem with which I have long wrestled.[13] Mass prosperity and leveling threaten more than just those who possess higher education and nonprofit jobs. Despite the specious displays of income distributions (before taxes and government disbursements) and of privately (but not corporately) held wealth in the United States, the standard of living of the privileged orders in America has obviously decayed steadily since the halcyon days of laissez-faire capitalism. All of the privileged—the executives, the professionals, the professors, even the schoolteachers—are not living as well as their predecessors did.

The quality of life of all of those on top is eroding. I have heard auto executives bitching about traffic congestion and Arizona land speculators complaining about the waning of the wilderness. These are enormous tensions, but they are more easily resolved in those elements labeled the New Class. Despite having the traditional upper-class interest in keeping the lower orders down, the entrepreneurs and managers have a conflicting interest in the profits and salaries that derive from mass prosperity and economic growth. Those in the nonprofit sector have only the much more distant interest in a healthy economy to support their pursuits, and their distance from production is so great that they are no more aware of it than a rentier shareholder is of the activities of his firm. As suggested by Wildavsky and Harrington, these social demands cannot be met through individual initiative, only through state action. So perhaps we can again adopt the Bazelonian formulation to suggest that the limits-to-growth publicists and activists are the most class-conscious part of the broad new New Class.

Obviously, the principal concern over the New Class has been political. One can reject the very idea of "class" yet recognize the necessity of coordinating the action or at least obtaining the votes of large numbers of people in order to achieve political goals on a national level. A significant chunk of the electorate (I would guess 10 percent) is the New Class, defined politically—the New Politics. Of course, the bulk of the people who voted for George McGovern would have voted Democratic if Attilla the Hun were at the head of the ticket.

The two political dissidents in the study, Michael Harrington and Kevin Phillips, are not optimistic. I think that Harrington's hope that some substantial proportion of this privileged New Class will, like himself, become converted to "properly understood" socialism does not even convince himself. Phillips' analysis is given considerable empirical support by Ladd's data, and his critique of alternative strategies seem plausible. But his New Right has no organization and no leadership (Wallace's 1968 campaign staff was the Ku Klux Klan in the South and the John Birch Society elsewhere; his aborted 1972 campaign only had a central core of personal henchmen very like those of J.E. Carter). Having examined the history of populism sympathetically, I regretfully conclude such movements lack staying power and their leaders have uniformly been charlatans and cranks. And I wonder if the disaffection is as deep as Phillips suggests. Take for example, the outcry over pornography—not so long ago there would have been not protests, but bonfires.

The political analyses agree in treating the Carter victory as a fluke, since he and his supporters fail to fit any ideological category—but this may be the new norm. Any prognostication will doubtless look silly in a few years, but it seems to me that, at least for the next few years, the situation in the United States will resemble somewhat the present Italian system: A policy so fractionated by organized groups, all capable of exercising veto power, that government is practically immobilized. Since government is now such an important player in the economic game, this situation permits the stifling of further economic growth, which has the effects upon education noted by Harrington, and upon the further growth of the New Class.

Oddly, it also brings into play another reaction. Expansion of government squeezes out the middling businessman who cannot afford to meet the paperwork, let alone the regulations, but it helps the small businessman who keeps his own books or perhaps no books at all. As in Italy, an increasing amount of American business is now being conducted in a "grey" market, and as a consequence, the economic and social data base for "planning" policy becomes increasingly fictitious. The State can build up the regulations to close all the loopholes in enterprise. Already, a powerful lobby within the bureaucracy is advocating national identity cards in order to keep better track of the presumed beneficiaries of social and economic policy. Another possibility is that we will give up on a lot of this regulation and taxation. Another faint possibility is that the system will gradually come apart, leading to the uglier possibilities Phillips suggests—we (and he) hope not. In this sense we are all "liberals."

Andrew Hacker was the only contributor to take up what I consider to be the most important issue. If history requires "the circulation of elites," would a new elite based upon education be competent to rule? Can an elite selected by its formal education and having that education influence its behavior rule effectively? Can it fulfill the needs of the entire society, and even do what is necessary to maintain itself? I can think of no way to approach this problem rigorously, but some anecdotal evidence might suggest difficulties.

Hacker refers to the U.S. performance in the Vietnamese war. Consider the nature of the debate over the war: one side said that we could bring the enemy to the bargaining table by adding another division of troops or bombing a bridge another few miles closer to Hanoi; the other side said we could bring the enemy to the bargaining table by stopping the bombing or withdrawing troops. Both were reasoned concepts. But the debaters, both the administration and its opponents, could not conceive of an enemy who was implacable, who would fight so long as he continued to get foreign supplies and the rate of young men coming of military age was sufficient to replace his losses, and who would only bargain for a surrender. The very idea of the bargaining table is very characteristic of the New Class; there, verbal skills presumably win victory. In retrospect, the "get-in-or-get-out" of the ill-informed working stiff seems like superb analysis.

The military performance was very strange indeed. The civilian leadership of the Department of Defense was so bedazzled with the systems approach that it persuaded the soldiers to forget how they had fought the Korean War. And the soldiers themselves were so taken up with bureaucratic struggle for position that combat performance was irrelevant.

About domestic policy, the less said the better. Again, the lessons learned in the New Deal on how to achieve desired social goals were forgotten. Worse, the system is now shot through with pseudorationality—the manipulation of pointless, usually fictitious numbers, jargon substituting for thought (what is "zero-base budgeting" but "why do we need that?"), and, as Jeane Kirkpatrick has pointed out, a media politics increasingly founded on abstract slogans.

Everett Ladd's poll data on the foreign-policy attitudes of educated Americans are especially disturbing. To *my* ideology these depict an elite incapable of defending a society or even themselves. To be sure, their ideas will change when directly threatened. Mayor Frank Rizzo was coarse but prescient when he defined a conservative as a-liberal-who-has-just-been-mugged, and it is unfortunate that people only lose their enthusiasm for "liberated values" when they have teenage daughters and for "progressive education" when their own children cannot count over ten without taking off their shoes. Campus unrest became less attractive when it turned against the university itself, and the benefits of affirmative action paled when applied to the universities. Socialism becomes tarnished when poets are jailed; revolution is ugly when the educated classes are exterminated. How sad that presumably intellectual people see a bird as dirty only when their own nests are fouled.

In 1978, the United States of America satisfied the claims of the Republic of Panama, just as England appeased Ireland in 1938. This situation will certainly change, but I fear, as I suspect do some of the other contributors, at the cost of some *other* country being obliged to make a "Christian sacrifice" for world peace. If not, the Russian New Class has a demonstrated capability for the resolution of these contradictions. Those Czech scholars mentioned by Harrington and Lipset have since reconsidered and recanted their views, persuaded by the more powerful arguments deployed to Prague by the clerisy of Marxist-Leninist orthodoxy—AK-47, T-55, and MIG-21 represent forms of universally comprehensible technological notation.[14] While you cannot kill ideas, raising their cost does seem to limit their sale.

To a large degree, America *has* become a meritocracy. A general is a West Point graduate who has attended the Command and Staff School and the Army War College and picked up a M.A. in International Relations—not a leader of troops. A professor is a Ph.D. who has published at least one vanity book—not a teacher or scholar. Not long ago, I was complaining about the incredible incompetence of publishers' employees to an editor, and she seriously replied, "But they are much more qualified now, you can't get in the door without a Master's." Civil servants, teachers, and "helping" professionals and technicians are admitted and promoted almost solely on credentials and written examinations. We deal now in words; in Bazelon's terms we work in a "paper economy." Perhaps overproduction has driven down the value of ideas. The idea-producing industries are shot through with shoddiness and slipshod practices (anyone who has had to deal with publishers knows exactly what I mean).

The least unlikely projection is more of the same, more credentialism and more educated people. The journalists will produce for those markets. The tiny band of intellectuals will maintain the pure flame of critical analysis of the society. Governments, foundations, international agencies, and all manner of nonprofit organizations will continue to provide suitable employment/sinecures for the superfluous members of the scholocracy. If they have it all their own way, they will fight among themselves; if challenged from the outside, they will unite against the threat, and, of course, some of them will defect and serve other constitutencies. Corporations and other institutions will increasingly find it necessary to deploy their own battallions of lawyers, public-relations men, government-relations specialists, and other staff to fight off the above. So long as social and political conflict is fought with New Class weapons, with words, nobody gets hurt and probably the New Class wins. This we may view as progress, or decadence.

Let me summarize the case:

1. No one claims that "class," however defined, explains everything.
2. Yet we do have a substantial and visible minority of the population that has been taking an adversary stance toward the existing economic, social, and political order on the avowed grounds that it falls far short of its potential.
3. Those dissenters are most obvious among a tiny group of highbrow journalists and communications entrepreneurs in a few large cities.
4. To some degree they influence middlebrow and even mass media.
5. But the only large audience for "the adversary culture" that we can certainly identify is the "soft" (humanities and social science) faculties of universities that are also highly productive of adversary ideas.
6. However, there is some evidence, but not so strong, that this audience might be found elsewhere among the highly educated, and we may reasonably project the faculty data as well as Ladd's analysis to suggest that these views are likely found among "word workers" or so-called "intellectuals."
7. We have some indication of cohesiveness among these journalists, these professors, and some elements in government, especially the social welfare and regulatory agencies, and their contractors.
8. We have weaker indications of sympathy among all highly educated people, whatever their source of income.
9. The study has not concentrated on "number workers" (scientists, engineers, etc.), but the evidence displayed might reasonably be interpreted as suggesting that they are not very disaffected and certainly not as much as the word workers.
10. We have some scraps of data and generally accepted theory to suggest that business managers are less firm in resisting the adversary position that entrepreneurs would be, and we have unquestioned evidence of the decline of entrepreneurship together with an increase of corporation staff, who in some sense are also word workers.
11. We need no data to tell us that in the last generation, place in American society has been more assigned on the basis of formal education ("credentialism") and less on family background or old-line free competition/performance.

12. We have had a respectable expansion of the high bureaucracy and an enormous expansion of government regulation of doing and a diminution of regulation of wording.

13. As in all things, there have been gainers and losers in these processes. Highly educated people have been major gainers especially in government, in universities, and other institutions, but the quality of their rewards has decreased, because the working people have also done rather well, at least until recently.

14. We have a perceived widespread alienation/resentment.

15. We have strong evidence of the persistence of greedy, selfish, snobbish, vicious, pretentious, hypocritical, and stupid behavior.

16. We have theories, economic or otherwise, of how these phenomena are related. Most of them cannot be proved in any rigorous sense, and are so highly politicized that agreement cannot be expected.

Have we a New Class? Well, from the above it seems clear that the Bazelonian New-Class-in-formation remains a formulation. These groups are incredibly fragmented and at one another's throats. They might conceivably make common cause against a common threat, e.g., economic growth, a foreign threat, or a populist upheaval. But today, as for the last decade, one can only understand national culture and politics in terms of conflict among several rival groups, an important one consisting mostly of well-paid (but more likely from tax than market sources) and well-educated (but more likely literate than numerate) folk who are secular, hardly averse to achieving their goals through government, and fiercely defensive of the autonomy of their personal behavior and economic institutions. If some want to call them a New Class, why not?

In best New Class fashion, let me respectfully conclude that much more research is called for.

NOTES

1. Richard Hofstadter, *Anti-Intellectualism in American Life* (New York, 1963), pp. 7-8, 19-21. (His tortuous wrestling only makes sense if it is realized that he is trying to construct an abstract definition of "the intellectual community," i.e., his circle.); S.M. Lipset, *Political Man* (1960; Anchor paperback, 1963), pp. 332-33.

2. On the readership of intellectual/liberal magazines see: Dwight Macdonald, *Memoirs of a Revolutionist* (Meridian paperback, 1958), pp. 26-27; David T. Bazelon, *Power in America* (New York, 1967), p. 338; Lewis S. Feuer, *The Conflict of Generations* (New York, 1969), pp. 377-78; Phillip Nobile, *Intellectual Skywriting* (New York, 1974), p. 260. Nobile quotes a publisher, "At least 80% of [*New York Review of Books'*] audience is academically oriented."

3. This line of thought was stimulated by R.H. Coase's "The Market for Goods and the Market for Ideas," *American Economic Review* (May 1974), which asks why economists opposed to government regulation of the market for ideas ("censorship") support the regulation of the market for goods. Since he is at the University of Chicago, I assume he meant to encourage other

economists to question the validity of regulation of the goods market, but it seems quite possible that regulation of other markets is in the economic interest of economists while the regulation of their own output is not. See also Malcolm Cowley, "The Literary Stock Exchange" in *The Literary Situation* (New York, 1958).

4. For example, "I had an ideological strategy too, which was to turn *Commentary*, as I myself had been turning, in the same leftward direction that I was confident the best energies of the sixties were also preparing to move." Norman Podhoretz, *Making It* (New York, 1967) Chapter 9. (Chapter 7 has some perceptive remarks regarding the sociocultural effects of the overproduction of English literature majors in the 1950s.) For a spritely but possibly unreliable account of another successful venture of the 1960s, see Nobile, *op. cit.*

5. E.C. Ladd and S.M. Lipset, *The Divided Academy* (New York, 1975), p. 136.

6. Suggestive is Richard Sennett, *The Fall of Public Man* (New York, 1977), pp. 301ff.

7. James Q. Wilson, *The Amateur Democrat* (Chicago, 1962), p. 13. (The index reads: "Professors; *see* Intellectuals.")

8. "Publius," *The Federalist*, numbers 78-81; Charles A. Beard, *The Supreme Court and the Constitution* (New York, 1912).

9. For example, Luke 20:46.

10. James T. Barry, "Social Origins and Values of Knowledge-Based Elites in Contemporary Society" (Ph.D. dissertation, Buffalo State University, February 1977).

11. J.K. Galbraith, *The New Industrial State* (New York, 1967), Chapter 15. Possibly because of the partial success of the strategy advocated by Galbraith, it is no longer as true that "the mature corporation is much less troubled by the social inventiveness of the educational and scientific estate."

12. See, e.g., the *Harvard Business Review* and *Business and Society Review*. George C. Lodge's *The New American Ideology* (New York, 1976) is apparently not a deliberate parody of this school.

13. B. Bruce-Briggs, "Against the Neo-Malthusians," *Commentary* (July 1974); review of Hirsch's *Social Limits to Growth* in *The Alternative* (August/September 1977).

14. The Czechs did not resist. "Intellectuals had . . . a class interest in nonviolence for its own sake." Christopher Lasch, *The New Radicalism in America* (New York, 1965), p. 169.

Appendix

ENUMERATING THE NEW CLASS

B. Bruce-Briggs

Looking for the New Class in the U.S. Census is a tedious business, made all the more so by the necessity of introducing the subject with an elaborate caveat. While not entirely new, the idea of the New Class is not yet established, and the statisticians of the Census Bureau have not been interested in the sorts of questions that concern this study. Their organization of social and economic data properly follows conventional lines, and, indeed, has to some degree shaped the analysis of social change in America.*

Normally, discussion of occupational change is accompanied by display of the data in Table A-1, to illustrate the shift to "white-collar" work and to the growth of "professional" groups. However, a closer look at the data reveals that the two most important trends are the decline in the number of farmers and the rapidly increasing numbers of women in the paid labor force, many of whom have been transient or part-time. If we examine only male workers and

---

*For example, the Ehrenreichs' "professional-managerial class" cited by Harrington is based on Census categories; better known scholars have made similar constructions.

exclude farmers, we find the distribution in Table A-2. Male nonfarm-occupational distribution has remained remarkably stable over the past generation; nevertheless, the most rapidly growing group is "professional . . ."

Table A-1
Occupational Distribution, 1950-70[1]
(in thousands)

	1950	%	1970	%
White Collar Workers	21,601	(36.6)	37,857	(47.4)
Professional, Technical & Kindred	5,081	(8.6)	11,561	(14.5)
Managers & Administrators	5,155	(8.7)	6,463	(8.1)
Sales	4,133	(7.0)	5,625	(7.0)
Clerical & Kindred	7,232	(12.3)	14,208	(17.8)
Blue Collar Workers	30,445	(51.6)	39,420	(49.4)
Craftsmen, Foremen & Kindred	8,350	(14.2)	11,082	(13.9)
Operatives & Kindred	12,030	(20.4)	14,335	(18.0)
Laborers	3,885	(6.6)	3,751	(4.7)
Private Household	1,539	(2.6)	1,204	(1.5)
Other Service	4,641	(7.9)	9,047	(11.3)
Farmers	6,953	(11.8)	2,448	(3.1)
Owners & Managers	4,375	(12.5)	1,428	(1.8)
Laborers & Foremen	2,578	(4.4)	1,022	(1.3)
TOTAL	58,999	(100)	79,802	(100)

More important, for our purposes, discussions of relatively privileged Americans concentrate on the two top occupational categories, normally referred to as "professionals" and "managers." But the Census Bureau is careful to label these more broadly. The latter is, in full, "managers and administrators," which was formerly "managers, officials, and proprietors," and before that "proprietors, managers, and officials." It includes not only "managers" as generally understood in common usage, but all manner of small shopkeepers and low-grade government officials, such as building inspectors, not to mention railroad conductors.

More important, "professionals" is a misleading abbreviation for the "professional, technical, and kindred" category, which includes many occupations not normally considered "professional"—e.g., nurses, health and dental technicians, draftsmen, dancers, and industrial technicians of all types. Most public-opinion research data lump the two top occupational categories together as "professional and managerial," and much social analysis considers this particular grouping as representative of the "elite" occupations in the United States—but this is obviously not the case.

Table A-2
Male Non-Farm Occupations, 1950-70[2]
(in thousands)

	1950		1970	
		%		%
White Collar Workers	12,974	(35.8)	19,428	(41.1)
Professional, Technical & Kindred	3,074	(8.5)	6,917	(14.6)
Managers & Administrators	4,456	(12.3)	5,386	(11.4)
Sales	2,715	(7.5)	3,378	(7.1)
Clerical & Kindred	2,730	(7.5)	3,748	(7.9)
Blue Collar Workers	23,228	(64.2)	27,807	(58.9)
Craftsmen, Foremen & Kindred	8,098	(22.4)	10,530	(22.3)
Operatives & Kindred	8,743	(24.1)	9,789	(20.7)
Laborers	3,740	(10.3)	3,440	(7.3)
Service	2,647	(7.3)	4,048	(8.6)
TOTAL	36,202	(100)	47,250	(100)

Furthermore, these two categories do not include all those Americans who might be considered well-off. Important occupational groups generally thought of as "business" are not in either of them. Self-employed artisans, such as plumbers and barbers, are counted in the "craftsmen" or "service" categories that are subsumed under "blue-collar." So a small businessman with a trade is considered a blue-collar worker while the proprietor of a mom-and-pop store is a "manager." The "sales and kindred" category contains a large business element; while it is largely sales clerks, it also includes real-estate and insurance agents, as well as stock-brokers and manufacturers' representatives, among the best paid and most characteristically entrepreneurial occupations. This is not to criticize the Census Bureau; any classification necessarily has an arbitrary element. But it is misleading to use the conventional overall gross occupational categories to define or delineate the New Class or any description of the American elite. So I have reorganized the Census data to suit the purposes of this study better by making some slight adjustments to improve consistency between years and by regrouping the occupational categories as follows:

Professionals—professional, technical, and kindred, less obvious technicians;

Officials—government-employed managers and administrators;

Salaried Businessmen and Nonprofit Managers—nongovernment, non-self-employed managers and administrators and sales workers, less sales clerks.

Independent businessmen—all self-employed workers, except professionals and farmers;

Farmers—farm owners and managers;

White collar—non-self-employed clerical and kindred, technicians, and sales clerks;

Blue collar—the remainder.

The resulting distribution, shown in Table A-3, leaves a good deal to be desired because it is not possible to split profit from non-profit employment in the private sector. Still, it does clearly illustrate several important trends. In addition to the decline of farmers and the rise of white-collar workers, we see substantial gains in a more narrowly defined professional group, as well as in government officials. However, the salariat has grown more slowly, and not only farmers, but other independent businessmen, have experienced a marked decline in relative *and absolute* numbers.

Table A-3
Revised Occupational Distribution, 1950-70[3]
(in thousands)

	1950	%	1970	%
Professionals	4,011	(6.9)	9,340	(12.1)
Officials	321	(.5)	819	(1.1)
Salaried Businessmen & Non-profit Managers	3,308	(5.6)	7,179	(9.3)
Independent Businessmen	4,459	(7.6)	3,752	(4.9)
Farmers	4,301	(7.3)	1,427	(1.9)
Salaried White Collar Workers	9,584	(16.4)	17,760	(23.1)
Blue Collar Wage Workers	32,567	(55.6)	36,528	(47.6)
TOTAL	58,551	(100)	76,805	(100)

Table A-4 details the numbers of the occupational groups that have been identified as being part of the New Class. Note especially the swelling numbers

Table A-4
Selected Occupations, 1950-70[4]
(in thousands)

	1970		1960		1950	
		*		*		*
Clergy	219	(2.7)	202	(3.0)	169	(2.9)
Lawyers & Judges	273	(3.4)	218	(3.2)	182	(3.1)
Physicians & Osteopaths	282	(3.5)	233	(3.4)	198	(3.4)
Dentists	91	(1.1)	83	(1.2)	76	(1.3)
Architects	57	(.7)	38	(.6)	24	(.4)
College Administrators	39	(.5)	11	(.2)⎫		
College Teachers	496	(6.2)	196	(2.9)⎬	126	(2.1)
School Administrators	173	(2.2)	99	(1.5)⎭		
School Teachers	2,786	(34.9)	1,797	(26.4)⎰	1,133	(19.2)
Librarians	124	(1.6)	76	(1.2)	56	(1.0)
Chemists (nonacademic)	110	(1.4)	96	(1.4)	76	(1.3)
Other Natural Scientists						
(nonacademic)	95	(1.2)	62	(.9)	43	(.7)
Statisticians	23	(.3)	14	(.2)⎫		
Economists	67	(.8)	27	(.4)⎬	36	(.6)
Other Social Scientists	44	(.6)	15	(.2)⎭		
Accountants	712	(8.9)	496	(7.3)	385	(6.5)
Engineers	1,230	(15.4)	871	(12.8)	535	(9.1)
Religious Workers	36	(.5)	61	(.9)	42	(.7)
Social Workers	221	(2.8)	95	(1.4)	77	(1.3)
Editors & Reporters	151	(1.9)	106	(1.6)	73	(1.2)
Authors	26	(.3)	29	(.4)	16	(.3)
Actors	15	(.2)	12	(.2)	18	(.3)
Personnel & Labor Relations						
Workers	296	(3.7)	103	(1.5)	53	(.9)
Vocational & Educational						
Counselors	108	(1.4)	32	(.5)⎫		
Computer Specialists	263	(3.3)	12	(.2)⎪		
Operations Researchers &				⎪		
Systems Analysts	81	(1.0)	23	(.3)⎬	96	(1.6)
Public Relations Men &				⎪		
Publicity Writers	76	(1.0)	31	(.5)⎪		
Radio & TV Writers	22	(.3)	16	(.2)⎪		
Research Workers, not specified	119	(1.5)	79	(1.2)⎭		
Federal Government Officials	278	(3.5)⎱				
State & Local Govt. Officials	540	(6.8)⎰	436	(6.4)	262	(4.4)
Other Salaried Managers &						
Administrators	4,390	(55.0)	2,946	(43.3)	1,853	(31.4)

*Per thousand work force

of academics, teachers, and personnel workers, and the appearance of the new occupations of computer programming, operations research, and systems analysis. However, in and of themselves, these changes would not appear to be sufficient to explain major changes in our society. This is especially true when these groups are considered relative to the entire labor force or population.

Discussion of occupational change is usually followed by discussion of the changes in industrial employment, often following the organization of the Anglo-Australian economist Colin Clark, who divided all industry into primary (extractive), secondary (manufacturing), and tertiary (services). Throughout most of history, most people have devoted themselves to the extractive industries, especially farming. The industrial revolution saw the rise of manufacturing. More recently has occurred the rise of services, which is held to be of fundamental importance.

In fact, as has been pointed out over and over again, the number of Americans engaged in extractive industries is not limited to those so classified by Clark's scheme. In addition to farmers, there are also the manufacturers and distributors of tractors and fertilizers, processors and distributors of produce, not to mention the agricultural scientists, extension agents, and ag school

Table A-5
Industrial Distribution of Employment, 1950-70[5]
(in thousands)

	1950		1970	
"Tertiary"		%		%
Public Administration	2,491	(4.5)	4,202	(5.5)
Public Education	1,547	(2.8)	4,472	(5.8)
Private Education	530	(1.0)	1,643	(2.1)
Health Services	1,609	(2.9)	4,246	(5.5)
Welfare, Religious & Other Nonprofit Membership Organizations	585	(1.1)	1,163	(1.5)
Other Professional Services (engineers, legal, etc.)	378	(.7)	1,987	(2.6)
All Other Services (transportation, trade, finance, hotels, etc.)	22,088	(40.1)	30,961	(40.4)
"Secondary" (Manufacturing & Construction	17,851	(32.0)	24,409	(31.9)
"Primary" (Agriculture, Mining, etc.)	7,945	(14.4)	3,471	(4.5)
TOTAL	55,804	(100)	76,554	(100)

teachers. So we are very quickly led back to the original occupational distribution mentioned above. Nevertheless, since certain industries are associated with the idea of the New Class, Table A-5 displays their changes in the past generation. Note that it is not overall "services" that have grown, but the Census categories of "public administration," "education," "health," and "other professional services."

A central idea is that the New Class is defined in terms of education. Here we have some very clear-cut and unchallengeable data. Even though educational statistics do not reflect the quality or the status of the education received, the measures are not disputable. There has been a large expansion of the highly educated population in the United States, as shown in Table A-6. (Unfortunately, it was not until the 1970 Census that separate data were shown for postgraduate education. However, using the U.S. Office of Education data on the numbers of college degrees awarded and assuming a forty-year active working life for degree-holders gives us the estimates in Table A-7.) These give substance to the widely held view that the amount of higher education has been expanding rapidly; nevertheless, the highly educated still constitute only a tiny proportion of the population.

Table A-6
Educational Attainment, 1950-70[6]
(in millions)

	1950		1970	
All persons 25 and over		%		%
not high school grads	58.3	(66.6)	44.5	(38.7)
high school grads	29.2	(33.4)	70.5	(61.3)
with some college	11.5	(13.2)	29.0	(25.2)
college grads (4 or more years)	5.3	(6.0)	15.3	(13.3)
Total	87.5	(100)	115.0	(100)
Experienced civilian labor force				
not high school grads	35.2	(61.3)	31.4	(39.2)
high school grads	22.2	(38.7)	48.7	(60.8)
with some college	8.7	(15.1)	20.6	(25.1)
college grads (4 or more years)	4.1	(7.2)	10.1	(12.6)
Total	58.5	(100)	80.1	(100)
College Enrollment	2.2		7.4	

Table A-7
College Graduates, 1950-70[7]
(in thousands)

40 year cumulative:	1950	%*	1960	%*	1970	%*
Doctor's	84	(.1)	165	(.2)	335	(.4)
Master's	653	(1.1)	1,262	(1.9)	2,525	(3.2)
Bachelor's or equivalent	5,148	(8.7)	8,096	(11.9)	12,822	(16.1)

*Percent of labor force

Census income data, especially of the higher earners, were examined closely. They indicate that the occupations of high earners are shifting toward the "professional" categories, but the proportion having high earnings is shrinking, so that the relative income advantage of professional occupations is falling. While I find these data agreeable to my (and Wildavsky's) thesis that some part of the New Class program is a response to a decaying standard of living, the same data indicate a precipitous drop in the income of proprietors. Remember, the Census can only report what the public tells it, and while education may now be the preferred route to status and position, in an increasingly taxed and regulated economy, the best way to *wealth* is to keep your own accounts and beware of all agents of government. Since I buy as much as possible in small shops, asking the proprietor, "How much for cash, no receipt?" I do not believe the census income data and do not display it. But, for whatever it is worth, the only high status occupations that increased their relative reported income during the 1960s were doctors, dentists, lawyers, and federal officials.

In summary, the published census data examined give substance to some widely recognized social phenomena:

— the relative decay of proprietorship;
— the expansion of salaried managers and professionals;
— the rapid growth of the health industry;
— a swelling of "number workers" (scientists, engineers, computer programmers).

In other words, the "old" New Class of Galbraith, Bazelon, and Bell.

But very little support is found for the appearance of the more limited neo-conservative New Class, unless we consider the following especially significant:

— the ballooning of academia, teachers, and college students;
— the appearance of well-paid federal officials.

These would not seem adequate to justify anything so grandiose as a "new" class, unless we turn from relative to absolute numbers. As suggested by Lipset's discussion of college radicals, it is possible that some sort of Marxistic "class consciousness" was generated in the 1960s merely from the increase in numbers. One deviant in a community is a trouble-maker, ten are a clique, a hundred a club, a thousand a pressure group, regardless of the absolute size of the community. Conceivably, a "critical mass" was achieved, but what that might be cannot be calculated from Census Bureau data.

NOTES

1. U.S. Census Bureau, *Historical Statistics of the United States: Colonial Times to 1970*, p. 139.
2. Calculations from ibid.
3. Calculations from 1950 and 1970 Censes of Population. Data for more recent years are not displayed because the Census estimates were based on a 5 percent sample of households, while intercensus estimates are based on a sample of less than 1 percent.
4. Ibid.; U.S. Census Bureau Technical Paper #26.
5. Calculations from 1950 and 1970 Censes of Population.
6. Ibid.
7. Calculations from *Historical Statistics*, pp. 385-86.

INDEX

301.44
N42   The new class?